My perspective of the Apostle Peter will never
inspirational and deep reflection of the life of F
It is a masterly woven account of the gospel th
life experiences to a most helpful application in today's world.

Archbishop Foley Beach
Anglican Diocese of the South, USA

Humans are *homo narratus* – storytellers. Following the footsteps of Jesus,
who was the storyteller *par excellence*, the Rev. Dr. Johannes van der Bijl has
gifted us with a remarkable story of Jesus according to Simon Peter. The author
captures the events so well – this is cinematic storytelling from the fine details
of movements and actions, to the broad, panoramic views of places, human
emotions and the characters of the disciples, who were like us. What the author
has produced is not mere speculation, but Scripture-shaped imaginings dipped
from its canonical entirety, historical background and theological vision. The
book also expresses the deep mystery of the divine through the struggles and
encounters of the disciples – all leading to the sense of wonder, loving adora-
tion and worship of the true God.

As I read this book, I felt the storyteller's sense of humor, inquisitive soul-
searching questions, prayer-soaked reflections, and flamboyant descriptions
of dramatic events – all these are interwoven with the story of Jesus, Peter and
the disciples. Johannes, a poet-theologian and iconographer, put his artistic
imaginations in the service of telling the biblical story as a single whole. This
book has both folkloric and visual iconographic sensibilities appealing to cultures and societies around the world, particularly in Africa.

Tekletsadik Belachew
Researcher at Tibeb Research and Retreat Center,
Addis Ababa, Ethiopia

We often learn more about what it means to follow Jesus from the lives of
others than we do from theological textbooks and Bible commentaries. In
this delightful book, Johannes offers us a fresh look at what it means to follow
Jesus through the life of the Apostle Peter. In doing so, he offers us hope in
our struggles and reminds us how we can follow Jesus today.

Rev. Winfield Bevins, PhD
Director of Church Planting,
Asbury Theological Seminary, Wilmore, Kentucky, USA

Dr. van der Bijl has given us an excellent insight into the teaching and life of Jesus that can only help us marvel afresh at Jesus's gracious purposes and ways of making disciples. Written through the experience of Peter and his brother Andrew, we catch a glimpse of the way Jesus fulfills and explains the Old Testament in a down to earth and personal way. There are many helpful background insights into the culture of Israel under Roman bondage which elucidate our Lord's teachings and calls for wholehearted allegiance. This book is a good, interesting and arresting read, drawing us into the drama of Jesus's mission and the disciples' struggles to comprehend its trajectory, challenges and joyful outcome. Drawing from the four Gospels, and focused on Peter's struggle to understand Jesus's call, this book makes an excellent introduction for anyone wanting to grapple with who Jesus is, what he demands, and how he graciously and patiently trains his followers. Worth reading and sharing.

The Rt. Rev. Peter Brain, DMin
Former Bishop of Armidale, New South Wales, Australia

In this amazing book we have numerous faith-building insights into the life of the Apostle Peter. Using his imagination, Johannes van der Bijl has cleverly woven together biblical information, and the outcome is inspiration. Personally I have been inspired to follow more wholeheartedly the Lord Jesus whom Peter loved and served. He is the One who transformed Peter's life. A hardworking fisherman became one of the greatest leaders in the history of the Church.

Johannes's book tells Peter's story in a new and refreshing way. He traces Peter's faith and failures, his progress and problems, his doubts and disappointments. He explores Peter's actions and reactions. He unpacks valuable lessons about growing as a Christian and a Christian leader. This book will help all who desire to grow in grace and truth and be more fruitful and faithful disciples of Jesus. I warmly commend it!

Bishop Ken Clarke
Former Mission Director,
South American Mission Society (SAMS) Ireland
Former Bishop, Kilmore, Elphin and Ardagh, Church of Ireland
Author, *Going for Growth*

I tried to speed-read *Breakfast on the Beach*, but couldn't put it down! Johannes van der Bijl manages a masterpiece of synergy between academic exactitude, historical chronology, biblical narrative, gospel synthesis, pastoral counselling, leadership training, and mission strategy all in one book! The author takes us up so close to Jesus and his intimate circle of buddy disciples that we feel incorporated into the group. This he achieves through the eyes of Peter, the disciple who most represents us – his failures, doubts, fears, passions – these become ours as with him we live through the call, conversations, teachings, life lessons, miracles and wonders that he gradually took in while in relationship with Jesus. We see how, in situ (the author's visit to Israel shows through as we visualize each physical site and scene), Peter asks the sort of questions we would ask, and fills in many of the blanks that the Gospels leave open.

The book is also a pastoral journey. We learn of camaraderie between unlikely people, storms, resuscitations, healings, exorcisms, hateful opposition, family rejection, and even a rebuke, addressing Satan, that nearly demolished Peter. The culmination comes with that dreadful denial. How could he recover? You need to read about that special *breakfast on the beach*.

The Rt. Rev. Alfred Cooper
Bishop, Evangelist and Church Planter
Diocese of Chile, South America

Crafted with care and told with passion, this story of Peter – however familiar – is a page-turner. It draws the reader into the world of lake water and hills, fishing boats and marketplaces, with an ease that belies the research that undergirds it. Watching Peter with Jesus, we cannot help but identify his story with ours. In that identification lies this book's capacity to move its readers to leave all behind and single-mindedly follow the hero, Jesus.

Havilah Dharamraj, PhD
Head of the Department of Biblical Studies,
South Asia Institute of Advanced Christian Studies, Bangalore, India

Johannes has introduced us into a wonderful exercise that we should do often when reading the sacred text, and that is to allow our imagination to fly and try to see what were the dialogues, the feelings, the fears and doubts of the biblical characters. This book has helped me to understand more the human side of the biblical story by paying attention to details that indicate to us that there is a story behind each verse, which helps us understand the text in a more enriching way. Students, preachers and teachers should learn from this book about how to take full advantage of the biblical stories in order to extract those truths sometimes hidden from the quick and easy reader.

Josué Hugo Fernandez
Regional Director LAC, Overseas Council

If the words of Scripture have become routine or too comfortable, then *Breakfast on the Beach* is a book for you. As I immersed myself in this imaginative retelling of the Jesus story, I encountered the words and actions of Jesus in a new way. The book places the familiar words of Scripture within a rich and detailed narrative, as told from the perspective of Simon Peter. Johannes employs both research and imagination to put himself into the shoes of the disciples; their wonderings, fears, hopes, and questions. As someone passionate about global mission, I am always looking for ways to share the gospel across cultures and in different ways. As Johannes notes in the introduction, storytelling is an effective way of communicating across cultures, and this book could thus serve as an approachable introduction to the person of Jesus.

Rosie Fyfe
National Director, New Zealand Church Missionary Society

A beautiful blend of storytelling mixed with a profound understanding of biblical, historical and cultural themes. The effect is like sitting down in a pub with a wise friend and listening as he unfolds his epic story. Peter and Christ come to life on the page.

Really a must-read by every disciple of Christ. Highly recommended.

Roger Griffin
Missionary in Mexico

The Lord wants disciples, rather than mere converts, to make up the redeemed community that he calls his church. But how does the Lord Jesus himself make disciples? Van der Bijl offers a very compelling answer. In *Breakfast on the Beach*, he shows how the Lord graciously chooses people who don't seem to be "disciple material" – plagued by doubts, trained in ways of thinking that are antithetical to the Lord's, and distracted by self-ambition – and then heals their waywardness through meditation on Scripture, communal accountability, and through learning to call upon God as "Father" in prayer. Written in a clear and engaging style as a kind of "story commentary," and imaginatively following Simon Peter through his first three years of discipleship, this book offers numerous helpful suggestions about how to understand the Gospels. But above all, a prayerful reading of the book is itself an entry into discipleship: an invitation to healing and reorientation to the Lord.

Jonathan Douglas Hicks
Missionary,
Society of Anglican Missionaries and Senders (SAMS-USA)
and New Zealand Church Missionary Society

What a delightful read! Johannes has made the story of Simon Peter's encounter with Jesus come to life in new and marvelous ways. Written in a narrative style of contemporary dramatic storytelling, you will be captivated from the first page as you explore the good news of Jesus afresh in *Breakfast on the Beach: The Development of Simon Peter*.

Rev. Charlie Holt
Founder and President, Bible Study Media

The *hakawati* (Arabic for "storyteller") in the Middle East captivates his hearers so they have no choice except to be back to listen to him day after another. Johannes is a skilful *hakawati*, who instead of telling a fictional story with imaginative characters and heroes, presents an amazing retelling of a real story. It is an authentic and genuine story focusing on a loving Hero through the eyes of another hero, Peter. If your passion is to enjoy Christ's company in Palestine in the first century then this book is indispensable. Bon Appetit as you dine with Jesus!

Rev. Riad Kassis, PhD
International Director, Scholars Programme, Langham Partnership

Van der Bijl wants to get under the skin of Simon Peter and into his sandals (p. xxvi). He offers us a wormhole that leads us into the first century and empowers us to see reality through the eyes of Simon Peter who discovered Jesus Christ and the path of conquering failure. As we go back in time, we smell the air, touch the fish, feel the weather, and understand the details of the biblical story as participants, not as observers. The book offers us a Theo-drama and invites us to be actors who continue the story of Simon Peter. It structures its progress through the metaphor of a seed that grows into a tree and paves the way for reproducing the blessings of the kingdom. The book is written as an exciting and inspirational story. It is pleasant and creative reading.

Rev. Yohanna Katanacho
Academic Dean, Nazareth Evangelical College, Israel

My friend and colleague Johannes van der Bijl has taken a simple concept from our training – How Jesus Discipled Simon Peter – and turned it into a work of art. He has expertly combined a harmony of the Gospels, a study in biblical backgrounds and a christological survey with a practical guide to how Jesus made disciples in everyday life – and all this in the beautiful historical narrative genre.

Johannes has also managed to immerse us in the socio-political, histori-cal, economic, and religious background to the Gospels, without making it feel like we are reading a Bible commentary or watching a history documen-tary. Johannes's writing style is simple, descriptive, humorous, and engaging. Ultimately, I love how all the characters in this story point to Jesus as a model and hero! This book will inspire you to enter our broken world as a broken vessel and make disciples who will transform the world with the good news that Jesus is restoring everything!

Jeremy Koeries
Country Leader, J-Life South Africa

This is a remarkable book: part novel, part biblical exegesis, part discipleship manual. Using his extensive knowledge of the geography, customs and tradi-tions of the time, the author has tried to get inside the heart and mind of Simon Peter as he tells his story from the time Jesus called him until the Ascension. *Breakfast on the Beach* will provoke the reader to further thought, discovery and discussion. It is a vivid and compelling read and is recommended for theologians and non-theologians alike.

The Most Rev. Dr. B. A. Kwashi
Bishop of Jos, Nigeria
General Secretary, Global Anglican Future Conference (GAFCON)

Johannes van der Bijl has written a biblically sensitive story that vividly por-trays in a cinematographic style the life and struggles of the Apostle Peter. In so doing, he touches the heart of the reader in such a way that we can identify with Peter's humanity and ever-strengthening and growing knowledge of Jesus as the Messiah.

Rev. Canon Dr. John A. Macdonald
Chair, Kenya Christian Education Partnership, an affiliate of ARDF
Vice-Chair, The Society of Anglican Missionaries and Senders (SAMS-USA)
Priest Associate, St. Martin's Anglican Church, Monroeville, Pennsylvania, USA

This is an insightful, biblically based and helpful compendium for mission, evangelism and discipling, especially in diverse contexts. Johannes van der Bijl captures big missiological concepts in an accessible way on the need to prepare the ground, to turn the soil, to ripen and sort out, to reap and to bear fruit. Read this book and be nurtured!

Thabo Makgoba, PhD
Archbishop and Primate,
Anglican Church in Southern Africa

I met Johannes van der Bijl and his wife, Louise, when they were missionaries in Ethiopia, and it has been my pleasure, early every morning for the past two months, to read carefully each page of *Breakfast on the Beach*. In this book, Dr. van der Bijl has carefully looked at the context of the words spoken by Jesus and has simplified the meaning of Jesus's message to Simon Peter – and us. Our respect for Simon Peter as the head of the church has prevented many of us from seeing his human side and how his faith progressively advanced until he became the person we know. Johannes shows us how Jesus's love and grace gradually changed Peter until he became Christ's strong witness. We, like Simon Peter, need the experience of the breakfast on the beach because we are human and we are all called to experience God's transforming power in us.

I have heard the gospel afresh as I read this book. It is a must-read for all. May God touch many lives through it!

The Rt. Rev. Francis M. Matui
Diocesan Bishop, Anglican Church of Kenya (ACK)
Diocese of Makueni

In this book, Johannes van der Bijl has brought Peter to life – the impetuous apostle also known for the mishap of denying his Lord. *Breakfast on the Beach* surfaces key biblical concepts and truth in a digestible and narrative form. The author is well aware the stories are irresistible to the human mind and are a powerful teaching tool. As a result, he fires your imagination and helps you find yourself in some sort of a mental movie. Most importantly, this book helps you not only follow Peter and his idiosyncrasies, but also reveals a Savior who is ever ready to leave the ninety-nine and go after the one lost sheep. You are sure to enjoy it.

Afrika Mhlophe
Pastor, Author, and Public Speaker

In this book, the Rev. Dr. Johannes van der Bijl is a wise mentor sharing his profound experience in his quest of the life of Simon Peter. In an attempt to get to know who Peter was, van der Bijl offers the reader a multidimensional view of the Scriptures. He helps us explore theological principles and cultural practices as well as archaeological probabilities. The book offers a message to all church leaders on how we can bring back those who might have failed to fulfil their call. As ministers, it is our responsibility to meet our fellow ministers at the point of their failure and provide necessary support to restore them back. If you are a church leader, consider reading this book once a year for the rest of your life.

Vicente Msosa
Bishop, Diocese of Niassa, Mozambique

Breakfast on the Beach by Johannes van der Bijl will be an invaluable resource for ministers (pastors, missionaries and lay leaders). It is an incredible treasure – a must-have for theologians, Bible schools and homeschoolers. This is more than just a book: it is wisdom distilled on Bible-rooted expositions. It reveals truths gleaned from many years of understanding the Bible. Van der Bijl has produced a much-needed resource for the Christian church today.

Ven. Lasarus Ngube
Archdeacon of Walvis Bay, Namibia

Breakfast on the Beach is a delightful read! The Rev. Dr. Johannes van der Bijl brings the story of the Apostle Simon Peter to life through his creative and winsome writing style. The reader easily begins to picture the scene and the characters, to hear the dialogue and envision the interaction of those present in these first-century encounters with Jesus, the Messiah. This book helps those who can't relate to biblical characters as the real flesh and blood humans that they were. *Breakfast on the Beach* helps the reader to enter the story so that the story of repentance, redemption and revival can enter the reader!

Jenny Noyes
Executive Director, New Wineskins Missionary Network
Global Mission Initiative Leader, Anglican Church in North America

Everyone loves Peter, often getting it wrong, but always trying his best for Jesus. Who better to provide the narrative focus for *Breakfast on the Beach*, an imaginative retelling of his-story. In 1986 Gerd Theissen introduced many of us to narrative theology as an accessible route into complex faith issues in *The Shadow of the Galilean*, and here van der Bijl picks up that tradition – always engaging, full of surprises, at times speculative, but deeply rooted in theological and historical research. Read it as a story, read it as theology, read it as a call to faith – it is all of these.

Rev. Mark Oxbrow
Director, Guided Study Programme,
Oxford Centre for Mission Studies, UK

Peter is one of the most identifiable characters in the Bible. In *Breakfast on the Beach*, Johannes van der Bijl uses his sanctified imagination to open up to us the person of Peter. While remaining true to the biblical text, we are introduced to the disciple in a new light. In one book, van der Bijl is able to craft a personally accessible commentary on the person and work of Jesus through the eyes of Peter. It is a compelling work because it does what all Christian books should do – point us to Jesus.

The Very Rev. Andrew C. Pearson, Jr.
Cathedral Church of the Advent, Birmingham, Alabama, USA

I have always enjoyed listening to Johannes as he expounds Scripture. He manages to bring it alive and enthrall me with his knowledge. Reading *Breakfast on the Beach* has been no exception. Simon Peter and the disciples have become as real to me as my colleagues are today. I feel as if I have lived and learned with them, albeit we are separated by two-thousand years of history. Such is the power of Johannes's storytelling and his carefully researched account of the life and growth in faith of Simon Peter. I commend this book to you. Read it and become as enthralled in it as I was.

The Rt. Rev. Luke Pretorius
Bishop, Diocese of St. Mark the Evangelist,
Anglican Church of Southern Africa

This is the wonderful story of the Gospels told by Dr. van der Bijl as he follows Jesus's life and ministry through Peter's eyes. This book is a picture full of colours and shades bringing together the Old Testament prophecies and "miracles, parables, and teachings of Jesus." There are encounters with the disciples every day from the call of Peter until Jesus's ascension. As we read the story of the gospel, one cannot fail to notice the spiritual depth, and the scholarly and academic ability. I recommend this wonderful book for preachers and those who want to meditate and live Jesus's story. Thank you Rev. Johannes for your insights which are a result of many years of meditation and preaching the good news of our Lord. I pray that this book will be a blessing to many.

The Rt. Rev. Samy Fawzy Shehata, DTh
Bishop of Egypt and Area Bishop of North Africa
Dean, Alexandria School of Theology, Egypt

Johannes van der Bijl has written a good story of the most significant and exciting succession of events that ever took place in this world. *Breakfast on the Beach* is a retelling of the story of the Man who turned out to be the God-Man, seen through the eyes of one who witnessed the whole thing – whose life was transformed by what he witnessed, and who went on to become the first leader of the Christian community. Readable, exciting, believable, refreshing – the author has given us something precious: a read which raises and answers questions, and leaves some for us to think about ourselves. Clearly, this is the work of one who has pondered deeply every part of Jesus's story.

David Seccombe, PhD
Former Principal,
George Whitefield College, Cape Town, South Africa

This book describes the life of Jesus through the eyes of Peter. With the author's serious research and storytelling ability, the life, words, and works of Jesus come alive through Peter. Van der Bijl's interaction with the Old Testament background in many areas of the story is particularly helpful. He also understands the social life of the first century. The interaction of Peter with his brother Andrew and other disciples comes alive in this retelling, and the description of stories, for example, with Peter and his wife, helps us understand the context of some incidents.

In the postmodern era, readers like to read stories. *Breakfast on the Beach* can help not only many young believers to know Jesus, but also mature Christians. With the narratives, it is definitely appealing to Asian readers as we value storytelling.

Joseph Shao, PhD
President Emeritus, Biblical Seminary of the Philippines
4th General Secretary, Asia Theological Association

The story of Peter reflects our own journey of faith. *Breakfast on the Beach* richly engages us as first-hand observers of this very human disciple and encourages us to open our eyes and see the work of Jesus around us. Dr. van der Bijl's vivid retelling of the gospel story shows deep understanding of the social, cultural, and political realities of the times, while guiding us to profound pastoral meditation on the text. A delightful and highly recommended read for all concerned to grow in their walk with Christ.

Perry Shaw, EdD
Researcher in Residence, Morling College
Author, *Transforming Theological Education*

The passion of my life has been to fully understand the "real Jesus" who walked on this earth. We are told over forty times to "walk as he walked," "do what he did," and follow "his pattern." In this book, Johannes van der Bijl has done an amazing job of looking at Jesus through the eyes of Peter and capturing the chronology of Jesus's life. I'd encourage you to read it with an open Bible, or better yet, an open harmony of the gospels, to fully capture the flow of Christ's life and the development of Peter's growing relationship with Jesus. You will enjoy the fresh look at Jesus's life through Peter's eyes. Fresh, inspiring, and full of unique insights – I highly commend this book to you.

Dann Spader, DMin
Founder, Sonlife Ministries and Concentric
Author, *4 Chair Discipling* and *Walk Like Jesus*

In this very engaging book, Johannes van der Bijl draws on years of experience of helping people live as disciples of Jesus in the face of daily challenges. He brings the gospel accounts of Simon Peter to life in a vivid way that provides numerous insights into what it meant for him to follow Jesus. Anyone who wants to follow Jesus today, and help others on that path as well, will find plenty of inspiration in *Breakfast on the Beach*. Do read it and recommend it to others.

Justyn Terry, PhD
Vice Principal and Academic Dean,
Wycliffe Hall, Oxford, UK

Breakfast on the Beach by Johannes van der Bijl is nonpareil for several reasons. It is on the one hand a fresh and accessible telling of Peter's story, but it engages the reader with a multidimensional exploration of what Peter may have felt and thought as he engaged Jesus day by day. Using his skills as both a fabulous artist and a good contextual exegete, van der Bijl dares to dive deeply into the character of Peter and paints an account that is both imaginative and tightly tethered to the biblical text. When recounting Jesus's encounter with the Pharisees regarding God's heart for mercy and not sacrifice, he expounds on the moment: "Had the birds stopped singing? There was an awe-filled silence. Simon produced enough saliva to swallow the dry kernels. Clearly, the Pharisees were dumbstruck" (p. 44). Van der Bijl, in a similar fashion, draws out the intense emotions when Peter prayed at the cross: "It felt like there were fingers around his throat . . . pressing harder and harder. His hands were cold and clammy. He tried in vain to regulate his breathing. He clenched his fists, digging his nails into his palms, trying to deal with the rising sense of panic" (p. 240).

This book draws the reader into the journey of the fisherman who questions his vocational competence as a fisherman at the outset and then evolves into a man focused and passionate in his pursuit of the mission bestowed upon him by his Master. This book is a gem.

The Very Rev. Henry Laurie Thompson III, DMin
Dean, President, and Associate Professor of Liturgical Studies,
Trinity School for Ministry, Ambridge, Pennsylvania, USA

I like to read the Bible and "walk in" the story and feel as much as possible what those characters felt and thus better understand the reality and message of each passage. Whenever I preach, I try to get people to do the same. *Breakfast on the Beach* has increased my perception of the attentive and impulsive gaze of Simon Peter, apostle of Jesus. I can visualize the events much easier now due to the deeply creative mind of the Rev. Dr. van der Bijl, to whom I am grateful.

The Most Rev. Miguel Uchoa
Bishop of the Diocese of Recife
Archbishop and Primate of The Anglican Church in Brazil

Jesus always made clear the importance of the church to be forming disciples . . . but life often imposes challenges which may lead many disciples to fail! The Rev. Dr. Johannes van der Bijl, with great sensibility, presents us this powerful tool in order to assist all of us in a restoration of injured disciples. Enjoy your *breakfast on the beach* – enjoy this banquet!

Rev. Geison Vasconcellos
Secretary General, Anglican Church in Brazil

Join in the journey of Simon Peter – with all his doubts and failings – in encountering Jesus. As Jesus draws Peter with restorative love, you too will be attracted through the power of this fresh, biblically grounded narrative. Through meticulous and sound biblical research, the Rev. Dr. Johannes van der Bijl fleshes out the story of Simon Peter so that as his walk comes alive on these pages, the reader is introduced to Jesus anew in a profound, heart-changing manner.

Breakfast on the Beach tells Simon Peter's story with passion and affability. As Peter's life is slowly changed through his time with Jesus, may others also partake in this transformative promise of loving encounter and extreme forgiveness. Drawing from the entirety of the biblical narrative, readers are introduced to Jesus through the eyes of the simple fisherman Simon Peter. In this journey of questioning and discovery as well as failure and restoration all may witness the deep, deep love of Jesus.

This book brought me to tears and laughter – occasionally concurrently! Jesus comes alive through Simon Peter's eyes!

Stewart Wicker
President and Mission Director,
Society of Anglican Missionaries and Senders (SAMS) USA

Simon Peter. There is hardly a more compelling and beloved character. Compelling and beloved particularly because he is one with whom it is easy to identify. You hold in your hands a story. This is a story of Jesus transforming and restoring the life of Peter, but overarching is Jesus. His love. His grace. His redeeming and restorative work. This is a story that shows how Jesus discipled his followers. A story that gives us a pattern to follow as we seek to make followers of Jesus.

I gladly commend this book to you because I gladly commend the author. Johannes has given his life to his Lord and following his Lord's leading, he has made disciples in countries and cultures around the world. May this book encourage you in your faith and equip you to go and make disciples.

The Rt. Rev. Steve Wood
Diocese of the Carolinas, USA

Breakfast on the Beach: The Development of Simon Peter weaves a wonderfully relatable story around the life of Simon Peter and his journey with Christ. But perhaps the book's greatest accomplishment is how it aptly explores Peter's character and mind, his inner and external conflicts, weaknesses and strengths – a true projection of humanness. This is an easy-to-read book for everyone who desires a visually captivating story with a unique glimpse into one of the Bible's most well-known personalities. You won't be surprised to find yourself endeared to Peter and drawn closer to Jesus Christ.

Bellah Zulu
Lusaka-Based Zambian Journalist and Communications Expert

Breakfast on the Beach

The Development of Simon Peter

Langham

PREACHING RESOURCES

Breakfast on the Beach

The Development of Simon Peter

Johannes W. H. van der Bijl

Langham

PREACHING RESOURCES

© 2021 Johannes W. H. van der Bijl

Published 2021 by Langham Preaching Resources
An imprint of Langham Publishing
www.langhampublishing.org

Langham Publishing and its imprints are a ministry of Langham Partnership

Langham Partnership
PO Box 296, Carlisle, Cumbria, CA3 9WZ, UK
www.langham.org

Isbns:
978-1-83973-207-2 Print
978-1-83973-529-5 Epub
978-1-83973-530-1 Mobi
978-1-83973-531-8 PDF

All Scripture translations in this work are the author's own and are based on the Nestle-Aland Greek text and William Robertson Nicoll, *The Expositor's Greek Testament*. Grand Rapids: Eerdmans, 1990..

British Library Cataloguing-in-Publication Data
A catalogue record for this book is available from the British Library

ISBN: 978-1-83973-207-2

Cover & Book Design: projectluz.com

To Louise,
my dearly beloved wife and my life partner on so many levels.
Like Jesus, you looked past the rough exterior of this sinful man
and saw the fisher of people God would make him.

Contents

Part IV: Reproduction and Replacement

Foreword

It is a great joy to introduce this remarkable book of the restoration of the Apostle Peter. Through this book my friend, the Rev. Dr. Johannes van der Bijl, who is also a gifted artist, paints for us a beautiful picture that embodies the love and the grace of our Lord Jesus Christ as he restores Peter on the beach.

This is a very inspirational book that teaches all church leaders how we can restore others who have failed to fulfill their call. Indeed, we need to meet our fellow ministers at the point of their failure and provide what they failed to understand. Indeed, this is a must-read book.

Johannes van der Bijl helps us to see how we can rekindle the agape love in a person by agape loving the person.

I thank God for Johannes and his wife Louise who love the Lord so much and have served him in a great way in many countries.

The Most Rev. Dr. Mouneer Hanna Anis
Archbishop of the Episcopal/Anglican Province of Alexandria
Diocesan Bishop of Egypt

Preface

Ever since I first met Jesus, it has been my heart's desire to make him known to others in ways that would make him more accessible and approachable. My experience at the time of my conversion was that all too often the church appeared to be a vehicle of morality as if Jesus was little more than another philosopher or lawgiver.

As I searched the Scriptures, I struggled with many personal questions and often wondered what the people portrayed in the pages must have been thinking at the time. There is such a gulf between my own cultural background and that of the biblical characters, that often their actions or reactions baffled or confused me. And Jesus was no exception. I could not understand why he seemed to go out of his way to antagonize these people called Pharisees, Sadducees, scribes, and Herodians as they appeared in the New Testament without explanation as to their origins or beliefs. It took me years to understand that there was a difference between their oral law, or "the tradition of the elders," and the Torah. With the advent of study Bibles, much has been unravelled in my mind, but the explanations were in notes at the bottom of the pages, or in boxes under various subject headings, and not in the text itself. As such, in the text, the person of Jesus continued to be largely veiled for me behind enigmatic idioms and riddles and allusions to cultural and religious practices of which I knew little. I still wanted a more three-dimensional Jesus than the one I read about on the pages.

Having worked with people from cultures and backgrounds very different from my own, ever since my personal conversion to Christianity, I began to explore methods of contextualization, reading books and articles and listening to various lectures on the subject. It was while on this adventure that I began to understand the true value of storytelling. Drawing people in, to experience as best they could, the realities of the life of the person of Jesus, whom I was seeking to introduce to them, often helped to produce a more positive response.

After I was asked to start a Theological College in Gambela, Ethiopia, I decided to put together a chronological PowerPoint presentation of the whole of the Bible in pictures and stories, including the Intertestamental Period. My aim was to make events and places come alive to those who had a radically different worldview and framework in which to make sense of the very foreign concepts of ancient Israel. Unfortunately, I only got to teach the Intertestamental Period, but that was enough to encourage me to find ways to use pictures and stories to convey the realities in the Scriptures to people in very different situations in life. Stories are such universally accepted and cherished vehicles of truth. So, I began a rather long journey of asking questions as I put together the stories of the Scriptures. Simple questions such as what was it like to live in that area, what was the climate like, what did people wear and why, and what did they understand about God in the thick of their daily grind?

In reading the Gospels, Jesus and his disciples remind me, in so many ways, of my times in academic settings with professors and, especially, students, debating and discussing what they were learning. And yet, in the Gospels the disciples are largely silent. I was left wondering what they were thinking and talking about when Jesus began to teach things that were hard to understand, much less accept and apply. Here and there we are told that they did not yet understand, but their characters remain largely flat and distant. If we could just explore their confused and conflicting thoughts and discussions in the light of what we know about the time, the culture, the oral law, and the like, perhaps they could help us come to terms with our own puzzlements.

After leaving Ethiopia, Louise and I began to work alongside an organization by the name of J-Life Africa in training both clergy and lay folk alike in the methods of Jesus as far as the making of disciples is concerned. Part of the first module uses Simon Peter as an illustration of how this method worked in the life of the most rounded disciple in the Gospels. I began to dig deeper and to add my own discoveries to the teaching and soon trainees and other trainers, and the J-Life leaders themselves, were encouraging me to write a book about the development of Simon Peter as a disciple.

And so, I began to research the life of Simon Peter as much as I could, to try to get a grip on who this man was in an attempt to get under his skin, or into his sandals, as it were. As good Jews, the disciples no doubt knew what we call the Old Testament well, and as followers of a first-century rabbi, these Scriptures would no doubt have been foundational to their learning and apprenticeship. They would also have known parts of the oral law, as well as the social practices of those they lived with from day to day, the Samaritans, the Greeks, the Romans, the Hellenists and others. Growing up and living in Galilee, they would have read Hebrew, and spoken Aramaic, Greek, and perhaps even a little Latin. And they lived in a certain part of the globe with a particular climate and topography, that must have had an effect on their travels.

Going to Israel opened up the Scriptures in ways not possible before. In spite of the fact that two thousand years lay between me and that land of the Bible, I was able to picture more or less what they must have seen, the mountains they must have crossed, the distances between towns and villages, and I began to appreciate the time it must have taken to move from one location to another.

Part of this book is my attempt to offer the reader a glimpse of what I was blessed to have learned and viewed myself. Using the thoughts of Simon Peter and the other disciples has helped me explore theological principles, cultural practices, archaeological probabilities, and geological practicalities or impracticalities, without making the book sound like a commentary.

It is my prayer that this book will offer a multidimensional view of the Scriptures to the readers, written from the perspective of an ordinary individual who, like so many of us, still struggles to come to grips with the reality of the person of Jesus. It is my hope to transport the readers back in time, by describing the cultural and religious realities of the day, and by providing vivid portraits of the landscape and climate so foreign to many of us today. I flatter myself to think that perhaps my rough sketches may provide others with material to make their own retelling of the story of Jesus come to life in ways that will captivate their listeners.

Ultimately, it is my deepest desire that people come to fall hopelessly and entirely in love with Jesus.

Johannes van der Bijl
Windy Corner
Villiersdorp, South Africa

Acknowledgements

Where does one begin to acknowledge the many people, places, books, articles, seminars, classes, podcasts, sermons, Sunday School lessons, and so many other things that have shaped my present understanding of who Jesus is, and what that means to me as one of his children and followers? When I first encountered Jesus through the necessary intervention of a dear childhood friend, I knew virtually nothing about him as a person, let alone as God incarnate. But I was told to read the Scriptures on a regular basis and, as an avid reader, especially of the English classics, I dived in and read it over and over again as one would read a novel. But I must confess that if God had not brought certain key people into my life, I would have continued to stumble along in my ignorance. These key people taught me the value of reading the Scriptures as one story, told through the struggles and triumphs of everyday people like me.

While these key people are too many to mention here by name, three men have played a monumental role in helping me see the Bible as a single cosmic drama in which the Creator personally interacts with his creatures in a bid to save them from their own devastatingly bad choices. The first is my former Hebrew and Old Testament professor from George Whitefield College and current Director of the Kirby Laing Institute for Christian Ethics, The Rev. Dr. Craig G. Bartholomew; the second is the late Rev. Dr. Kenneth Bailey, and the third is an Old Testament scholar and current Ministry Director for Langham Partnership, the Rev. Dr. Christopher J. H. Wright.

Then there are the many friends that helped me write, check, edit, rewrite, and publish this book – too many to mention by name. I am grateful to each and every one of you.

I also wish to acknowledge my debt of gratitude to my wife, Louise, our two sons, Hanno and Heyns, their wonderful wives, Lauren and Hanna, and our adorable grandchildren, Jeremiah, Rophe, Amelia, Addy, and Everett, as they have walked most of this journey with me.

To God, Father, Son, and Holy Spirit,
my rock, my light, my life,
be all glory, and honour, dominion, and power,
both now and forever.
Amen

Preamble

Blisters. He actually had blisters on both his hands. It had been a long time since he had handled the nets. Too long. His body ached all over. In the humid predawn, rivulets of sweat streamed down and collected in little pools at his feet in spite of the fact that he had stripped earlier on in the evening. Had he lost it? Had he lost the ability to catch fish? When he was younger, he could fish all night long and then still stay up until his nets were washed and mended. But what was he thinking? He was still young . . . it was just over three years ago that he had left his nets to follow . . . no, he didn't want to think about that. It was too fresh . . . too painful. It just deepened his sense of failure . . . that he did not measure up to his own expectations, not to mention the expectations of others, for that matter. And he thought he knew himself so well! How could he have been so mistaken? He was once so sure of himself . . . now he only had doubts and confusion.

Simon looked out over the lake. It was still fairly dark, but he could see the shoreline. The lake always brought back memories . . . myriads of memories, some good, some not so good. Like the memory of one night in particular . . . that night when he called him to come to him on the water. At first there was nothing but certainty . . . he didn't even think twice. Why did he take his eyes off him? Why did he look down? Maybe he ought to have walked away then and saved himself the humiliation of . . . no, he was not going there. He was sure that if he thought about this more recent awful night he would sink into darkness and never resurface.

He had once been so sure . . . so sure of everything he did . . . but now? Now he couldn't even catch a single fish. Failure. Nothing but a failure.

What was that sound? Was someone shouting to them? Yes, there was a voice coming from the far shore. He could just see the outline of a man standing on the beach. The others gathered around Simon and strained to hear what the man was saying. "Children, have you caught any fish?" The voice sounded familiar . . . was it one of their regular customers?

"No," they shouted back.

Another failure, Simon thought . . . another disappointment. What kind of a fisherman can't catch a single fish?

What was that? Did the stranger tell them they should cast their nets on the right-hand side of the boat? Yes. That's exactly what he had said. "Then you will catch some," he said. Really? Simon looked at the water . . . he couldn't see anything moving beneath the surface. Aside from that, the sun was about to crest the mountain . . . it was getting too late for a catch. But a certain resignation overcame him. Why argue? He was so tired . . . tired of trying to prove himself . . . tired of always trying to be right . . . tired of always trying to be better. Just do what the man says. Besides, what did he have to lose?

And then . . . the nets had hardly sunk down when the water began to bubble and swirl. Fish! Lots and lots of fish! Instinct kicked in and Simon began to pull at the ropes. As they emptied the net into the boat, fish flapped furiously all around him, drowning in oxygen. Thinking back later, Simon could not quite recall when it dawned on him that something about this event felt ever so familiar . . . as if this had happened before. And then he heard John say, "Simon, it is the Lord!"

The Lord? The Lord! Simon suddenly felt naked . . . exposed. That voice! In some sense, Simon felt that the voice was indirectly calling out to him. "Simon, where are you? Simon, what are you doing here?" Simon was the one who had tried to convince the others to return to their old vocations. There was nowhere to hide. This awkward meeting was unavoidable. He felt trapped . . . and yet . . . he felt elated as well. Yes, elated and somehow free . . . he had already hit the bottom of the deepest pit in his life. What could be worse than that? He threw on his outer garment, plunged into the sea, and swam to the shore where Jesus was waiting for him.

Simon stumbled out of the water and straight into the arms of his Lord. For a moment he simply clung to Jesus since he was completely out of breath after the swim. The others were still struggling with the fish-laden nets.

There was already a fish on the fire along with a piece of bread. How did he . . . where did he . . . ? Simon thought.

"Simon, bring some of the fish you have just caught," Jesus said.

The fish he had caught? If it wasn't for Jesus, he would still have had an empty net!

He climbed back into the boat to help drag the net to shore. It was full of fish . . . one hundred and fifty-three in total. But astoundingly . . . the net was not torn or damaged.

"Come," Jesus called to them from near the charcoal fire, "let's have breakfast."

Breakfast on the beach? How wonderful. I'm famished, Simon thought. He did not yet know that it would be a breakfast that would change his life completely.

Part I

Preparation and Planting

"I will turn the soil and prepare it with compost."
Luke 13:8

1

Tilling and Sowing

He was tired. Ever since Andrew and John had left to look into the ministry of John the Baptizer, he and his partners, Zebedee and his other son, James, had worked long and hard. They even had to employ extra hired hands to help with the sorting, salting, and drying of the fish. Still, he did not regret giving his brother leave to go. So many unanswered questions hung in the air . . . was John the Messiah? Was this the moment they had longed for all their lives . . . dreamed about . . . yearned for? Liberty! The Roman stranglehold was tightening around the throat of the nation and many were crying out to God for a saviour . . . a deliverer like Moses . . . a warrior like the great Gideon . . . but while there had been a few promising individuals, the Romans had crushed them like snails between the thumb and forefinger.

Simon heard himself sigh. Was he despondent? Life sometimes seemed so endlessly pointless, like a wheel simply turning around and around until, one day, it would abruptly stop. And what would all the toil and the struggle amount to in the end? As the suffering sage once said, "Man is born to trouble as surely as sparks fly upward."[1] So what if he owned a boat and had a big compound? He wondered what his parents would have thought had they witnessed his apparent success. Would they be proud of their son? He worked so hard . . . but so much of what he earned was eaten up by Roman taxation. Every fish . . . a different levy for each kind . . . it was all so tiresome. The tax-collectors waited on the harbour walls like vultures. Scavengers, the lot of them! And yet, there was one who seemed to be fair. Simon always tried to steer to where Levi, or Matthew as some called him, had set up his booth. Although he was still a collaborator with the Roman scum, somehow this man seemed to have a conscience.

---

1. Job 5:7.

"Oh, dear Lord," Simon silently prayed. "Is there no mercy, no balm for the weary and the downtrodden? Have you abandoned us forever? Have you rejected us? Forgotten your people? Why is your anger so intense? Why . . ."

"Simon!" Someone was calling his name. "Simon!" He looked up. Andrew? Yes, it was Andrew. He watched as his younger brother came bounding toward him. Fear suddenly clutched at his heart. What had happened? Was someone sick? Had someone died? Was there trouble in Israel? But no, Andrew's voice did not sound like he bore bad news . . . it was urgent and yet carried a note of joy. "Simon!" Now Andrew was waving frantically and smiling. "Simon! Brother! We have found the Messiah!"

The messiah? Another one? Another radical who would raise the hopes of Israel only to have them dashed against the seemingly immovable Roman monolith. His initial joy at seeing his brother suddenly changed. What did he feel? . . . Was it unbelief? Fear? Cynicism? Irritation?

"Simon!" Andrew fell into his brother's open arms. He was laughing even though he was totally out of breath, like an athlete who had just won a marathon. Simon untangled himself, held his brother at arm's length, and looked into his eyes. They were filled with hope.

Oh, Andrew, Simon thought, have you been tricked into believing yet another zealous madman? Images of so many young men flashed through his mind . . . once they too had been filled with the same fervent hope in a self-proclaimed messiah figure, but they had been slaughtered by their oppressors, leaving behind only gut-wrenching sorrow and despair.

"John, the Baptizer? He is the Messiah?" Simon enquired.

Andrew's smile melted into a look of amazement. "John? No! No, he himself told us that he was not the Messiah. In fact, he made it quite clear that he was only a messenger preparing us for one who was far greater than he. One who was to come after him. He said that he wasn't even worthy to tie the sandals of this man."

"Ah," Simon said, turning away slightly from his brother and fiddling with the nets absentmindedly, "this must be an important man indeed, if the great John the Baptizer would stoop lower than the lowliest slave."

Andrew heard the scepticism. In fact, he could feel it . . . smell it. Its stench eclipsed that of the pungent rotting fish entrails that permeated the air around the harbour. What had he expected? He knew how hard Simon had worked to provide for them, to drag them out of the abject poverty of their youth. In some ways, Simon had been more like a father to him than a brother since their parents had died.[2] But the years had taken their toll and Simon had grown increasingly distant and quiet. It was as if the fiery dreams of his youth had slowly been extinguished. How could he convince Simon that this man was different? Different from the many others whose defeat had blurred the vision they once had.

Had they not left Bethsaida because of its godlessness? The Romans had all but taken over the town, building their baths and their places of idol worship. Had they not come to Capernaum because they believed that there was more to life than what they had witnessed thus far? True, they were not completely free from bondage and oppression, and Capernaum appeared to be as ungodly as Bethsaida, but at least they had the synagogue and their friends and their family . . . and their livelihood . . . and the rather large compound they shared with Simon's in-laws and their partners. Things were not altogether bleak.[3] Andrew gazed at his brother's shoulders. He had not noticed before how stooped Simon had become. And now . . . now it seemed that his joy was adding another heavy burden on his brother.

But Andrew could not contain the conviction that bubbled up inside him like a spring after a good downpour of rain. "Simon . . . Simon, just come and see. Come with me and just . . . just meet him. I told him all about you. I told him all about your bravery and your strength and how you have carried our family on your shoulders for so many years."

Suddenly, there were tears in Andrew's eyes. His gratitude for his brother's many sacrifices rose from the depths of his being and broke out in a quickly stifled sob. Andrew wasn't an emotional person normally, but he was tired, and his guard was down. Besides, he had been thinking about their parents. What would they have thought about their sons had they still been alive?

"I told him how your positive outlook kept us going even through the darkest of our storms. I told him how pugnaciously persistent you are and

---

2. Cf. Markus Bockmuehl, *Simon Peter in Scripture and Memory* (Grand Rapids, MI: Baker Academic, 2012), 168.

3. If the archaeologists are correct about the large insula in Capernaum being Simon and Andrew's home (cf. Mark 1:29), then he must have been a fairly astute businessman. It seems probable that this home was occupied by several families: Peter, his wife and her parent(s), Andrew, and perhaps the Zebedee family including James and John as they were partners (Luke 5:10). Cf. also, Vassilios Tzaferis, "Capernaum," *New Encyclopedia of Archeological Excavations in the Holy Land* 1:292. https://www.google.com/url?sa=t&rct=j&q=&esrc=s&source=web&cd=5&cad=rja&uact=8&ved=2ahUKEwiil7v4h4jnAhXSgVwKHfxCCfUQFjAEegQIBRAB&url=https%3A%2F%2Fwww.academia.edu%2F15651558%2FCapernaum_Village_of_Nahum_from_Hellenistic_to_Byzantine_Times&usg=AOvVaw0OnpLxFhDgaN1hX_ZpVkkM, and https://en.wikipedia.org/wiki/Capernaum.

how firm you have remained in spite of it all. What a sure foundation, what a steadfast rock, you have been to us."

Simon turned to him, his mouth slightly ajar as he tried to process Andrew's words. Was this what he meant to his brother? A sure foundation? A rock? How then could he snuff out the burning wick just because he was despondent? No, that would be wrong . . . almost unforgiveable.

"Simon," Andrew pleaded, "Simon, just come and see for yourself."

The big fisherman sighed. "Alright, Andrew. I will come and see this man. But you have not told me his name."

"His name is Jesus."

"Jesus! Well, he certainly has a good name for a messiah . . . deliverer, rescuer! Where is he?"

"He is where I left him. Close to Bethany . . . that is, Bethany beyond the Jordan."

"Bethany? But Andrew, that is a three-day journey!"

Andrew grinned. "Two, if you run and walk fast."

Simon heard himself sigh yet again. What was the matter with him? He sighed more than an old grandmother these days! "Alright, Andrew. Let me speak to Zebedee and make sure that he will be willing and able to continue in my – in our – absence."[4] He smiled at his younger brother. How he loved him! How he wanted to see him happy!

"You can go home and greet everyone first. Then eat and wash . . . and pack some provisions too!" But Andrew was already gone, loping along like an ungainly camel . . . where did he get those long legs from?

Simon walked over to speak to Zebedee. He would have to choose his words carefully and wisely. Like him, Zebedee had seen his fair share of disasters. But Simon worried needlessly. As he approached his partner's boat, he heard the shrill excited voice of John, Zebedee's younger son, the brother of James . . . the one who had gone with Andrew to meet with the Baptizer. Would that boy's voice never break? "We have found the Messiah!" John squeaked like an overexcited girl. When their eyes met, Simon knew Zebedee would understand. That's what fathers do.

---

4. This is speculation on my part. In Mark 1:21–22 we are told that James and John were with their father, Zebedee, when Jesus called them to follow him. However, Luke 5:7 and 10 indicates that James and John were also fishing partners with Simon and Andrew. As both sets of partners had their own boats in this passage, I am assuming that Zebedee was part of the partnership. Another possible scenario is that James and John became partners with Simon after the initial call, but this seems unlikely for various reasons. It also seems probable that the business continued after the two sets of brothers left to follow Jesus as it appears to have been relatively easy for them to pick up where they had left off after the resurrection, cf. John 21:1–3.

* * *

"So, tell me more about this remarkable encounter." Simon and Andrew had been walking in silence for a while now. They had skirted around the western side of the Sea of Galilee, avoiding Magdala and Tiberius, choosing rather to walk along the more arid and less populated Jordan valley. For Simon, it had been difficult to leave his wife and his extended family. He knew their thoughts . . . they too were weary. But deep inside, everyone secretly longed for release . . . for freedom . . . for liberty. There had been so many unspoken prayers in their home that morning. God had heard their ancestors before . . . why not now? Why not through this man? Dear merciful God, let it be true. Simon's wife had fussed over them, packing far too much food for the journey, but also not forgetting to give Simon a long list of the provisions he was to bring home from Judea.

"Well," Andrew said, "there we were, on the banks of the river Jordan, when suddenly John the Baptizer looked up at this man walking past . . . I wish I could describe the look on the Baptizer's face . . . it was certain . . . it was clear. 'Look,' he almost shouted, 'there is the Lamb of God!' This wasn't the first time the Baptizer had mentioned the Lamb of God . . . the first time he added that the Lamb had come to take away the sins of the world. I don't know why it took us so long to respond." Andrew had begun to talk faster, and his voice had risen an octave. "Brother, you know what John meant? He was talking about the Passover! The Exodus! The Conquest! And he was speaking right there, close to Jericho where Joshua crossed over the Jordan to take the Promised Land! Close to where they celebrated the Passover when their wilderness wanderings were over. The Lamb . . . dear brother . . . John called the man the Lamb. The spotless Lamb whose blood covered our doorposts so that the angel of death would pass us by. The Lamb slaughtered before our release from bondage . . . the Lamb slaughtered before the Conquest!"

Simon attempted to stifle a laugh but failed. "Yes, dear brother, I know the meaning of the Passover lamb. I preside over the ceremony every year, remember?"

Andrew looked embarrassed, but just for a moment. Then the flames of excitement shone in his eyes once more and he plunged into another monologue. "Yes, the lamb of Passover . . . but this man, the Baptizer said, is the Lamb of God who takes away the sin of the world! This is far greater than the exodus of our ancestors! John had told us that he had seen God's Holy Spirit descend on the man like a . . . like a bird . . . like a dove . . . yes, a dove . . . like the Spirit hovering over creation in the beginning. Brother, you know some of the first words we learned from the holy Scriptures were that the 'Spirit of

God was hovering over the face of the deep.'" He looked at Simon expectantly. "You know the words, brother?" Simon snorted indicating that his brother ought to continue the story and avoid the endless theological speculations and arguments that were so rife among the Pharisees and Scribes. "But then there was also a dove after the great flood, remember? Not that Noah's dove was the Spirit, but . . . it just made me think of it, you know? Water, new life . . . something like a bird."

"Andrew, stop! Please! What did John the Baptizer say?"

"Oh . . . oh, yes . . . well, he said that the Spirit descended on this man as he came up out of the waters of baptism. But that was not all, brother! God had told him beforehand that the one on whom the Spirit rested would be the one who would baptize with the Holy Spirit!"

"Baptize with the Holy Spirit! What does that mean?"

For a moment it seemed as if Andrew was lost for words, but then he said, "I don't know . . . but brother, surely it must mean that there would be something . . . something new . . . something great . . . something like a new creation . . ."

"Andrew, please. Stick to the story. What did John say next?"

"Well, he said that there was a voice from heaven."

"A voice?"

"Yes. God's voice. And God said something like, 'This is my dearly loved Son, in whom I am well pleased.' At first John thought it was just thunder, but there were no clouds in the sky . . . and the voice was far too clear."

"God's Son?"

"Yes . . . you know . . . like a king . . . like the Messiah. Simon! He *is* the Messiah! Don't you see?"

Simon sniffed loudly. "Go on." Was he ever going to get all the information out of his brother? Would it take three days . . . or two, considering the rate that he was being dragged along by Andrew.

"Well, then I . . . that is John[5] and I . . . we followed him. At some point he must have heard us or sensed that we were behind him, so he turned and asked us what we were looking for."

"And you said . . . ?"

"Well," Andrew blushed at this point, "I really didn't know what to say. So, I just asked him where he was staying."

"Well, that was very polite, even if a bit indirect. How did he respond?"

---

5. Most scholars assume that the other disciple was John.

"He was ever so gracious. He simply smiled and said, 'Come and see.' But there was an urgency about his statement, as if we hadn't a moment to lose . . . as if we had to heed him that very minute." Andrew fell silent, reliving that moment.

"So, you went?"

"Yes, and we talked and talked and talked . . . it seemed we talked for hours. We spoke about messianic expectations . . . about the prophecy that the Messiah would be born in Bethlehem, for one. This was important to us because clearly he was from Galilee. Then he told us he had been born in Bethlehem, but because of Herod, the family fled to Egypt. Later, on returning, they found out that Herod Archelaus was reigning in Judea, so they relocated to Nazareth. Interesting, don't you think? Nazareth. Didn't the prophet say that there would be a branch coming from the stump of Jesse?[6] But he also asked us questions . . . about our family and . . ."

"And you told him all about me?"

"Well . . . yes. Isn't that right? I mean, you really are my hero in so many ways and, besides, I wanted him to know that I come from a good, devout family." Andrew paused. "But then he let us ask him questions again."

At this point Andrew's chatter turned into almost incomprehensible babble. He talked so fast, Simon almost couldn't take it all in. He gave more reasons why Jesus met all the biblical requirements of the Messiah, and how he fulfilled all the prophecies.

"And so, I was . . . well, we were . . . we were convinced that this man was who John the Baptizer had said he was . . . that he was the Messiah!"

"And then you came to find me?" Simon smiled.

"I *ran* to find you." He paused for a moment, as if to muster courage to say what he wanted to say. "Brother, I . . ."

"It's alright Andrew. Just allow me to form my own opinion. Please. Promise me that."

"Alright, I promise, brother. Actually, all I want you to do is to come and see him. You will know the moment you meet him."

Would he? Simon wasn't so sure. Would this man be able to overcome the doubts that tormented him like a festering wound inside his soul? Would this light that he could clearly see in his brother's eyes dispel his own darkness? But he had given his word. He would come and see for himself. That much he could do.

---

6. Some speculate that the Hebrew word for branch "*netser*" used in Isaiah 11:1 is why Matthew said that it was prophesied that Jesus would be "called a Nazarene," cf. *Archeological Study Bible*, 1561, 1623.

2

First Impressions

There!" Andrew was pointing at a group of people talking with what some would call an unimpressive looking individual.[1] There was nothing unusual or outstanding or unique about this man. He looked like any other labourer. And yet the small huddle around him appeared to be mesmerized.

The two brothers stood at the fringe of the group waiting for an opportune moment to make their presence known. They didn't have to wait for long. Jesus turned around, acknowledged Andrew with a nod and a smile, but then he fixed his gaze on Simon. After what felt like an age he simply said, "So, you're Simon the son of John!" Suddenly Simon had the uncomfortable feeling of being exposed by this man's piercing gaze . . . like his heart lay open before him . . . as if all his desires were known to him . . . none of his secrets hidden. But then Jesus smiled and put his hand on Simon's shoulder. "But, in time, you shall be called Cephas."

Cephas! A rock! The was the same word Andrew had used to describe how he felt about his brother's dogged steadfastness during the lean, difficult years. His parents had named him after the great Simon Thassi, second son of Mattathias and brother of Judas Maccabeus. Clearly, they had hoped to see an end to the Roman occupation of their land in their lifetime, but they had not.[2] Now here was a man who seemed to indicate future greatness for their son: "You shall be called Cephas." Simon couldn't help but recall God's words to the Patriarch: "I am changing your name. It will no longer be Abram. Instead, you will be called Abraham, for you will be the father of many nations." And Jacob . . . Jacob's name was also changed. "From now on," God had said, "you will be called Israel, because you have fought with God and with men and have

---

1. Isaiah 53:2.

2. This is pure speculation on my part. But cf. Bockmuel, *Simon Peter in Scripture and Memory*, 21.

11

won." Cephas! Rock! There must be a reason why this man said he would be called by a different name . . . in time. What was it that he could see that Simon was unable to see for himself?

"Brother?" Andrew looked concerned. "Brother, are you well?"

"What? Yes. Yes, I am well. I was just lost in thought . . . a little distracted."

Andrew smiled. He knew that Simon too had felt the charisma of Jesus. That sense of urgency, that compulsion. They followed him to where he was staying.

Simon's mind was spinning. When the man had indicated that one day he would be called Cephas, the Rock, he, like Andrew, did not know what to say. He felt stupid. The least he could have said was "thank you," but it was as if he had been struck dumb. Those eyes! There was something about this man . . . that much he was willing to concede. But . . . the Messiah?

* * *

"Today, we must go to Galilee," Jesus announced.

What? But we just got here, Simon thought. He had done some hasty bargaining with a few sellers in the area, but he had not yet been able to locate some of the items his wife had wanted. The small group was already moving, however, so he too headed in the same direction. He would explain the situation to his wife later.

He didn't say much along the way . . . his mind was too preoccupied. "Cephas. Rock . . . what could that mean?"

As they came closer to Galilee, Simon saw a familiar face in the crowd coming towards them, but before he could raise his hand in greeting, he heard Jesus say, "Come, follow me." Philip? He and Philip had grown up together in Bethsaida. How did this man know Philip? Why did he want Philip to follow him?

It didn't take long for Philip to be impressed by Jesus in the same way that Andrew and John had been. The statement, "Come, follow me," sounded more like a compelling command. Simon hardly had a chance to talk to Philip, to enquire as to the wellbeing of his family, and to engage in the customary pleasantries, before Philip took off to find an old friend of his named Nathanael.

Oh, the fickle nature of youth, Simon thought. Or no, that was unkind. Not fickle . . . impetuous perhaps, or naïve maybe. Just like he had been before the harshness of life had robbed him of his dreams.

Later Simon found out that Nathanael had been sceptical too, wondering out loud if anything good could come out of Nazareth. Simon had been taken aback when told where the Rabbi hailed from, but as Andrew repeatedly reminded him, Jesus had been born in Bethlehem, just as the prophet Micah had foretold.[3] He wasn't sure what to make of the visit of the Magi,[4] the shepherds and the angels,[5] the flight to Egypt and the subsequent angelic redirection to Nazareth on the family's return from their exile.[6] Simon could understand the choice of Nazareth in a sense. Nazareth was an insignificant backwater town, a good hideout, as it were, but what alarmed Simon more than anything else was that the Nazarenes were known to be a hot-headed, proud and fanatical group of people. Was this man Jesus possibly a product of their misguided zeal to see the Messiah come from their ranks?[7]

But Nathanael had quickly changed his mind, even going so far as to declare Jesus to be the Son of God, the King of Israel! This sudden, seemingly over-the-top political and religious outburst did not seem to bother the Rabbi. He simply smiled and predicted that Nathanael would experience even greater things. Greater things! In his reply to Nathanael Jesus had compared himself to Jacob's ladder . . . angels ascending and descending on him. It sounded absurd. Was he saying that he was somehow a divine link between heaven and earth? That is what it sounded like to Simon.

"This man," Simon said to his brother, Andrew, "this Rabbi of yours, sounds a little . . . he sounds a little . . . different."

Andrew seemed disappointed. "Why don't you at least call him by his name, brother. You know his name."

Simon sighed. There was that sigh again! Oh, was there nothing that could lift him out of this joyless, dismal pit of despondency and doubt? "Yes," Simon said. "I know his name. But to call him Jesus,[8] sounds so . . . so . . ."

"Hopeful?" Simon looked at Andrew briefly. As he turned to walk away, Andrew quickly blurted out, "We've been invited to attend a wedding with him. In Cana. Will you come?" Simon hesitated for a brief moment, then nodded and walked away. He needed time to be alone.

---

3. Micah 5:2.

4. Matthew 2:1–12. It is probable that the Magi were descendants of those over whom Daniel ruled (Daniel 2:48) and thus they would have been acquainted with the prophecy of Balaam (Numbers 24:17).

5. Luke 2:8–20.

6. Matthew 2:13–23.

7. Robby Gallaty, *The Forgotten Jesus: How Western Christians Should Follow an Eastern Rabbi* (Grand Rapids, MI: Zondervan, 2017), 99.

8. The name Jesus, Yeshua in Hebrew, means to save, deliver, or rescue. It is the same name given to Hoshea in Numbers 13:8 and 16, so one can only imagine the political and religious overtones this name carried.

* * *

This man . . . this Jesus . . . seemed to be so intentional in all he did and said. He had a habit of silently removing himself from the group and seeking out a place to pray. But when he wasn't praying, he was engaging everyone . . . no one seemed too small or insignificant . . . he treated everyone with dignity and sincerity. And he was kind to men, women, and children alike. There was a soft firmness about him, Simon thought. And he had a wonderful sense of humour . . . a gentle teasing, if you will. Like at this wedding.

Simon didn't really want to go . . . he felt he was neglecting his duties as a fisherman, a husband, a business partner. And he needed time to reflect on all he had heard and seen in the past few days. The last thing he needed was noise and gaiety. But here he was, laughing and smiling with the best of them.

Then the mother of Jesus, an extraordinary woman by the name of Mary, approached her son with an urgent and yet somehow indirect request. "They have no more wine," she simply stated. Later, when he thought back on this occasion, Simon wondered if Mary had learned by experience to leave her requests open-ended . . . she knew that her son knew what to do and he always did what was best.

"Dear woman," Jesus replied in a playful tone, "that's not our concern!" And then in a softer tone, he added, "There's a time for everything in life, mother, but this is not my time." Simon watched her carefully. She playfully tossed her head to the side and said to the servants, "Do whatever he tells you to do." And then she was gone . . . moving from one person to another, one group to another, chatting with everyone. Like her son, she appeared to love engaging people in conversation.

Simon suddenly became aware that he was standing on his own. The others had followed Jesus inside the house. Simon turned and saw Jesus instructing the servants to fill the six stone water jars. They filled each one to the brim. Then Simon heard one of the servants gasp. He heard the word "wine" being whispered amongst the group. Had the water turned into wine? But those stone water jars were usually used by devout families for religious cleansing rituals, not for drinking. What was Jesus doing? Water in purification jars turned into very good wine? Why?

Simon watched the master of ceremonies tasting the wine. He saw his eyebrows shoot up . . . then Simon saw him hurry over to the bridegroom and with a voice filled with sheer amazement, he asked him why he had kept the best wine for last.

Simon quickly looked over to Jesus, but he was behaving as if nothing out of the ordinary had happened. The servants were talking in excited yet hushed tones with each other. He could see they were as perplexed as he was. And the others who had come along with them . . . they too looked as if they had just witnessed a . . . a miracle? Yes, a miracle. That is what it was. God had provided water and manna for his people in the wilderness. That had been a miracle. But now . . . now Jesus had provided wine . . . the best wine . . . from water. This was a miracle too. Simon shook his head as if to wake himself up. What had he just witnessed? Why the purification jars?

Simon felt he had been right all along. This man was different. Jesus did things differently . . . and that bothered him . . . but in time Simon learned that Jesus always had good reasons for doing and saying what he did.

Years later, in a very different setting, in a guest room in Jerusalem, Simon would remember this day . . . wine, purification . . . another ceremony. But for the moment, he just could not wrap his head around it. So he buried his thoughts and went home . . . home to where simple folks like him belonged. He felt comfortable in Capernaum. He felt in control of his life. Things were predictable and understandable and non-threatening. Water, wind, fish . . . these were things he was accustomed to. This was where he wanted to stay. Let the younger ones follow the risky one . . . this man . . . this Jesus. No, for himself, he preferred to have both feet anchored firmly on the ground. Simon smiled to himself. The ground? No, rather he preferred to have his feet anchored firmly on the floor of his fishing boat.

3

Misgivings

"Simon!"

Ah, so they were back from Jerusalem. Finally! Simon too had been there for the annual Passover celebrations, but had returned early. One of the partners had to continue their business, he reasoned.

"What news, little brother? What has the rabbi . . ." Simon caught himself. He knew how much Andrew disliked him referring to Jesus as the rabbi. So, he quickly added, "What has Jesus been up to this time?"

"Simon, brother, oh what a time we all had! What to say . . . what to think!"

"That doesn't sound like news to me, brother. It sounds like the babbling of an over excited young man! Tell me the news!"

"Yes, well . . . let me collect my thoughts . . . and catch my breath! As you know, we went to Jerusalem for the Passover."

"Yes. I was there, remember?"

"Well, yes, but you weren't with us when we went to the temple. You know how those scoundrels exploit the people in the courts, selling animals and exchanging coins at inflated prices. Some even say they do it to fund the zealots. . ."

There he goes again, Simon thought. Speculating. Always speculating and seeing a conspiracy under every rock and around every corner. "Yes?" He tried not to sound impatient.

"Yes, well, Jesus chased all the sellers out with a whip of ropes."

"I heard something about that . . . but tell me more."

"He chased them out. He overturned their tables. He scattered the coins of the money lenders. 'Get out of here!' he told them. 'How dare you turn my Father's house into a den of thieves!'" Andrew laughed nervously. What would his brother think of such a radical act?

But Simon smiled a crooked smile – and continued to mend his net. "And . . . ? What did those crooks have to say about that?" he asked.

Andrew was encouraged to continue. "They questioned him, of course. No, actually, at first they shouted something like, 'What do you think you're doing?' But then they asked for some sort of assurance that he had authority to cleanse the temple precincts . . . I guess that in their hearts they knew that this behaviour was unacceptable. But then . . ." Andrew's voice trailed off.

Simon turned and looked at his brother. He was so young, yet there seemed to be a maturity about him lately. Maybe following Jesus was good for him. "Yes, Andrew? And then?"

"Then . . . then Jesus said something strange."

"Oh, brother, just spit it out! Getting answers out of you is like dragging an overfilled net to shore!"

"Well, I just don't want you to worry. I don't want you to think . . . less of me . . . or of him, for that matter."

"Andrew, I love you. I will always do what is best for you. Have no fear. I am not your judge. I am just your brother."

"Yes. Well, Jesus said . . . 'Destroy this temple, and in three days I will raise it up.'"

"He said *what*?"

"Simon, you promised!"

"Yes, yes . . . but did he say how he would rebuild a temple that has taken forty-six years to build, and even now is not yet complete?"

"That's what the leaders all said . . ."

Simon wasn't so sure that the comparison between him and the sceptical leaders was a positive one. For a moment, neither of the brothers said a word. Neither of them knew what to make of this strange statement.

Simon finally broke the silence. "So, what happened then? Did the whole of Jerusalem declare him mad and turn their backs on him?"

"No, actually quite the opposite. Many began to hang around him, but for some reason or other, Jesus didn't trust them. He said he knew human nature only too well . . . he knew what was in their hearts."

Simon suddenly remembered that feeling of standing exposed in Jesus's presence . . . as if his very inner core had been laid bare before Jesus. Then he simply stated, "He is a wise man, your Jesus."

"*My* Jesus? Simon . . ."

"Yes, yes, Andrew . . . I know, I know. Forgive my negative attitude. Go on . . . tell me more. I will listen . . . just talk."

Andrew went on to tell his brother all about a Pharisee by the name of Nicodemus who had come to speak with Jesus under cover of darkness, more than likely because he feared his peers. Jesus had spoken to him in riddles . . . something about being born again. The poor Pharisee at first took him literally and expressed doubt, wondering how a grown man could re-enter his mother's womb to be born a second time.

At this, Simon laughed out loud. "Yes!" he chuckled, "that would be difficult!"

But Andrew failed to see the humour. He became quiet and then said, "Brother, I think what he meant was that we need to be changed inwardly . . . spiritually . . . as if we were newly born . . . as if we were new people. The prophet said that God would cleanse us with water and give us a new heart and a new spirit and place his Spirit in us.[1] A new beginning . . . a spiritual rebirth. That's the only way that we can find true and lasting freedom."

Simon didn't know what to make of his little brother's statement, so he said nothing. Later, he would speak. It was always easier to understand these hard sayings of Jesus when looking back and reinterpreting them in the light of what they learned over the years as they walked with him. But at the time, these sayings were just puzzling riddles.

Andrew continued. "Jesus then told Nicodemus that God has shown his love for the world by sending his son into the world . . . not to judge it, but to save it through him. He said that there's no judgment for those who believe in him . . . that he is the light that dispels darkness."

Light! Light that dispels darkness. That was what Simon craved more than anything . . . to have this heavy fog lifted from him . . . this doubt that was crippling him.

"And John the Baptizer? What does he have to say about this? Does he still believe that Jesus is the Passover Lamb?"

"He still believes, yes." Andrew replied. "In fact, we heard it said that he believes Jesus has been sent by God and that he speaks God's words because God has given him his Spirit without limit."

"That is high praise, indeed."

"Yes, and John also said that if *we* believed in Jesus, we would have eternal life. Simon, I don't understand all these things, but I do believe that Jesus is the Messiah! I really do!"

Simon gazed out over the waters. How tranquil it all seemed . . . silent . . . peaceful. But the wind could whip up the sea in an instant. That was what he

---

1. Ezekiel 36:24–27.

felt was happening in his heart at that moment. His brother's words, like the wind and the ripples, were beginning to have an effect on him. Where was this headed? Was his brother in danger?

"There's more . . ." Andrew hesitated.

Simon sensed that what Andrew was going to say would be even more puzzling than what he had already disclosed. But he had promised to listen, so he nodded for him to continue.

"We went through Samaria."

That was more than Simon could take. "You went through Samaria! What on earth were you thinking? Have you washed?"

"Have I what?"

"Have you washed? Have you purified yourself? You walked over unclean land and were in the presence of unclean people! You have defiled yourself! Please tell me you didn't eat with them!"

"Simon, please, brother . . . you need to hear what I have to say."

Simon snorted loudly and was about to get up and storm off, but his brother grabbed him by the arm and pleaded. "Please. You promised to listen. You said you were not my judge. Why are you judging me now?"

"Is Jesus not concerned about the laws of purity, brother? Tell me. You know we do not have anything to do with Samaritans and for good reason. They are an unclean people . . . a mixed race with a misguided religion!"[2]

"Yes, but Simon, is there anything too hard for our God? Is there anyone beyond his reach? I know you are going to say something like a leopard can't change his spots, but Simon . . . anything is possible with God, right?"

Simon said nothing. In his heart he was at sea . . . a stormy sea . . . a dark, troubled sea. But he held his peace and let his brother continue.

"We stopped at Jacob's well. There was no one there . . . just us. It was noon and it was hot. Jesus was tired. We were all tired and hungry . . . so we went into the village to find food."

He saw Simon was about to protest yet again, so he started to speak louder and faster. "Jesus stayed behind. It was as if he wanted us to go . . . to leave him there. So, we went, but when we returned, we found him . . . well, we found him talking with a woman."

---

2. Samaritans were descendants of some of the northern tribes left in Israel after the Assyrian conquest. Their religion had already been tainted by Jeroboam from the time of the division of the kingdoms into north and south, but it became even more mixed after the remaining Jews intermarried with the foreigners settled in the land by the Assyrians. Over time they developed their own version of the Jewish faith and their own temple on Mount Gerizim. For a helpful short history see: https://margmowczko.com/a-brief-history-of-the-samaritans/.

"A woman! At that hour? No decent person goes to draw water at that hour! And no self-respecting rabbi talks to a woman ..."[3]

"That's just the point, dear brother. You know how Jesus talks to everybody. He's not like our leaders ... in fact, he's not like anyone I've ever met before. He touches those everyone else avoids ... he talks to men, women and children as if they are all equal in his eyes. It is as if he sees past the present ... past the exterior ... it is as if he sees what they can be, not what they are."

This last statement touched Simon deeply. Yes, he had sensed that too ... experienced it. He too had felt as if Jesus saw what could be, rather than what was. He seemed to see the positive possibilities of the future and not the mistakes of the past with their consequences in the present. It was as if, through his gaze and thoughtful words, he encouraged people to hope again ... to dream again ... to see things as they might be ... to realize that while one is alive, nothing is hopeless. Yes, he had felt that, and now he wondered if this woman had felt that as well ... misguided as she may be.

"And what were they talking about?"

"Well, we missed part of the conversation, but apparently it had all started when Jesus asked her for a drink of water. We all thought it was an odd way to start a conversation with a stranger, but ..."

"Actually, that was a brilliant move on Jesus's part," Simon interrupted.

"Sorry?" Andrew couldn't believe that Simon seemed to see this as a positive thing ... he had expected some objection.

"By asking her for a drink of water, he put her at ease."

"How so?"

"He requested something from her that she could freely give. Something he did not have. That gave her a dignity of sorts ... an importance. She is probably used to being ignored or shunned by those who know her. By doing this, Jesus probably broke down her defences and gave her the freedom to talk freely without fear. He did not shut her down with rejection ... he opened her up with respect."

"That's exactly what happened, brother! At first, she had some sort of theological discussion with him. She felt free to talk to him, just as you said. But then ... Jesus said something about 'living water.' I think she misunderstood at first. She thought he meant it literally, like an endless stream of some kind. So

---

3. The usual time for drawing water at a well was early morning or early evening. Only those hoping to avoid others would draw water at the hottest time of the day. There were strict rules of separation for men and women at this time. Today, in orthodox circles those rules are still enforced.

she asked him to give her the water he was talking about. Maybe she felt that if she had access to this inexhaustible resource, she would never have to face the accusing looks of her people again. It would be as if she had never lived a life of wickedness . . . she could keep her past to herself and not be reminded of it every time she had to go to the well."

"True, but she would still have to live with her own thoughts . . . her own darkness. She could not escape from that. What did Jesus say then?"

"He confronted her with her sin."

"Sounds like he ambushed her! It reminds me of when Israel lured the Benjamites into a trap and attacked from behind when they least expected it.[4] Quite a brilliant tactic, actually. What did Jesus do then?"

"He asked the woman to get her husband. When she replied that she did not have a husband, Jesus surprised us all by stating bluntly that she was right! She has had five husbands . . . five! And the man she is living with at that moment is not her husband! You should have seen her face! It was like when the wall of Jericho fell! She gulped for air, but I suspect she has learned how to recover her composure quickly given that she probably hears worse from others. She tried to deflect the focus off herself by opening up yet another theological debate."

"Ah, yes . . . that always works. Trick your opponent into taking another path away from that which leads directly to the heart of the matter at hand."

"Simon, here Jesus said one of those things that leaves me . . . no, all of us . . . puzzled. He said a time would come when it would no longer matter whether we worship in Jerusalem or someplace else. He said that God was looking for those who would worship him in spirit and in truth, regardless of where they might be. We were talking about that along the way. Did he mean that we would no longer be required to go up to Jerusalem every so often?"

"Did you ask Jesus?"

Andrew shook his head. "No . . . we didn't dare. It would seem disrespectful to question him. Besides, I don't want to be the one asking the questions. He might think I am slow to understand."

"Oh, Andrew, haven't I taught you anything? It is by challenging others, by asking them to explain what they have said, by asking questions that one learns the truth."

"The rabbis and Pharisees and scribes don't like anyone asking them questions."

---

4. Judges 20:29–36.

"That is because they feel threatened. They are proud and pompous. They think just because they went further with their studies than we did that we are unlearned men! Ha! Unlearned! We know the Torah by heart, and you know many of the other holy books, too. And we can read Hebrew and speak Aramaic and Greek because we grew up in Galilee of the Gentiles! But they feel that because they can quote other learned men – sages and rabbis from the past – that somehow that makes them superior to us! So, when you . . . an unlearned man . . . ask them questions, they think you are being impertinent."

"Jesus is so different . . ."

"I am learning that . . . slowly, I admit . . . but I am learning. There's something about him that . . . that . . . well, go on. What happened next?"

"The woman seemed to understand Jesus better than we did. She had been told that when the Messiah comes, all would be made clear. And then, without really asking him directly, she managed to get him to say it!"

"Say what?"

"That he is the Messiah! It was actually at that point that we made our presence known. We heard him say clearly, 'I am the Messiah.' We all looked shocked . . . we *were* shocked . . . that he was telling her things we hadn't heard him say directly to anyone else before. And she was shocked that he . . . the Messiah . . . had spoken to her at all . . . a woman of ill repute! Then, she just ran away. She was in such a hurry to get away that she left her water jar beside the well."

"She just left?" Simon sounded disappointed. "That's it?"

"Well, no . . . she came back. But in the meantime we tried to get Jesus to eat some of the food we had bought, but he wouldn't."

"Hmm . . . was it not clean?"

"No, it wasn't that. He said something about having food to eat that we didn't know about. So we wondered if someone had brought him food during our absence. Oh, Simon . . . we really are slow to understand."

"So, did someone bring him food?"

"No, he meant that his nourishment comes from doing the will of God . . . that is what sustains him. Yes, I know . . . it's puzzling. I'm still not really sure what that means. Surely, he must have been as hungry as we were! But at that point we heard a crowd coming. The woman had told the townsfolk about this man who had revealed her life to her and that she thought he was the long-awaited Messiah. Imagine that! This woman . . . this very unlikely person . . . brought the 'living water' Jesus had spoken about just moments before, to the very people who had shunned her. And when Jesus saw the crowd, he likened them to a ripe harvest field. Oh, what a joyful harvest it was! The whole village believed in him – they all accepted that he was the Messiah. They begged him to stay . . . and so we stayed there for two days."

"Samaritans! Who would have believed it?"

"Yes, they said that they believed that Jesus was the Saviour of the whole world. Imagine! Most Gentiles call Caesar the saviour of the world!"

"These Samaritans seem to be more perceptive than most people, including our own. How odd it is that Jesus has come to us . . . to his own . . . and most of us have not accepted him, but they have!"

"Simon? Brother? May I ask you . . . ?"

"No, you may not." Simon stood up. He wasn't ready to make any major decision about anything, let alone about the Messiah. There was too much at stake. What would he do with his fishing business? How could he leave Zebedee? Who would provide for his family? No, he was not ready to make any decision . . . positive or negative. He needed time.

"Where is Jesus now?" Simon asked.

"In Cana."

Cana. That was where Simon had seen Jesus change water into wine . . . into the best wine . . . in six stone water jars used for purification rites. An uneasy feeling came over him. How much more evidence did he need? This Jesus did and said things that no man in living memory had said or done. Surely . . .

"Simon! Andrew!" A government official rushed up to them, totally out of breath, looking as if he had seen death face to face. "Where is Jesus?"

"Why?" Andrew asked, understandably suspicious. He knew who this important man was . . . everyone did . . . but what were his intentions?

"My son," the man gasped, "my son is dying. I have heard that Jesus has healed others . . . perhaps he can heal my son! Where is he?"

"He is in Cana," Simon replied, looking sideways at Andrew who seemed to be reluctant to give any information about Jesus's whereabouts.

Without another word, the man flew about and began to run in the direction of Cana.

"Shall we follow?" Simon asked. "Or shall we wait for Jesus to return with the man?"

"Yes, brother! I mean no, brother. Let's go quickly! Before he gets too far ahead of us!" Andrew was beaming, smiling from ear to ear, every tooth gleaming in the sunlight.

What a joy it is to see him smile, Simon thought. "Let me just tell everyone where we are going . . . give me a moment," Simon said out loud.

"I will help, brother!"

Something was stirring in Simon. Was it that he wanted to see yet another miraculous healing? Was it that he needed yet another confirmation of something he already knew but wasn't willing to admit?

"Brother! Quickly!"

"Yes, I'm coming," he said, as he hurried to tell his partner Zebedee that he was leaving once again. "Tell the family, Andrew, and grab something for the road!"

* * *

"We've lost him!"

"We'll catch up brother . . . he can't have gone far."

"He was running when he left us. He's desperate, Simon. His son is dying."

Yes, Simon thought. I would also be running if it was my son. Desperation makes people do strange things. No man with an ounce of dignity in him would run anywhere. The official must love his son very much to not care what others think of him. A whole day had passed and they had seen no trace of the government official. Cana wasn't that far from Capernaum. They should have met up with him by now. Although they had been delayed on the road as they had looked for him in the crowds and the usual resting places.

"Wait! Simon, there he is . . . he is coming back! Look!"

Andrew was right. The man was coming towards them, walking fast but not running. He seemed deep in thought. Just then, a group of men ran up to him.

"Master! Master! Come quickly! Your son lives! He is well!"

The man's legs could no longer hold him up. He folded like a wet rag and fell to his knees, sobbing uncontrollably.

"Master!" The servants were laughing and weeping at the same time. "He is well. He has recovered!"

"When?" The man seemed to regain some of his composure. "When did he recover?"

"Yesterday afternoon at about the seventh hour."

The man's shoulders shook as he sobbed once again.

"He was right. Jesus was right. We will not believe unless we see miraculous signs. As Moses said, we are a stiff-necked people. I tried to force him to come with me, but all he said was, 'Go back home. Your son will live.' What choice did I have? I had to believe him. And now . . . and now . . ."

Simon and Andrew walked up to the man.

"And now Jesus has healed your son from a distance," Andrew said. "He didn't even need to touch him." Simon realized that Andrew wasn't asking a question . . . he was making a statement . . . some sort of statement of faith.

"Yes," the man sobbed. "Yes." Then he grabbed the arms of his servants as he lifted himself up. He looked at them intently. "He is the Messiah. You must believe! I can't wait to tell my family. I believe! They will, too, when I tell them what happened. It is a miracle . . . nothing less than a miracle." With that the group bounded back towards Capernaum, praising God as they went.

Simon stood motionless, rooted to the spot. "Yes," he thought, "we must believe!" This is the second sign he'd seen now. First the water into wine and now this . . . healed without a touch. Come to think of it, Jesus hadn't touched the water or the stone jars either . . . the servants just did what he told them to do. The official now believes. His servants believe . . . he is sure his entire household will believe. It even sounds as if Andrew believes. "What is wrong with me?" Simon thought. "Why am I struggling to trust Jesus? Why can't I believe in him?"

4

Changes

"Where is Andrew?" Simon was concerned about him after hearing the news of John the Baptizer's arrest.

"He is resting." Simon's wife replied. "Leave him be. He is really tired and not just physically."

"This must be quite a shock for him."

"Yes."

"Did he tell you anything?" asked Simon. "I heard that Jesus had been threatened too. Did someone hurt Andrew? If someone hurt him, I'll . . ."

"Simon, Simon. Enough. He is unharmed. But I think he is a bit shaken by everything that has happened."

"What? What happened? Tell me!"

"Let me speak! And lower your voice. He needs to rest."

Simon gave his wife a look of exasperation.

"Well, apparently Jesus healed a lame man at the pool of Bethesda . . ."

"Jesus heals lots of people," Simon interrupted. "What was so different about this healing?"

"It was on the Sabbath."

"The Sabbath! Why? Couldn't the healing not have waited a few hours? You know, Jesus really does push the limits. It is almost as if he purposely does things to annoy and alienate himself from the leaders of our nation. He ought to be winning them over, not offending them!"

"Hush! Not so loud! You will wake Andrew up! It seems the healed man told the leaders who had healed him. They had stopped him in the street because he was carrying his mat home on the Sabbath. They recognized him because he had been lying there by the pool every day for years. After that, the leaders began to harass Jesus for breaking the law. But then . . ." Simon's wife drew closer to her husband and her voice dropped to a whisper. "Then

27

Jesus . . . well, perhaps it is better to say our leaders *thought* that Jesus . . . was making himself equal with God because he spoke about God as his Father."

"No need to whisper, Gisa.[1] I'm awake." Andrew stood leaning on the doorpost.

Simon rushed up to him and held him tight.

"You must promise me, little brother, promise me this will end now. No more following Jesus."

"Brother." Andrew's muffled voice could be heard coming from Simon's chest. "Not so tight." Simon released his grip but still held on to his brother's shoulders. He took a deep breath and looked him squarely in the eyes.

"Andrew, many other young men your age were killed in the past because they followed a self-proclaimed messiah or a would-be liberator. I do not want an empty seat at my table . . . or an empty room in my home."

"Jesus *is* the Messiah! Of that I am convinced. Yes, this was frightening, but think, brother! What if he is telling the truth? If we turn away from him now . . ."

Simon sat down heavily, holding his head in his hand. He rubbed his forehead.

"Just tell me what happened."

"The leaders were questioning Jesus because he healed the lame man on the Sabbath."

"That much I know."

"Well, he then tried to explain to them that the Sabbath does not restrict God in his working."

"Andrew. Did he call God his Father?"

"Yes, he did. But brother, he was trying to point out that he could only do what God showed him to do . . . or empowered him to do. Perhaps a better way of explaining it would be to say he was only able to do that which God was already doing . . . as though he somehow is participating in God's work."

"And how does Jesus know what God is doing? The prophets of old didn't always know what God was doing. How does he know? Or more importantly, how do *you* know that it is *God* who is leading him?"

"Simon, you know how Jesus speaks to God all the time, not only when he is alone. I've watched him. It's as if he is always listening . . . waiting for direction. He says he only does what God tells him to do. He speaks to God

---

1. Gisa is a term of endearment for a sister-in-law. We do not know the name of Simon's wife.

as if he were his Father. He speaks to God like . . . well, like I speak to you. He says the Father loves his son and shows him everything he is doing."

"Sounds like he was attempting to absolve himself."

"Not at all! How can you say that? Saying what he did was the opposite of an attempt to excuse himself . . . in fact, he further fanned the flames of their indignation."

"And now? Will they ever recognize him as Israel's Messiah?"

"He *is* the Messiah, brother, whether they recognize him or not. They may have stood in judgment over him that day, but a time will come when the tables will be turned. He will be the judge of them. Simon, he told us that the Father has given him the right to give eternal life to those who listen to his message and truly believe in God. He said . . . he said that the day has come when the dead will hear his voice and live! Not at the end of the age . . . then too . . . but he was speaking about now! The resurrection of all will come later, but *now* the dead – the spiritually dead – will hear his voice, and those who hear will live!"

"You are beginning to sound just like Jesus."

"Brother, I *have* heard his voice. In so many ways, I once was like a dead person, but now . . . now I am more alive than I have ever been!"

Simon said nothing. He was a witness to the truth of that statement. Andrew was more alive now than ever. Simon had never heard such conviction – such certainty – in his brother's speech before.

Andrew continued. "John the Baptizer testified of him when he called him the Lamb of God. Our leaders tolerated John for a while . . . they were even excited about his message. But even John said that Jesus was greater than him and *that* they don't believe."

"They are educated men, Andrew. Sometimes too much learning can make one blind."

Simon looked at his wife with amazement. Did she just say that?

"That is exactly what Jesus said, Gisa. He said that they search the Scriptures because they think they hold the key to eternal life . . . but those self-same Scriptures speak of him . . . they point to him like a signpost."

"Well, he is not going to win their approval by antagonizing them this way." Simon surprised himself. He thought his voice sounded unnecessarily harsh.

"No? Well, he says he doesn't need their approval. He has God's approval. Besides, if we believe Moses, we ought to believe Jesus."

"How so?"

"Because Moses wrote about him. If we believe what Moses wrote, we will believe what Jesus says."

"And now John the Baptizer is in prison. He, at least, spoke out against the breaking of the law! Yes, he annoyed the leaders by calling them broods of vipers . . . that's true . . . but why did Jesus have to heal on the Sabbath? How long until the leaders turn against him . . . and you, too?"

"Are you afraid for me, brother? Or is there something else you are afraid of?"

Such a direct challenge! And from Andrew, no less! But he was right. Simon was afraid at that moment . . . but he was more afraid of what he might say . . . that he would live to regret words spoken in anger . . . so he chose to remain silent . . . and silently he turned away and left the compound.

∗ ∗ ∗

The news spread quickly. Jesus, the wonder-working, yet controversial, rabbi had been rejected in his own hometown. At first, he was praised by everyone. He taught in the synagogues and people flocked from miles around to hear him speak. Everyone had wanted him then. They were like children with new whistles or spinning tops. When he first claimed to be the fulfilment of the prophecy of Isaiah, people were amazed. They wondered how a common labourer could speak so eloquently and powerfully.

But then, Jesus seemed to go too far yet again. It really was as if he didn't want fame or fortune . . . he certainly wasn't there to please people. Why talk about the widow of Zarephath and Naaman the Syrian?[2] It was a slap in the face. How dare he suggest that God would pass by his own people and only bless the Gentiles! No wonder the people of Nazareth tried to throw him off a cliff. How he managed to walk away was a mystery. Maybe what he said to Mary at the wedding was right . . . his time had not yet come.

But now, Jesus was in Capernaum!

There will be no keeping Andrew away from Jesus now, Simon thought. Things had been going so well. He and Andrew were fishing together again, and business was good. Why did Jesus have to come to Capernaum?

Simon and Andrew had decided to cast their net from the shore that day and were about to pull it in when Simon suddenly became aware of the fact that Andrew was standing rigid, staring at something or someone behind them. Simon turned, and his heart sank. Jesus had appeared as if from nowhere.

"Come, you two. Come, follow me and let me show you how to fish for people." Simon looked at his brother. There was a bright gleam in his eyes. He knew Andrew wanted to go . . . and perhaps they should. Why not? It wasn't a

---

2. 1 Kings 17:7–24; 2 Kings 5:1–27.

permanent commitment. And at least, he would be there to see that no harm came to his brother. He noticed that Andrew was holding the net loosely, like he was ready to drop it and leave it behind. Simon nodded to their hired hands. They would see that the nets were cleaned and mended and returned home. And James and John could take care of the business while they were travelling.

But that was not to be. Jesus called James and John to follow him as well. Simon would never forget the look on Zebedee's face as he watched them leave. The small band walked into town slowly, talking all the way. Only Simon said nothing. What would he tell his wife? How long would this take? Who would provide for the family while he was gone? There was only so much he could expect from Zebedee, especially since his sons were leaving too.

* * *

But that Sabbath . . . in many ways it was a turning point. Jesus taught in the synagogue and kept everyone spellbound. Simon, Andrew, James and John were blown away by his teaching. But the crowd? They listened with rapt attention, but they seemed to be more interested by the healing of a demoniac. The news that spread like wildfire through every village in the region was not about his teaching . . . it was about his healing.

Looking back later, Simon wasn't exactly sure how it happened. One moment they were standing outside the synagogue and the next they were walking into his home. True it was very close by and convenient, but had he invited Jesus? Surely not. He knew his mother-in-law was ill.

After they had exchanged customary pleasantries and everyone's feet had been washed, there was an awkward silence. Simon's wife kept giving him annoyed looks. Simon could not recall later who spoke first, but soon everyone was begging Jesus to heal Simon's mother-in-law. It all happened so quickly. One moment Jesus was at her bedside . . . the next she was healed! With a simple rebuke from Jesus, the fever left her. It was as if she had never been sick! She was back to her old self and was soon serving them and fussing over every dish and drink. Only the best was good enough for Jesus.

The whole family loves him, Simon thought. Am I the only one who sees what might happen if things go wrong? Am I the only one who remembers . . . Theudas, Judah . . . how many others?[3]

But he didn't get to think for long. At sunset, the sick and demon-possessed came from the town and surrounding villages . . . once the Sabbath was over,

---

3. Flavius Josephus, *Antiquities of the Jews*, 17.10: "Now, at this time there were ten thousand other disorders in Judea . . ." See also Acts 5:36–37.

people were free to walk as far as they wished. They came in droves with their family members and friends, until the entrance to the compound was blocked. As the demons were cast out, they would scream, "You are the Son of God!" But it seemed as if Jesus did not want the truth to be known . . . he hushed them and commanded them to be silent.

Why? Simon thought. If Jesus is the Messiah, why not tell them all plainly?

* * *

The following morning, Jesus was gone before the rooster crowed. Simon and his family were early risers, but, it appeared, Jesus was earlier still. People searched for him everywhere. They finally found him in a solitary place and Simon, still caught up in the excitement of the previous evening, begged Jesus to come back quickly. People were looking for him . . . wanting him. But Jesus was reluctant to stay in Capernaum. He wanted to preach in other Galilean towns, he said, because that was why he had come.

Why? Simon wondered again. Why? If Jesus is the Messiah, why is he intent on keeping it hidden? But he held his peace and made ready to take his leave with the small group. His wife was all in favour of his going . . . her only regret was that she could not go along with them. Simon regretted that too. Maybe, one day, that too would change.[4]

They travelled throughout the region of Galilee. Jesus was teaching and healing as they watched. People were flocking to him from everywhere . . . Syria, Decapolis, all over Galilee, Judea and Jerusalem, and even east of the Jordan. It was a gigantic wave of humanity. They all came to be healed . . . demon-possessed, epileptics, paralytics. He had compassion on them all and healed each one.

---

4. 1 Corinthians 9:5.

5

The Turn of the Tide

It took Simon three whole days to recover after they returned from the trip. How did Jesus do it? Where did his energy come from? He stayed up late at night, praying to God, whom he called his Father . . . and before anyone else was up, he was praying again by himself in a remote place. He slept so little and yet did so much . . . and no one was about to give him any rest.

The trip was over. They had followed him closely . . . they had learned a lot, seen a lot, experienced so much first-hand. At times Simon felt like he had been caught in a whirlwind, so many things were hitting him from all sides. But now they had to knuckle down and get some real work done.

It was good to be back in the boat again that night. There was something about the rhythmic lapping of the small waves against the hull that calmed him. Simon realized that part of his exhaustion was that he had been nervous. He was never sure about what he ought to say or do. He knew what he thought about the Messiah, or at least what he had been taught about the Messiah, but Jesus seemed to be so different from what he had imagined and from what he believed the prophets had said about him . . . the coming one who would be like Moses. He really did not know what to make of Jesus.

Andrew, on the other hand, appeared to be quite at ease. He didn't seem to see the many possible scenarios, the many different ways things could go horribly wrong. Simon knew he was being overly vigilant and that he tended to anticipate problems where often there were none. But he felt responsible for his brother whom he thought was too trusting and naïve.

But soon Simon's troubled thoughts were soon replaced with a different concern. Where were the fish?

By morning, they had still caught nothing. They were tired, but there was still much to be done before they could go to bed. It was while they were cleaning their nets in the warm currents from the springs,[1] that Jesus came and asked Simon to let him use his boat as a platform to speak from. At first Simon was suspicious of this request. Was Jesus trying to recruit him? Or was he trying to make it appear as if he already had? But he thought, Why not? As long as Jesus didn't ask him to do anything else, he was content.

So Jesus taught the people from Simon's boat. Due to the shape of the harbour, with people standing on the curved piers on both sides, Jesus's voice carried as if he was on the stage of a Roman amphitheatre. Simon began wondering if Jesus may have helped his father build the amphitheatre in Tzipori.[2] But he was only listening with half an ear . . . his mind was focused on getting the nets ready for the next catch as fast as he could.

"Simon," Andrew said.

"What?"

"Simon, the Master is speaking to you." They had taken to calling Jesus "Master" while on the trip. It just seemed fitting . . . respectful.

Simon looked up to see Jesus looking directly at him. "Simon, let's go fishing."

Was the irritation that welled up inside Simon just the result of his tiredness? Or was it because a non-fisherman was telling him to do something every professional fisherman knew was ludicrous? Thinking that Jesus would change his mind once he explained how fishing worked, especially that they had tried in vain to catch fish all night long, Simon muttered as calmly as he could, "Master, we have been fishing all night and we haven't caught a thing."

When no reply was forthcoming, Simon glanced up. Jesus was still looking at him. Was that a hint of a smile on his face? He was beckoning with his head for him to come. Was he mocking him? Everyone was looking at him . . . what was Simon the fisherman going to do now? All sorts of thoughts were racing through his head . . . the water changed into wine, the son of the official healed, his mother-in-law healed, the many healings and exorcisms . . . could it be? Oh, what did he have to lose other than his sleep . . . and perhaps his pride and stubbornness?

---

1. The Sea of Galilee is fed by several warm springs as well as the upper Jordan River.

2. "Bible scholar and archeologist Jerome Murphy O'Connor believes that after returning from Egypt, Joseph and Mary settled in Nazareth precisely because of its proximity to Sepphoris. After 3 BC, Sepphoris was the center of a building boom, providing work opportunities for artisans such as Joseph. Did Jesus have a hand building the theater of Sepphoris, just reconstructed for us? Perhaps." https://www.itsgila.com/highlightssepphoris.htm.

"Well, if you say so . . . we can try again." Simon pushed the boat away from the dock.[3] Andrew and the hired hands had already hopped on board, filled with anticipation. Simon knew he was alone in his doubt and disbelief . . . so what? Someone had to be a realist.

But no sooner had they cast the nets into the lake than the water came alive with the furious flapping of fish. And the nets! They were beginning to tear due to the abundance of the catch! Simon shouted to his partners, James and John, for help. But even with their boat, there was still not enough room for all the fish.

And then it happened. Simon felt like he had been struck by lightning. It was one thing for Jesus to change water into wine . . . another for him to heal people, even his mother-in-law . . . but this . . . this hit home. Simon knew in the depths of his being that what he had just witnessed could not be explained rationally. In fact, what he had just witnessed was impossible, humanly speaking. He had dared to argue with Jesus, and he had been proved wrong. In many ways, he had been wrong all along.

The second bolt of lightning came almost simultaneously. This meant he had no more excuses. He had to believe. Jesus was who he claimed to be . . . the holy one of God. Holy! He, Simon the fisherman, was standing in the presence of someone . . . how had the Baptizer put it? . . . of someone whose sandal he was unworthy to untie. And then he felt it . . . a flood of deep unworthiness . . . a profound nakedness . . . a crushing sense of sinfulness. While he could now acknowledge Jesus as Messiah, there was no way he was worthy to be his follower, his disciple. He fell to his knees before the one he had resisted for so long.

"Lord." That was a more fitting term of address than Master. "Lord, please. Just leave me be. I am not what you need. I am not what you are looking for. I am not disciple-making material. I'm a plain man, a sinful man . . . feeble and frail. I will not do you justice . . . I will fail you . . . so, please. Please, leave me and look for another." He felt like he was babbling, so he stopped trying to speak. Perhaps a reverential silence was what was called for anyway.

Then he looked up. Those eyes . . . Simon looked right into those eyes that had bored into his soul the first time they had met. Once again Jesus was looking deep into his inner being, seeing something Simon himself could not see . . . and he was smiling that smile again.

---

3. For an insightful article on the harbour where this more than likely took place see: https://biblearchaeologyreport.com/2019/07/08/footsteps-three-things-in-capernaum-that-peter-likely-saw/.

"Yes, Simon. I know," he chuckled. "You are not now what you will be. But I will make you what I know you can become, a fisher of people. Don't let doubt and fear keep you from what you have been called to be. I am with you. Just follow me . . . walk *with* me . . . walk *like* me."

As soon as the boat reached the harbour walls, Simon, Andrew, James, and John knew what they needed to do. True, they didn't know where they were going – they didn't even know what they would do – but that no longer mattered. If Jesus could provide an abundance of fish at a time when there was not one for the catching, they had no reason for any form of apprehension. So, they left it all and followed Jesus.

Part II

Nurturing and Nourishment

"The seed I planted was watered by Apollos,
but it was God who made it grow."
1 Corinthians 3:6

6

Learning to Follow

Trust does not come easily to some. Large crowds had been following Jesus for quite some time, and Simon, at last, was one of them. There had been many reasons for his paralyzing reluctance. Simon was a hardworking, practical man. Nothing had come easy to him . . . and he was responsible for a family. There was too much to lose in following an itinerant, penniless preacher. There was also the deep-seated fear that this following might lead nowhere, which is what had happened to the others who thought they could liberate Israel from the tyranny of Rome.[1] The Romans had crushed them as if they were fleas on a donkey's back. There was no guarantee that Jesus's followers would not all meet the same violent end.

But it seemed to him that his own sense of unworthiness had held him back too. What could he do for a rabbi? True, he knew the Scriptures fairly well. He had learned the Torah, the first five books of Moses, by heart before the age of ten, but he was not eloquent nor was he persuasive. Some of his friends had gone on to study the Scriptures further and had learned the interpretations of the different rabbis of old . . . but Simon had had to take care of a family. Further education had been denied him. He did not know the finer aspects of the law, and he could not quote famous men from the past.

But Jesus had been relentless in pursuing Simon. Jesus was different from other rabbis. He did not look for perfection in his followers. In fact, the longer Simon followed him, the more it seemed that Jesus intentionally called the imperfect . . . like that leper, for instance. While everyone else scattered and held their hands before their mouths, Jesus not only stopped to listen to the man, but he actually touched him! No one had ever done that before! Simon knew the story about Naaman being cleansed by Elisha. Elisha had not even

---

1. Flavius Josephus, *Antiquities of the Jews*, 17.10: "Now, at this time there were ten thousand other disorders in Judea . . ." See also Acts 5:36.

bothered to look on the commander from Aram, much less touch him! But Jesus *did* touch this leper . . . both physically and through his words which were so kind . . . so reassuring. And the man was healed immediately. As usual, Jesus's only request was that the man tell no one . . . he had only to show himself to the priest so that he might be allowed to return to his home, his society, and to his family.[2]

It was this difference . . . this otherness . . . this selflessness . . . that chiselled away the protective and impenetrable wall of mistrust that Simon had built around himself. While there was still much that Jesus said and did that left Simon puzzled, he simply could not argue with the fact that Jesus was a remarkable man and that, if he would only stop sending people away and telling them to say nothing about what he had done for them . . . he might well be the one who would restore the kingdom of Israel to them.

No one could deny that there were many who followed Jesus – perhaps for the wrong reasons – but at that moment it seemed to Simon like the whole world was right there in his home . . . all around Jesus, listening, learning. In fact, there was no space to let even one more onto the compound![3]

As Simon was reflecting on what he had already seen and what the future might hold, he heard a scraping noise above him. As he looked up, he saw a piece of his roof move. What on earth was happening? he wondered. As he rose to check, the light of the sun broke into the room and blinded him for a moment. He felt something brush against him as it was lowered down from above. He looked down and saw that it was a man on a sleeping mat in front of him. The friends who had lowered him were chattering loudly from above . . . explaining something about how they could not get in through the doorway because of the crowds and that the man was a paralytic. They wanted Jesus to heal him. Before Simon could protest, Jesus simply smiled and said to the paralyzed man, "Son, your sins are forgiven."

"This man blasphemes!" Simon couldn't help overhearing the hissed objection from one of the leaders. "Only God can forgive sins!"

Yes, Simon thought. That is true! Only God can forgive sins. He felt an all too familiar flutter of doubt again in his heart.

But Jesus was smiling. Even though it was not possible that he had heard the comment, Simon knew well enough that somehow, Jesus always knew what was going on in the minds of his opponents. "What is easier?" Jesus asked. "To

---

2. Leviticus 13:6, 13, 17, 23; 14:1–32.

3. For an interesting article with illustrations on the House of Simon Peter see: https://madainproject.com/house_of_saint_peter.

say to this paralytic, 'your sins are forgiven,' or 'get up, take your mat and walk'? But that you may know that the Son of Man has authority to forgive sins . . . I say now," and he looked directly at the man, "get up and walk."

The atmosphere was tense. The man first wiggled his toes . . . and then he shifted his legs. Clearly, he had feeling where just moments ago there was nothing but numbness. He shifted to the edge of the mat. Then with one fluid movement, he stood before them all. Apart from an initial collective gasp, no one said a word. The man bent over, rolled up his mat, and with grateful tears washing over his face, he walked out through the crowd. As he passed through the door, the silence was replaced with loud proclamations of praise to God.

What just happened? Simon wondered. He forgave the man's sin. He healed him, too. And he called himself the Son of Man. Somewhere, Simon had heard that term before . . . from one of the prophets, he was sure. But what did this all mean? Who was Jesus really? And . . . but wait! Where was Jesus going now?

Simon and the others jumped up quickly and followed Jesus. Simon knew he could repair the roof later. The crowd followed Jesus, too, all the way to the sea and, as he walked, he continued to teach them. But no amount of teaching could have prepared them for what Jesus did next. Sure, everyone liked the tax collector, Levi son of Alphaeus, or Matthew as some called him, because he treated them fairly, but still . . . he was a collaborator with the Romans! Every fish . . . every single fish Simon caught had been taxed. Simon simply couldn't believe what he was hearing Jesus say to Levi! "Come. Follow me."

Simon was still reeling from the shock of it when he realized that things were actually going from bad to worse. Jesus had just agreed to have dinner at Levi's home together with his disciples and all of Levi's friends! What would the leaders say about this? What would his own friends say? His reputation would be gone forever. Imagine! Eating with collaborators and with sinners! True, these men were Jews, but they were not the right kind of people.

And sure enough, that is exactly what the leaders did say. Capernaum was a small village where everyone knew everyone else and everyone knew everyone else's business. After all, what else was there to talk about unless Herod or the Romans did something atrocious? When Simon and some of the others stepped out of Levi's home into the street for a breath of fresh air, some people from the village cornered them. "Your rabbi! Why does he eat with tax collectors and other worldly people?"

At that very moment, Jesus appeared in the doorway. Apparently, he also needed a bit of air . . . or did he? He always seemed to be at the right place at the right time. Smiling, he firmly stated, "It is not the healthy that need a physician, but the sick. I did not come for those who live rightly, but for those who do not."

That is so right! Simon thought to himself. So, that is Jesus's methodology! To bring the *wayward* back in line. And then when everyone was following the law of Moses as they should, that would be the time when God would act on behalf of his people again! Was that not the story of Judges? When the people repented and turned from their wicked ways, then God heard from heaven and sent a saviour! Yes, that must be what Jesus was doing.

With a newfound spirit of camaraderie welling up inside him, Simon barged back into Levi's house and embraced his new fellow follower. Levi was startled at first, if not a bit bewildered by this very visual and physical show of acceptance, but it took only a moment for him to return the embrace. The sense of belonging was exhilarating to Levi . . . it was as if he had suddenly been found after wandering in search of something he could not find.

But if Simon thought he was alone in his questioning of the way Jesus did things, he was wrong. On the way home that evening, some of the people milling about asked Jesus about fasting. "John's disciples fasted," they said. "The Pharisees fasted. Why are your disciples always eating and drinking?" At first Simon was offended, but the feeling of offense quickly turned to guilt. The question somehow made him doubt himself again, as if others were better than he was . . . more righteous, more holy, more worthy.

But then he heard Jesus speak. "Have you ever heard of the guests of the bridegroom fasting while he is with them?" He chuckled. "Of course not!" But then a cloud seemed to pass over his face. Jesus looked past them all as if he was looking into the future. After a short period of silence, he added quietly, "There will come a time when the bridegroom will not be with them and then they will fast." Was that sadness Simon detected in his voice? But looking up suddenly, Jesus smiled again as he said, "No one sews new cloth onto old clothes, nor do they put new wine in old wineskins. In both cases they would tear. No, both must be new." With that he turned and walked away.

Simon was quiet. He did not understand. What did Jesus mean? True the things he did and said could be described as new . . . even revolutionary. Speaking to Samaritans, touching lepers, calling tax collectors to follow him . . . all very new and very different. But Jesus was pouring this new teaching into them . . . and they were not new. Simon did not feel very new at all. In fact, he felt very old and tired. Oh, would he ever understand?

7

Mercy, Not Sacrifice

It felt like they had been walking and talking for hours. Jesus had a habit of using the simple things of nature to illustrate spiritual truths . . . lilies, birds, various trees . . . as they trekked across the countryside. And as he looked around him, Simon had to admit that the scenery was breathtakingly beautiful. He had never had the time before to simply walk about enjoying the scenery, not that he would have noticed many of the beautiful things that Jesus pointed out to them as they walked.

They had just entered a grain field and the grain was full and ready for harvest. Sheaves upon golden sheaves waved in the light breeze. Without thinking, Simon picked a few heads, rolled them in his hands, and popped the kernels into his mouth. They were all hungry . . . the others did the same.

"Rabbi!" The shout came from behind them. They turned to see a few red-faced Pharisees glaring at them. "Your disciples are breaking the law of the Sabbath!"

Simon looked at the other disciples, the grains turning dry in his mouth. Really? What law? Simon couldn't recall a law forbidding the eating of grain on the Sabbath. Or was it that he had rubbed the grain in his hands? He knew there were many rabbinical interpretations of the scriptural commands. Was that what they were citing? The rabbis had multiplied the requirements and the restrictions of the law in their efforts to force people to keep it . . . but how were ordinary people like Simon to know what was right and what was wrong when the rabbis could not agree amongst themselves? He looked at Jesus. His face was serene and peaceful. The accusations didn't appear to irritate him at all.

"Did you read what David did when he and his men were hungry?" Jesus asked. Simon was trying hard to remember the story, but he was so preoccupied with trying to swallow the dry wheat kernels in his mouth that he couldn't think. "In the days of Abiathar, the high priest," Jesus continued, "David went into the house of God and took the consecrated bread and he and his men ate it. That wasn't lawful, was it? The bread was there only for the priests, correct?"

The Pharisees looked confused. They had not heard teaching like this before and they had not prepared an argument against it.

Jesus continued. "You have read in the law that the priests in the temple desecrate the Sabbath day, and yet they are innocent, haven't you?"[1] Then his voice took on a different tone . . . a solemnity, an authoritative firmness. He took a step toward them and stood between them and his disciples. "I tell you truly, one greater than the temple stands before you."

The look on his face had changed. It seemed as if his eyes were on fire. His voice was stronger, louder . . . almost like a thundering flood of water. "If you really understood God's intentions you would not be so quick to judge and condemn the innocent. God said: 'I desire mercy, not sacrifice.' Remember?"

Had the birds stopped singing? There was an awe-filled silence. Simon managed to produce enough saliva to swallow the dry kernels. Clearly the Pharisees were dumbstruck. Then Jesus said, softly but clearly, "I tell you, God gave the Sabbath for the service of humanity, not humanity for the service of the Sabbath. Do not make the Sabbath to be more than what it is." Then he added, "But know this – the Son of Man is Lord even of the Sabbath."

There was that phrase again. The Son of Man. Simon so wanted to ask Jesus what he meant by calling himself the Son of Man, but he was afraid he would appear foolish to the others, so he held his peace. It sounded like Jesus was saying he was a son of Adam . . . like all of humanity . . . but when Jesus applied the term to himself, he gave the impression that it meant something more specific . . . that he was someone greater than just an ordinary human being. Maybe Simon could ask him sometime when they were alone . . . But they were moving again, this time toward the local synagogue, with the silent, angry, and embarrassed Pharisees following.

As they entered through the synagogue door, Simon noticed a man with a shrivelled hand sitting on the ground to one side. Why did their leaders always have to treat people with deformities with such disdain? Especially in a holy place! Jesus's words echoed in his head. Mercy not sacrifice. Mercy. The word seemed to fly in the face of what these teachers of the law believed. They hounded people, always finding fault, always accusing. And today was no exception. No sooner had the Pharisees come inside the building, when they pounced on the unsuspecting man and turned him to face Jesus.

"Is it permitted to heal on the Sabbath?" they asked.

---

1. Matthew 12:5; Leviticus 24:8; Numbers 28:9–10.

Jesus walked past them and sat down at the far end of the synagogue. Looking at the people gathered there he said gently, "Your sheep falls into a pit on the Sabbath day. What do you do? Will you leave it there or lift it out?" It was a rhetorical question of course, but Simon couldn't help wishing that someone would state the obvious. Of course, they would take it out! Mercy. It would be the merciful thing to do.

Jesus turned and looked at the man with the shrivelled hand. He looked so pathetically sad. Simon couldn't understand how the Pharisees could be so cruel? It was bad enough that he had a deformity and that they treated him so unkindly, but to use him as . . . as bait . . . like bait for catching fish. They were using him as bait to catch Jesus! Surely that was not an act of godliness?

Then Jesus's voice seemed to fill the whole space. "Stretch out your hand!" For a moment the man simply looked at his tormentors as if waiting for their approval. But then he shook off their grip and moved slightly forward. He stretched out his hand and, as he did, it was healed. Mercy. Mercy, not sacrifice – not rules and endless regulations. Mercy.

The Pharisees left the building as one man. Later someone told Simon that they overheard these very men plotting to kill Jesus. How lawful was that? Simon thought. But then again, he was a simple man.

But the threat did not stop Jesus, although he and his followers did withdraw from that place. He continued to heal the sick, constantly reminding them not to make any speculative claims about him. Jesus was merciful and gracious and humble. What was it that the prophet Isaiah had said about the Messiah? He struggled to remember. It hurt his head to try to recall things he had learned in his youth. Something about a servant whom God himself had chosen. Yes! That was right. He remembered now. "See my servant! I will uphold him. He is my chosen one and I delight in him. I have put my Spirit on him, he shall bring about justice for the nations. He shall not cry out or shout out loud, or make his voice heard in the street. He shall not break a bruised reed or snuff out a smoking wick. He shall bring about a new and true way. He shall not falter or fail until he has founded the true way on earth; and the coastlands shall wait for his teaching."[2]

Jesus did not parade himself before anyone. And he was always kind to the broken, the dispirited, the downtrodden, the marginalized. Mercy, not sacrifice.

---

2. Isaiah 42:1–4, my own translation.

8

Narrowing the Focus

When Jesus came down from the mountain that morning, he did not look like someone who had spent the whole night in prayer. Rather, he looked revitalized. There was a certain gleam in his eye . . . a gleam like that of someone who knew something no one else did . . . something good he was about to share.

Simon had come to learn that when Jesus went to pray on his own, he was not simply reciting prayers learned from the rabbis. No, Jesus did as much listening as he did talking . . . and when he listened, he heard the very voice of God. How he did that, Simon had no idea. But lately, experience was causing him to believe things he did not understand . . . and Jesus's prayer life was one such experience. He didn't feel the need to question it . . . that was just the way it was.

By this time, Jesus had gained quite a following, but it seemed to Simon that he now wanted to narrow his focus. For a while now, Jesus had been spending more and more time with a smaller group – to Simon's delight, with him, and his old fishing partners, James and John. At first, Simon had wondered if this would be a problem for Andrew. After all, this personal journey had started because of Andrew, not because of him. But it seemed that Andrew had learned not to question Jesus . . . he appeared to be content with the fact that his brother was beginning to take the lead again, as a big brother should.

But why? Simon thought. Why is he singling us out? What does this mean? Cephas. Jesus called me Cephas when he first met me. A Rock. Simon knew what it was like to be in a partnership, and while this was not exactly an equal partnership, it was as if he was being drawn in closer . . . prepared perhaps for something larger than himself. That worried him.

"Simon."

"Yes, Lord?"

Jesus placed his hands on Simon's shoulders and looked directly into his eyes. "I want you to be a part of a closer community. My community. A commissioned community who will represent me to all, a community who will follow me in every way . . . be like me . . . think like me . . . act like me. The time has come for you to become an active participant in this ministry."

Before Simon could say anything, Jesus had moved on and was saying the same things to James and John . . . and Andrew and Philip – the original small group – but also to Levi, Bartholomew, Thomas the twin, the other James, Thaddeus, Simon the zealot, and Judas Iscariot. Twelve in all. Twelve! Like the twelve tribes of Israel! Was that significant at all? Was this the beginning of some sort of a renewal of the nation?

Then Jesus turned to them and said, "I now designate you apostles. You will go wherever I send you. You will have my authority to do and to say what I do and say. But come, the crowd is gathering to listen." With that, he went back up the mountain and sat down to teach.

Later, Simon wished he had been more attentive, but his mind was reeling. An apostle? With Jesus's authority? To do and say what he did and said? How? He was a fisherman, not a speaker and certainly not a healer or exorcist! But then again, wasn't that Moses's argument with God at the burning bush? Not me God . . . send someone else.[1]

"You are blessed," Jesus was saying to the crowd, "when you know that you cannot rely on your own strength. The kingdom of heaven will be populated by those who know they cannot earn a place in it. You are blessed when you are deeply troubled by your sin, because when your sin is covered, you will be comforted. You are blessed when you are humble – the earth is God's to give to the meek, not the mighty. If you desire to live the kind of life you were made to live – if you seek after that like a starving and thirsty person – you will be blessed because you will be living in harmony with yourself and your Creator. If you are merciful to others, you are blessed, because you, too, will receive mercy."

Mercy, Simon thought. Mercy not sacrifice. Not rules and regulations that humiliate and shame people.

"You are blessed when your heart is pure because then nothing will obscure the face of God. You are blessed when you are peacemakers because then you will be doing what your Father does. You are blessed when you suffer mistreatment from others because of what you believe and practice . . . the kingdom of heaven belongs to you. You are blessed when people insult you,

---

1. Exodus 3:11.

revile you, persecute you and accuse you falsely because you are associated with me. Remember, they did the same things to the prophets of old."

Simon felt like he was back in Hebrew school, listening but not always comprehending. These sayings were so different . . . the wrong side up, as it were . . . turned around . . . the exact opposite of what he thought it meant to be blessed. Oh, how was he going to be an apostle when he understood so little? Suddenly, he was aware that Jesus was looking at him . . . or perhaps he was looking at the twelve. After all, they were seated together now as a group.

"Salt that is no longer salty is useless, right? How does one make saltless salt salty again?"

Someone in the crowd laughed.

"You." Now Jesus *was* looking directly at them. "You are the salt of the earth. Think about a lamp. Who would light a lamp only to hide it under a basket?" He chuckled. Clearly no one would do that.

Simon looked at the crowd. They hung on Jesus's lips, mesmerized by the profound and yet simple words pouring from the healer's mouth. Like him, they had never heard such teaching before.

Jesus continued. "Just like a city high on top of a hill cannot be hidden, so you too must not be hidden, because you are the light of the world. Just like a lamp must be placed on a lampstand, so your life must point people in the right direction – above, not below – to God, not to yourself or any other. You see, when people witness your selfless way of life, then they will give glory to your heavenly Father. So, shine out your light in the world."

Simon was intrigued by this teaching. It was true that every rabbi served as a model for his disciples to emulate. But Simon was no rabbi. He was a fisherman. And yet Jesus very clearly intended these comments to apply to him and his companions. They were salt. Along with all their ceremonial offerings, this people had been taught to offer salt as well. It was part of the burnt offering for sin and of the incense offering which represented the prayers of the people. In that sense, salt was a blessing. But they were also commanded to sow the conquered land of their enemies with salt so that it would be difficult to grow crops there later. In that sense, it was a curse. Was Jesus saying that they were a blessing and a curse to the world? Like Abraham was a blessing to all who blessed him and a curse to all who cursed him? Is that what they were? All the families, all the people groups, all the nations were to be blessed through them? They were the salt of the earth.

But also, light. For Simon, that image was clearer. Light illuminates. Light exposes. Light dispels darkness. So, by copying the way Jesus was showing them, others would look past them and see God. They were not to be like their leaders who wanted people to look at them and praise them. No, they were to live in a way that would make people look at and praise their heavenly Father.

Father. It was the first time Simon had applied that intimate word to God, even if only in his thoughts. He had always spoken of Abraham as the father of the nation . . . not God. But Jesus had indicated earlier that those who believed in him were somehow reborn in a spiritual sense . . . and therefore, their origin was no longer purely earthly, but rather heavenly. So, he ought not to call any man "father" – not even their great founder Abraham – because he had God as his Father. This was all so new . . . like fresh fruit picked in the early morning . . . refreshing and sweet.

"Do not misunderstand me." Jesus had now turned his attention back to the crowd. "My purpose is not to abolish the Law or the Prophets."

So, it is not new after all, Simon thought.

"The Law and the Prophets remain valid. They are God's words . . . not one jot or tittle can be removed or changed. The reason I have come is so that I might fulfil their true meaning and intention . . . to accomplish their purpose. If you disregard the least of the commandments and teach others to do the same, then you will be regarded as the least in the kingdom of heaven. The reverse is equally true. If you obey, you will be called the greatest."

Simon was puzzled. Isn't that exactly what the Pharisees . . . the teachers of the Law . . . do. Don't they obey the smallest details? Haven't they created myriads of extra rules or explanations to make sure they never break the smallest commandment?"

"But I must warn you," Jesus continued. "Unless your integrity exceeds that of the teachers of the Law, you will not become citizens of the kingdom."

Simon's puzzlement turned into confusion at this point. The Pharisees excelled in virtue. They were determined to be righteous and to live according to strict rules and regulations. How could he, a simple fisherman, be more virtuous than that? Simon looked up to see Jesus looking at him with a crooked smile on his face. How did Jesus know what he was thinking?

"You have heard it said . . ." Jesus emphasized the word "said" as if Simon was to read something into the word. Then it came to him like a bolt of lightning. That's it! Said. You have heard it said! Jesus did not say, "You have read it written . . ." He was addressing the oral law . . . the teaching of the Pharisees and scribes. He was telling them that there was something wrong with their exposition of the Law and the Prophets!

Then Jesus went through a number of misapplications of the Scriptures . . . on anger, adultery, divorce, vows, punishment for law breaking, and hating one's enemy. In most cases he broadened the application of the law. Like when he spoke about love. What Simon had learned in the synagogues was that love was only to be extended to like-minded neighbours. Enemies were to be hated and, if possible, exterminated. That was what the Zealots believed. But Jesus taught the exact opposite. They were to pray for a blessing on those who persecuted them because God blessed all humans equally. He blessed them all with sun and rain. He was no respecter of persons. He was kind and so those who believed in him ought to be kind. That raised the standard yet again. They were to be like God in every way. Indeed, Jesus said they ought to be perfect even as he was perfect.

"Don't do good things just so that other people will praise you and honour you." Jesus taught a lot about private righteousness, saying that the inner relationship with the Father mattered more than outward appearances. The opinion of humanity was not to be their primary concern. It was a matter of the heart. God saw all and knew all. So why pretend? Giving, praying, fasting – all the things that the leaders paraded before them to show how holy they were – Jesus said should be done quietly . . . privately.

Like prayer. Prayers were something they were taught to recite from memory – over and over and over again – as if the repetition would finally wear God down to the point where he would grant the petition out of total exasperation. They had prayers for everything. Prayers for waking, prayers for sleeping, prayers for eating, prayers for drinking . . . endless, repetitive, monotonous prayers. But Jesus was showing them through his own example how they could talk to the Father directly . . . because he already knew all about them anyway. Praise first – to focus the heart on the one addressed – and then petition. Praise helped raise the level of petition from a limited earthly context to a limitless heavenly one.

Jesus also spoke about forgiveness a lot. Simon knew well enough that oppressed people carry a lot of resentment and thoughts, if not deeds of revenge, were always close to the surface. But Jesus taught them a different way . . . the way of forgiveness. He taught them to ask God to forgive them as they forgave others. Simon noticed a few people shake their heads and walk away. How did one forgive? How did one forgive like God? Was that even possible for a human? Simon thought about the resentment he had allowed to fester inside him. He would need to talk to Jesus about this . . . get more clarity. Surely there was a limit as to how much one could forgive another.

"Where are your treasures?" Jesus was asking. Simon immediately thought about his wife . . . his home . . . his family . . . his business. Those were treasures that had kept him from following Jesus a long time ago. "Moth and rust destroy things stored on earth, and thieves break in and steal them. So, rather than accumulate things that have no eternal value, store up treasures that do . . . treasures in heaven. Because wherever your treasure is stored, that is where your heart will be."

How does one store up treasures in heaven? Simon wondered. Were these treasures their tithes and offerings that they were meant to bring to fill the treasury rooms of the temple? There was little chance of that happening now that he had partially given up his livelihood. Surely that could not be what Jesus meant. They had a little put away just in case they needed that in the future . . . but it was so little. He often worried about how he would provide for their needs.

"Don't worry about everyday life," Jesus was saying. What? How did he know? "Don't worry about what you will eat or drink or wear. Life is far more important than food."

A flock of common sparrows flew overhead. Jesus pointed to them and added, "Look at those birds in the air. They don't store away provisions, do they? And yet they never lack food. Your heavenly Father takes good care of them." He directed his gaze once more to Simon. "You are of far greater value than they are."

Value. Was he really of greater value to God? Simon struggled with this thought. He was a nobody . . . an obscurity . . . easily overlooked. He paused in his thinking and looked at Matthew. Matthew returned his gaze and smiled a weak smile. He obviously still felt as if he did not fit in with the group. Simon smiled back. Yes, he may be overlooked by many, but he was rarely overlooked by the tax-collectors! He was of value to them! But surely this was not how God would value him. Jesus went on to point out the wild poppies growing in abundance all around them. They really were beautiful. And Jesus was right. Even Solomon's robes could not rival them. "So, if God clothes the fields so luxuriously," Jesus continued, "don't you think he will clothe you as well?" There was that smile again. "O, you of little faith. Don't be anxious for the things that dominate the thoughts of unbelievers. Your Father knows all your needs. Rather spend your time thinking about how to live in the kingdom of God and allow the King to take care of your needs. Live life in the present moment . . . think about tomorrow only when it arrives."

From that point on, Simon knew he was only listening with half an ear. It was that idea of value that kept his mind occupied. Jesus was speaking about judgment and persistent prayer . . . something about a narrow gate and a bad tree . . . and then something about a house built on bedrock.

A house . . . built on a rock. He knew he had learned something about that in his studies at Hebrew school years ago. Wasn't that what David had said near the end of his life? That God was his Rock and that God had built up the house of David? That would then apply to the Messiah as the descendent of David, but now Jesus seemed to be applying the image to them.

He would have to think about that later. He was still thinking about the concept of value, especially his value before a God who had created all he could see . . . the entire earth belonged to Him . . . what was he, a mere man, that God Almighty would place any value on him?[2]

Simon was roused from his reflections by the murmuring of the crowd. He heard quite a few people express amazement at the authoritative nature of Jesus's teaching, comparing his style with that of their leaders. Yes, Jesus was different. His teaching was different. But the difference lay in the fact that he seemed to take them back to the original intention of the Scriptures, not to the speculative ruminations of men, however wise they might be.

* * *

It was a slow walk back to Capernaum. Simon kept looking at the poppies in the field, and every bird that flew overhead reminded him of what Jesus had said about him having value. He, a lowly fisherman, was of greater value than many birds. The Almighty God was mindful of him.

As they walked into their village, a Roman centurion hurried toward them. Simon's hand instinctively moved to the fishing knife in his belt. Was this trouble? But no, the man looked grieved . . . a number of the Jewish leaders were with him.

"Lord," the man was out of breath. "Lord, please. My young servant is suffering terribly. He is confined to his bed, unable to move, and he is in a great deal of pain."

Servant! This man values his servant? Remarkable, Simon thought. And he is a Roman soldier . . . a Gentile! I haven't seen any one of our rulers care that much for their servants!

The Jewish leaders began to talk all at once. "This man loves our people!" "Look! He helped build our synagogue!" "If anyone is deserving of your attention, it is him!"

Simon was amused. Did they care as much about his servant as he did? Or did they care about what this man could do for them?

"I will come and heal him." Jesus said simply.

"Oh, no, Lord!" The centurion's voice broke through the babble. "No, Lord! I am not worthy for you to enter my household. I am a Gentile. You are a Jew.

---

2. See Psalm 8.

I didn't even think I was worthy to come into your presence. That's why these friends are with me."

So, he knows the law, Simon mused. He was a humble man for sure. He didn't seem to be offended by the implications of the law of separation . . . on the contrary, he appeared to understand the ramifications of his request in the light of their respective cultures. Many tongues would be loosed if Jesus entered his home.

"Lord, I understand how authority works," the centurion continued. "I am under the authority of those greater than me and consequently when I give a command my subordinates listen and obey. So, simply speak the word of healing and I know my servant will be healed."

Was that shock on Jesus's face? It looked as if this statement had taken Jesus by surprise.

"I've never witnessed faith like this in all Israel," Jesus said to the crowd gathered around them. Then he added solemnly. "Mark my words, many Gentiles will come from all over the world to feast with Abraham, Isaac, and Jacob in the kingdom of heaven. But many of those for whom the kingdom had been intended will not be there. They will be cast out into the darkness and there they will wail with regret."

Gentiles will come to feast with Abraham, Isaac, and Jacob in the kingdom of heaven? Gentiles? The idea of Gentiles being included in the kingdom had never occurred to Simon. They had been taught that the Messiah would restore the kingdom to Israel . . . there had been no talk of Gentiles.

Turning to the centurion, Jesus told him, "Go home. It is as you have believed."

The centurion did not hesitate. He believed. It seemed as if he harboured no doubt in his mind. Later, they heard that the servant had been healed at the very moment that Jesus spoke the word. Simon wondered why they were surprised by the news. If the centurion did not doubt, why did they?

Simon lay awake that night thinking about what he had learned that day. There was so much to process. Thankfully, Jesus had a tendency to repeat his lessons, so there would be other opportunities to learn. He listened to the soft rhythmic breathing of his wife next to him. She had been with him for many years now . . . he had not really known her before they were betrothed to each other . . . but his parents had chosen wisely. She was of more value to him than a thousand other women. Value! Yes, surely that's how it was. If he could value his wife, as well as his brother Andrew, and his extended family, and his friends . . . and if a Gentile centurion could value his servant . . . then yes. God could value him . . . *did* value him. And that thought gave him great comfort. He smiled and calmly drifted off to sleep.

* * *

They had been walking southwest of the lake for a while. Jesus was teaching them as they walked, but periodically, he would stop to address the large crowd of people walking with them.

They heard the wailing before they saw the funeral procession. Coming out of the gate of the small village of Nain was a woman being supported by those with her as if she was unable to carry herself. She was clearly inconsolable.

"Who is she?" one of them asked as they came closer.

"She is a widow," the villagers replied. "God took her husband, and now he has taken her only son as well. Oh, such a tragedy! Who will take care of her in her old age?"

Jesus did not hesitate. Simon could clearly see that he was moved with compassion. He walked right up to the devastated women and gently said, "Do not weep." The woman stared at him blankly.

Oh Jesus, Simon thought, the young man is dead. She will weep many more bitter tears before she joins him in Sheol.[3]

But Jesus had moved to the side of the stretcher on which the body lay, wrapped in spices and cloth. He touched the body and the bearers stopped. The woman turned around, alarmed at first, but then, as she saw the form of her beloved child, her sorrow overwhelmed her once again and a deep sob escaped from her chapped lips. Never before had Simon seen such utter despair chiselled into the face of another fellow human being.

"Young man," Jesus said.

Was he addressing the dead? He was speaking to the corpse as if he were alive!

"Young man, I tell you, get up."

Simon felt himself go weak at the knees. The widow stopped weeping and ran to the stretcher where the wrapped-up body of her son was wriggling in an attempt to sit up. The stretcher bearers hastily set down their charge and stood to one side in awe. The mother quickly removed the linen bands that covered her son's face. There were no words spoken between them at first. Indeed, neither could speak. She held his face in her hands and kissed him over and over again, gently rocking him back and forth as one would a baby.

---

3. The Hebrew word for the collective place of the dead.

There was only a gasp from the crowd. A great fear gripped them. They had never witnessed anything like this before. The young man had been dead. Dead! But there he sat, still wrapped in his grave cloths, but very much alive. How? It was one thing to heal the sick . . . it was another to raise the dead. Elisha had raised the Shunamite woman's dead son to life . . . and there was that corpse that came to life after touching Elisha's bones in his tomb . . . but those were just stories from long ago. Or were they? This was something completely foreign to their life experiences.

"A prophet!" someone cried out. "A great prophet has come to us! God has visited his people this day!" They all repeated the cry, scampering away to tell everyone they could. Their mourning had turned into rejoicing.

This ought to get Jesus a few more followers, Simon thought. Who can deny that he is God's Messiah now? The eyes of all Israel may yet be opened. Yes, the movement was gathering momentum. Soon, even the leaders would acknowledge Jesus as the Coming One.

But he was wrong.

* * *

Although Simon had hoped that all Israel would believe following this great miracle, he was sorely disappointed the very next day.

"Are you the one we were expecting, or should we be looking out for another?" This was the question of a delegation from none other than John the Baptizer. John had been arrested once again and was languishing in Herod's prison.

Of course, no one could blame John. Everyone had been expecting a more militant Messiah, someone who would lead them out into battle against their Roman overlords like the great judges, kings, and warriors of old. People repeated the stories of the Maccabees over and over again to their children, hoping that one day God would send them another Judas Maccabeus. At every Festival of Lights this hope would be rekindled.

But Jesus. He was so different . . . different from what they all believed the prophets had said, or at least different from what they had been told the prophets had said. And what about the pronouncements of John the Baptizer? Where was "the axe laid to the roots?" Where was the "winnowing fork" and the "fire"? John was not alone in his confusion.

In response to the delegation's question, Jesus merely smiled . . . that gentle and compassionate and understanding smile . . . and said, "Go, tell my cousin what you have heard and seen. The eyes of the blind are opened, the ears of the deaf are unstopped, the lame leap as deer, lepers are cured, the dead are raised back to life . . . and words of liberation are preached to the oppressed."

He was quoting from one of the prophets, of that Simon was convinced. Jesus had strung together a number of statements from different parts of the scroll, something Simon had heard rabbis do before. The idea was to make the hearer recall the whole prophecy and not just a part of it. And surely this prophecy had to do with the Messiah.

"It is the prophecy from Isaiah," Andrew whispered in his ear.

Yes, Andrew had gone further than his brother in his studies . . . Simon had seen to that. One of them had to learn the Scriptures.

"If you look at the prophecy in its entirety, and not just in parts, it validates Jesus's ministry," Andrew explained.

Simon looked at his younger brother. Effort well spent, he thought.

Then Jesus added, "No one will be happy if they stumble because of my ministry."

Simon knew what he meant. The style of Jesus's ministry was so different from what he had imagined of the Messiah . . . he himself had stumbled along in the beginning because of this difference. Indeed, Jesus's character – his humility and gentleness – seemed inconsistent with the image the Baptizer had conjured up for them. But now, the teaching and the signs . . . and these prophetic words of Isaiah . . . certainly validated his ministry. It may be different, but it was divinely empowered. Surely, Jesus could only do what he did because God was with him.

The disciples of John left. They appeared to be convinced by what they had seen and heard.

May they provide comfort for the Baptizer, Simon thought. It would be a sad day if a great man like John was to lose his faith in Jesus at this point in time.

As if reading Simon's thoughts, Jesus began to speak well of John. It was a eulogy of sorts. "What kind of a man did you go out into the wilderness to meet?" Pointing to the reeds dancing in the shallow waters he added, "A flimsy reed, swayed by the gentlest of breezes?"

A reed? What a strange comparison. But wait! Simon pulled a coin of Herod Antipas from his purse. There was an image of a reed on it! Was Jesus trying to tell them that they ought not to be looking for an earthly ruler like Herod?

"Or were you seeking a man dressed in all manner of finery? Of course not! You know people dressed in fine clothing live in palaces."

He *was* comparing John with Herod! Once again, in his own enigmatic manner, Jesus was forcing them to think outside the parameters of what they had been told and what they had come to believe. Not a king . . . they should not be expecting an earthly king . . . Neither John, nor it seemed, the Messiah, would be an earthly king.

"So, what did you go out to see? A prophet?"

No one said a word. Everyone seemed to be too preoccupied trying to get a grip on this new frame of reference.

"Yes! Yes, you went out to meet a prophet! But I tell you, John is *more* than a prophet. He is a messenger, *the* messenger spoken about by the prophet Malachi. He is the forerunner sent to prepare the way of the coming one. Of all the great prophets of the past, none was greater than he."

Interesting, Simon thought. Their leaders spent a lot of time decorating the tombs of the great prophets, but they were reluctant to accept John's message.

People were nodding in agreement with Jesus. They were beginning to understand. John was the herald . . . that is why he had identified Jesus as the one on whom the Spirit of God had rested.

"And yet," Jesus paused as if thinking how to continue. "And yet, even the most insignificant in the kingdom of Heaven is greater than John."

Simon scratched his head. What did *that* mean? Just when he thought he was following the thread he lost it again. Lately he spent a lot of his time in the evenings rethinking things that Jesus had said during the day . . . like a cow chewing the cud, over and over again . . . but unlike the cow, all too often Simon could not swallow. He just did not understand.

"Since John began to preach, the kingdom has moved forward . . . but it is the ordinary people that are storming into it!" Jesus looked at his followers and the crowd.

That's true. What a bunch of misfits we are, Simon thought. Many in the crowds are from the lowest level of society. And yet . . . and yet Jesus had said that even the most insignificant was greater than John! Simon felt excitement overtake him. That's it! The forerunner was not born to Israel's finest, nor was the Messiah . . . and neither are the citizens of the kingdom. This is a kingdom unlike any other. It is not a political creation, nor is greatness measured here by pedigree or hierarchy. It is measured simply by unmerited inclusion.

"The law and prophets looked forward to this kingdom," Jesus said, drawing this eulogy of John to a close, "but John is the one who has ushered it in. He is the Elijah you expected . . . he is the herald of the great day. Think on these things. The truth demands attention and wise listening!"

But then, as if he had neglected to say something important, Jesus added, "To what shall I compare this generation?"

Simon noticed that a group of scribes and Pharisees had arrived and were standing at the edge of the crowd.

"This generation is like children trying to play a game in the marketplace with friends who are totally uncooperative. So, the children complained. 'We played merry music, but you did not dance. We played sad music, but you did not mourn.' John led an austere life, neither eating nor drinking as others do, but you said he was possessed by a demon. The Son of Man, on the other hand, does eat and drink with his followers – all his followers – and you say he is nothing but a glutton and a drunkard and a lover of sinners . . . one who keeps company with the unclean tax collectors and law breakers."

It seemed the whole crowd had become aware of the presence of the religious leaders . . . and the leaders, in turn, had become aware that these words were meant for them. Disgruntled, they moved away.

"You may condemn wise action now, but in the end you will be proved wrong."

Suddenly Jesus stood up. It was as if he was disturbed in his spirit.

"Oh, what sorrow awaits you, unrepentant cities . . . Chorazin and Bethsaida! If I had done the same signs in Tyre and Sidon as I have done in you, they would have mourned their sins in sackcloth and ashes. Truly I tell you, the day of judgment will be easier for them than for you."

Jesus's voice was thick with emotion. "And you, Capernaum!"

Simon swallowed hard. Chorazin and Bethsaida he wasn't too concerned about . . . but his hometown?

"Do not think that you, Capernaum, will be honoured in heaven. Certainly not. Instead you will go to the collective place of the dead. Sodom would still be here today if they had witnessed the works done among you. They too will be better off in the judgment day than you."

Was that a tear Simon saw glistening on Jesus's cheek or was it sweat? This abrupt condemnation seemed to be softened with a tone of sadness.

Suddenly, Jesus broke into prayer. "Father, Lord of Heaven and Earth, thank you for veiling the truth from those who think themselves wise and important . . . and for making it clear to the simple and the childlike. Thank you that this is what you have seen fit to do."

Turning to his disciples he continued, "My Father has entrusted everything to me. No one really knows the Son except the Father and no one knows the Father except the Son – and those to whom the Son chooses to reveal him."

Then to the crowd he said, "Come to me . . . you are exhausted and weary of trying to obey the many religious rules with which you have been burdened.

My yoke . . . my teaching . . . is not cumbersome. So come, let me show you a more meaningful, humbler, and gentler way of life."

He held out his hands as if in invitation. Who could hold back? Those whom others had discarded were accepted and loved by him. As one man, the crowd surged forward, and the sombre mood was broken with peals of laughter. Simon smiled. Who needed the high and mighty when you had the crowds? He would later learn to reject that philosophy.

9

A Sense of Confusion

Simon felt like he was at sea . . . a rough sea . . . cresting a wave only to plunge into the trough the next moment. Just when he was certain the leaders had all turned against Jesus, he heard that one of the Pharisees by the name of Simon had invited Jesus to a meal. Jesus had accepted and they were all going. It seemed so positive.

But things did not start well. Providing water for the washing of guests' feet was considered the minimal demonstration of good hospitality. Simon, the Pharisee, neglected to do so. He also neglected to greet Jesus with the customary kiss . . . nor did he anoint Jesus's head with olive oil. Perhaps he was afraid of being censured by his peers . . . or perhaps he was intentionally rude or provocative. It was hard to say, for certain. However, if the intention had been to insult Jesus, it failed. Jesus neither appeared to take offense nor did he show the slightest sign of annoyance.

Then a woman . . . a notoriously immoral woman . . . entered the house. Kneeling behind Jesus, she began to weep uncontrollably. Her tears fell on his feet and, as they did, she let down her hair to wipe them. Everyone was horrified. No self-respecting woman would let down her hair in public! And if Jesus were a prophet, thought the guests, he would not allow her to touch him, because it was clear that she was a sinful person. Could things get any worse?

But, quite calmly, Jesus turned to his host and said, "Simon, I want to tell you something."

"Please, proceed, teacher." The Pharisee was clearly uncomfortable with the continuing spectacle unfolding at his dinner.

Jesus proceeded to tell a simple story about two debtors, one owing much and the other less. Neither was able to repay his debt, and both were graciously forgiven, their debts cancelled. "Now, which one of the borrowers do you think would love the lender more?"

"Well, I suppose the one who was forgiven more," came the answer.

"Exactly!" Jesus replied. His eyes lit up like flames. Turning to the woman, he continued. "Simon, when I entered your home, you neglected to show me even the most basic form of hospitality. You neither had my feet washed nor did you provide me with water so that I could wash my own feet. But this woman has not ceased to bathe my dust-covered feet with her tears. She has humiliated herself in front of you all by using her hair to dry them. You did not anoint my head with olive oil, but she has been anointing my feet with costly perfume!"

Jesus gave the Pharisee a withering look. "Like the one borrower who owed more, this woman, though her sins are real and many . . . this woman, because she knows that her sins have been forgiven, has shown me more love than you." Looking at the woman directly, he added, "Your sins are forgiven."

"How can he forgive sins? Who is this man?" Simon and the disciples heard the sharp, cutting complaints, but Jesus was not disturbed.

"Go in peace, dear woman. Your faith has saved you." And with that, Jesus rose and left without another word. So much for winning over the leaders!

* * *

As was his custom, Jesus took his disciples along with him when he toured the villages around Galilee. It was a good apprenticeship model. They could watch him at work and listen to his teaching and then, under his supervision, they would do and teach what they had seen and learned. This was not unusual. Simon knew that other rabbis did the same with their disciples . . . but once again, Jesus was different.

Jesus included a group of women in his close circle. Some of them he had healed, others he had delivered from demon possession. Simon felt that he had been prepared for this through what Andrew had told him about Jesus's dealing with the Samaritan woman. He had treated her kindly and respectfully . . . like an equal . . . and had thus restored her dignity and, later, her social standing.

In turn, some of the women served Jesus and his disciples in practical ways. A few were women of means, like Joanna, the wife of one of Herod's stewards. She had crossed a wide social chasm to become one of Jesus's followers. And, indeed, for Jesus to be associated with one from the Herodian group was equally scandalous. But while these women sat at Jesus's feet just like the other disciples and learned the same lessons – in many ways their relationship with Jesus was the exact same as that of the men – they were prevented from engaging in more visible parts of his ministry because of the cultural practices and social norms of the people. Most men would not even speak to women in public. Would Jesus bring about change in the future? Simon wasn't sure. But Jesus was certainly breaking down barriers on so many levels.

* * *

Jesus had just healed another demon-possessed, blind and dumb man . . . the crowds pressed in to see more, and he and his disciples retreated into the house. They didn't even have time to eat. People were beginning to speculate openly. "Could this be the Son of David? Could Jesus be the Messiah?" When Jesus's brothers heard what was being said, they tried to take him away . . . they thought he was out of his mind. How they would change their opinions later!

This type of public praise of Jesus did not sit well with the Pharisees. They were still licking their wounds from previous encounters with him and were becoming increasingly bitter. "It is no wonder that he can cast out demons," they scoffed. "He is empowered by Beelzebub, the prince of demons."

As always, these words, never spoken to Jesus directly, but in private where the Pharisees could gather support from like-minded people, were known to Jesus. He was tired and in need of rest, but he felt he ought to address this latest accusation before it infected a larger group.

"Think about it," Jesus said. "Any kingdom rent asunder by civil unrest will eventually cave in on itself, right? Of course! So, in the same way, if Satan was divided against himself, his own kingdom would soon be no more. Correct?"

The silence indicated that the crowds were thinking about the logic.

"Now, let's take this a step further," Jesus said. "If I am casting out demons by the agency of Satan, what are your own exorcists doing? They cast out demons too, don't they? Surely you stand condemned by their actions!"

Murmurs of agreement could be heard from the crowd.

"But if . . ." Jesus paused. He waited until he knew everyone was listening. "If I cast out demons by the Spirit of God . . ." He paused again. The suspense was palpable. "If I cast out demons by the Spirit of God, then the kingdom of God is here among you right now."

Right now? Simon thought. It was true that the presence of God's Spirit would reveal the identity of the Messiah . . . the prophets had said so. But could the kingdom of God be with them now? How could that be?

"Who is able to enter a strong man's house and plunder it?" He let them ponder the question for a moment. "Surely only one stronger than him, right? Someone who could first overcome him and bind him and then take whatever he pleases."

Simon was struggling to follow the train of thought. Was Jesus saying that by casting out demons, he was proving that he was greater than the Prince of demons? Yes, that had to be what he meant. And plundering Satan's house surely meant that those trapped in his grasp . . . the demon-possessed . . . were being released and set free. A greater kingdom plundering a lesser kingdom . . . the kingdom of God plundering the kingdom of Satan. Was that what Jesus was teaching? But if that was the case, then who was Jesus that he was able to bind the strong man and to plunder his house?

"Anyone who is not with me is against me," Jesus said bluntly. "Anyone working against me is not with me. Instead of gathering together, he is scattering the flock."

That was simple enough to understand. There could be no neutral ground in this scenario. The prophets spoke about God reclaiming his scattered people, and one was either working with him or against him.

But Jesus was not finished. "Listen carefully to what I have to say now. There is nothing that cannot be forgiven . . . every sin and every blasphemy . . . except the blasphemy against the Holy Spirit. That cannot be forgiven. Anyone who speaks against the Son of Man can be forgiven, but not the one who speaks against the Holy Spirit. Such a person will not be forgiven . . . not in this world or the next."

Simon mulled the thought over in his mind. Yes, if one was so blind as to think that the work of the Holy Spirit was the work of the prince of demons, then how could anyone be forgiven? It was like saying God was the devil! That was blind, indeed! And if Jesus was casting out demons by the Holy Spirit, then what the Pharisees had said . . . could that be forgiven? Were they that blind?

The tone of the discourse had become tense. It was now obvious to everyone who Jesus was targeting with his rebukes.

"A tree . . . are you listening? You all know that a tree is identified by its fruit. If it is a good tree, then its fruit will be good. If it is a bad tree, then its fruit will be bad. You know a tree by what it produces."

This was challenging the crowd. They had to choose a side. Both could not be right. This was like Joshua challenging the people to choose who they would follow . . . like Elijah challenging the people before the prophets of Baal.

"You spreaders of poison! Do you think evil people like yourselves can ever speak what is good and right?"

Simon suppressed a nervous laugh. The faces of the Pharisees were crimson, their eyes as round as full moons.

"Your words reveal what is in your hearts!"

Simon nearly choked. Didn't the psalms and the proverbs warn them to guard their hearts? What did *Simon's* words reveal about *his* heart? Jesus's words did not only apply to the Pharisees . . . surely this was a word for everyone.

The prophet Jeremiah said the heart of humankind was desperately wicked and that only God could truly understand it[1] . . . what did God see when he looked at his heart?

"Good things come from good hearts and evil things come from evil hearts," Jesus continued. "You had better listen to what I tell you now! On judgment day you will all give account for every idle word you speak . . . and your own words will either clear you or condemn you."

Were the Pharisees still within earshot? Had they heard what Jesus had said? This is true, Simon thought. Words do reflect the innermost person. Bad words serve as irrefutable evidence against the speaker . . . they expose people for who they really are.

But Simon was troubled. What did his words say about him? He was so quick to speak before he thought through the implications. What was in his heart? He determined to be more careful with his words in the future. Better still, he needed to examine his heart. He did not want anyone to think he was a bad tree.

* * *

The Pharisees are relentless . . . you have to give them that, Simon thought. Just the other day, they stormed off after being exposed for what they were . . . bad trees bearing bad fruit . . . and now here they were again, this time demanding that Jesus validate his ministry by showing them miraculous signs. Simon was quite taken aback. What about all the previous miracles? What about the healings, the exorcisms, not to mention the raising of the widow's son? Were they not signs enough?

Jesus was seated as he taught the crowd of people crammed into the house. He looked up at these sign-seekers and simply stated, "A wicked and adulterous generation seeks after miraculous signs. They will only be given one – the sign of Jonah."

Simon quickly recalled the story of the reluctant prophet . . . Jonah had been called by God to go to Nineveh to warn them of impending doom . . . but he chose instead to go by sea in the opposite direction! But God would not be thwarted. He sent a storm . . . the superstitious sailors cried out to their gods for help and cast lots to find out which one of them had brought this calamity upon them by angering their god. When the lot fell to Jonah, he told them what he had done and instructed them to throw him overboard. The terrified sailors at first tried to save him, but eventually they did as he said. The storm

---

1. Jeremiah 17:9–10.

ceased – the sailors were saved . . . but, so was Jonah . . . he had not drowned. Swallowed by a huge sea creature, he remained in its belly for three days and three nights . . . and there he repented of his disobedience. That was the story as he remembered it, but what was the sign of Jonah?

"Just as Jonah was in the belly of the sea creature," Jesus explained, "the Son of Man will be in the belly of the earth for three days and three nights."

There he goes again, Simon thought. Who is able to understand such round about riddles?

Jesus sighed deeply. "The Gentiles of Nineveh will judge this generation. Unlike you, they repented at the preaching of Jonah. And I tell you . . . one greater than Jonah is here."

The Pharisees were breathing heavily, but they stood their ground. What were they waiting for?

"The Gentile Queen of the South came from the ends of the earth to seek out the wisdom of Solomon. She too will condemn this generation. I say it again . . . one greater than Solomon is here."

One of the Pharisees opened his mouth as if to protest, but Jesus did not give him the opportunity.

"An evil spirit, when it has been cast out of a person, goes to find another host. If it finds no vacant place, it will return to its original host and, finding it unoccupied, clean, and in order, it invites other evil spirits more wicked than itself to move in with it. And this last infestation will be much worse than the first. That is how it will be with this generation . . . that is how it will be with you."

No one said a word. Had Jesus just indicated that their leaders were evil? Even the Pharisees were stunned. Thankfully, someone broke the awkward silence. "Rabbi, your family is waiting for you outside. They want to talk with you."

Simon turned and craned his neck to see over the heads of the crowd. There were so many people . . . no wonder the family could not get into the house.

"Who is my family?" Jesus replied. "Who is my mother, and who are my brothers?" He pointed at his disciples. "All who follow me are my family, my mother and my brothers. Everyone who does the will of my Father is my mother, brother, and sister."

Simon knew what Jesus meant. Those who followed a rabbi believed that they collectively entered into a new familial relationship that transcended bloodline . . . and that new relationship demanded as much allegiance as any other, if not more. The same situation arose when Elisha was called to follow Elijah . . . there was a severing of bonds that took place before the following could commence.[2] Total commitment. Genealogical ties were temporal . . . spiritual ties were eternal.

Nevertheless, Jesus went out to speak with his biological family as he walked towards the lake. Simon thought they seemed concerned and rightly so . . . Jesus was making as many enemies as he was supporters. But that day, such large crowds gathered to hear him that he again had to get into a boat to teach the people.

Jesus spoke to the crowd in parables. These were not always easy to understand, and it seemed that was what he intended . . . only those who had ears to hear would hear. Much of what Jesus had to say was the opposite of what they had been taught. Simon was beginning to understand that the reason many of the leaders would not see was because they could not see . . . they had ears, but they did not listen . . . they had eyes, but they did not see . . . their hearts were closed, not open . . . they could not receive anything.

The first parable Jesus told them seemed to illustrate this truth. He spoke about a sower who scattered truth like seeds. But although every seed had the same properties and the same potential for growth, the soil on which the seed fell determined whether the seed would be eaten by the birds, or germinate but not reach maturity, or be choked by weeds, or grow up to produce a bumper crop.

This is surely a lesson for us, Simon thought. The problem lies not with the sower nor with the seed . . . the problem is whether the seed is received and nurtured. He could see this now . . . that was the difference between those who followed Jesus . . . his family, if you would . . . and those whose calloused hearts prevented them from seeing the truth in spite of clear evidence. This insight helped Simon understand why Jesus appeared to be failing to bring in all of those in Israel. Like weeds growing in the fields of wheat, those who opposed the truth would always be there as long as the evil one roamed the earth . . . as long as the strong man, as Jesus had called him, was in command of his house.

But ultimately, Jesus proclaimed, the kingdom of God would triumph in spite of apparent setbacks. Although at the moment the kingdom appeared to be small and insignificant, especially in the eyes of the mighty and the wealthy, it would grow, and many would find their rest in it. Simon thought of his beloved wife when Jesus spoke of mustard seeds and yeast. How many times had he watched her prepare meals for the family, using those very same ingredients? He would never watch again in quite the same way.

---

2. 1 Kings 19:19–21.

Jesus then spoke of the kingdom using the images of treasures and a pearl of great value. He explained what lay behind the rejection of such a great prize – hardened hearts and the presence of evil in the world. But the day would come when falsehood would be exposed . . . when wheat would be separated from weeds . . . good fish separated from bad fish . . . with eternal consequences.

This is serious, Simon thought to himself. A great responsibility has been placed on our shoulders. Jesus has called us his "sent ones" . . . his representatives in the world. We will experience rejection . . . that is to be expected and anticipated . . . if some reject the Lord, they will surely reject us as well. Simon let that thought percolate for a while. He found it strangely comforting. It was not their task to ensure that the seed would be properly received . . . it was their task to sow . . . to plant the mustard seed . . . to knead the leaven into the dough . . . to cast out and to pull in the dragnet. This is a treasure Jesus has gifted to us . . . a treasure that must be shared.

Jesus touched his shoulder. "Simon, let us go to the other side." It was already evening, and Jesus was clearly exhausted . . . they were all exhausted. Dealing with the enquiring crowds and the challenging leaders had taken its toll on them as a group.

This is very different from physical labour, Simon thought. This tiredness is far deeper. Perhaps crossing to the other side of the lake into an area where the majority of the people were gentiles would mean they could rest. They would be far from the demanding crowd.

* * *

They had hardly entered the boat when Jesus fell asleep on a cushion in the stern.

Rest well, Master. We will take you to where you can renew your strength, Simon thought, suddenly realizing that he not only respected Jesus, he actually cared for him. He smiled to himself. I belong here . . . with him . . . with them. This is my family.

They were in the middle of the lake when Andrew sounded the alarm. "Simon! The wind!" It was still a breeze, but sailors knew that the winds coming over the eastern mountains could change the sea from a tranquil body of calm water into a frenzied, seething mass of foam-headed waves. They quickly pulled in their oars and trimmed the sail as the winds hit. There was nothing they could do now but ride it out, letting the wind carry them whichever way it wanted.

But this was a storm like none other they had experienced before. The wind tore at the folded sail, threatening to break the mast and split the ropes holding it. The waves tossed them around like a piece of driftwood, battering the sides of their boat. Plunging down into the depths of each trough, they hardly crested the next wave before it broke over them. They could not bail fast enough. Experienced as they were, they were filled with terror. They knew the sea well . . . they knew their boat well . . . and they knew that this boat could not take this kind of onslaught for very much longer. They would sink and, given their current location, they would more than likely drown.

No! Simon thought. Not now. We cannot perish now! We need more hands to bail out the water.

Surprisingly, in the midst of this fierce and frightening storm, Jesus was still asleep. How was that even possible?

"Teacher! Wake up! We are going to drown! Aren't you concerned?"

They spoke about what happened next for years afterwards. It was clear that Jesus did not share their sense of terror. He simply stood up and said in a firm voice, "Quiet! Be still!"

And the wind simply stopped. The huge waves that had threatened to engulf them flattened out . . . the silence was palpable. They all stood frozen, staring at Jesus in total disbelief and awe. What had just happened?

He looked at them with a sternness Simon had not seen before. "Why are you so afraid? Do you still have no faith?"

The terror they had experienced during the violence of the storm was now replaced by another, deeper fear . . . a fear produced by the calmness. It was one thing to heal a person, another to drive out a demon . . . even another to bring a dead person back to life. But to command the unpredictable and uncontrollable forces of nature? Who could do that? Only one who was Lord over the created order itself.

"The psalm," Andrew whispered in Simon's ear.

"Psalm? What psalm?"

"Don't you recall? 'By his word he raised a strong wind that made the waves surge. Mounting up to the heaven, then plunging down into the depths, they reeled and staggered like drunken men, all their skill useless. In their terror they cried to the Lord, and he saved them from their troubles. He reduced the storm to nothing; the waves were stilled.'"[3]

"Yes . . . yes, I remember! 'They rejoiced when all was quiet, and he brought them to the port they desired.' But the psalm is speaking of God . . . it was God who stilled the storm."

"So that means . . . ?"

"I don't know, Andrew. I just don't know."

---

3. Psalm 107:25–30.

10

Beyond the Borders

Jesus calmly returned to his spot in the stern and went back to sleep. The incessant whispering of the flabbergasted disciples obviously didn't bother him. When they reached the region of the Gadarenes, Jesus was one of the first to climb out of the boat. It appeared to the disciples that the calming of the storm had not had any effect on their Master. He was just the same as he always was, as if nothing out of the ordinary had taken place.

But they had little time for reflection. Suddenly, out of the tombs, above them, came an unearthly howl and two wild and stark-naked men came rushing up to them. As soon as they saw Jesus, they collapsed in heaps of what looked like nothing more than skin and bones. They were the foulest looking individuals the disciples had ever laid eyes on. Simon wondered why had Jesus come here? Why to this God-forsaken Gentile area? One man lay writhing on the ground, whimpering like an injured animal. The other shrieked, "Why have you come here, Jesus, Son of the Most High God?"

Several thoughts ran through Simon's mind at once. Indeed, why *had* they come here? He wanted an answer to that question himself. This was an unclean place. Pigs were roaming nearby. There were tombs. And now these men. But how did this wretch know Jesus? And why did he call him the Son of the Most High God?

"Come out, you foul spirits!" Jesus's voice thundered above the shrieking of the men.

"Please!" The ghoulish scream made them all shudder. "Please, do not torture us!"

Simon wondered. Was it his imagination or was this plea spoken by many voices? Surely not. There was only one man speaking.

"What is your name?" demanded Jesus.

"We are legion . . . legion, for we are many," came the reply.

Ah! So, there are many voices speaking through one mouth! Simon realized. But a Roman legion was 6,000 men strong! And these powerful dark forces of the spirit world, were crying out for mercy. Jesus possessed something that caused these demons to tremble in abject terror . . . something that they who had walked with him for a while now had not seen until that moment.

"Please! Jesus! Do not send us to the bottomless pit. Send us into that herd of pigs over there! Yes, yes, send us there! Please!"

The multiplicity of voices sounded otherworldly . . . unnatural . . . evil. Simon noticed that Jesus did not appear to be alarmed. He was in total control of the situation . . . just as he had been the previous evening. But that was a natural storm . . . this was a storm of an altogether different type. This was unnatural. The past evening, the disciples had learned that Jesus had authority over the seen world . . . now they were learning that he was also Lord over the unseen world.

"Then go!" That was all Jesus said. There was no argument, no further conversation. Just a simple command . . . and the demons left and entered the herd of pigs. Up until that moment, the pigs had been grazing quietly, but they became frenzied when the demons entered them. Their terrified screaming was not unlike that of the men only moments before. Then the herd turned and, as one, hurled themselves over the cliff into the waters below. The swineherds fled, yelling abuse at Jesus as they ran.

The disciples all stood in awe. No one dared move or break the silence. What had they just witnessed within a very short space of time? First, there had been the calming of the storm, and now, this incident with the Gadarene demoniacs. These experiences were far greater than any story they had ever heard from their teachers . . . greater than Gideon's three hundred against 135,000[1] . . . greater than Judas Maccabaeus against the forces of Antiochus[2] . . . this was one man against a diabolical legion.

Simon could not recall who stepped in first to clothe the two men . . . but he remembered how the shivering fleshed skeletons sat silently weeping tears of joy. They looked at the disciples one by one and then settled their eyes on Jesus.

"Take us with you," one of them said.

Who could tell what these men had been through . . . how they had come to be possessed by so many foul spirits. What had the local pagan population done to them? They had bruises . . . chain marks . . . on their arms and legs.

---

1. Judges 7.
2. 1 Maccabees 6.

At that moment they heard the shouting. A mob had gathered just above them. They kept their distance but made it plain that they wanted Jesus to leave their district.

How sad, Simon thought. They cared more for their pigs than for their kin.

As Jesus turned to get back into the boat, the one man grabbed hold of the edge of his garment. "Please, Lord. Take me with you."

Jesus smiled at the man . . . that same kind and compassionate smile. "No," he said gently. "No, you must go tell your family and your friends what God has done for you."

Without another word, the man rose and helped his friend up from the ground where he sat, weak and afraid. "Yes," he said simply. "They need to hear that there is a God in heaven who cares."

Simon watched them walk gingerly up the hill on their bare, blood-encrusted feet. "Blessed are you, Lord God of all creation," he prayed silently. "Grant your blessings to these two men. You who blessed our ancestors, Abraham, Isaac, and Jacob . . . bestow your blessings upon them, too. Have mercy on them, and graciously restore their health and strength. Open the eyes, and ears, and hearts of all they encounter."

"Brother?" Andrew stood beside Simon. "Brother, we need to go."

Without another word, they got back into the boat . . . each one captive to his own thoughts. Had any one of them thought that this was what it would be like to follow the Messiah? What kind of a man is Jesus? What kind of power does he possess? There was yet so much to be understood, but this they knew . . . Jesus was no ordinary human being.

* * *

They had sailed in silence, but the quiet was broken even before they managed to dock the boat on the other side. A large crowd had gathered . . . news travelled quickly in and around the lake district. Jesus was swamped from the moment his feet touched solid ground.

"Please, let me through!" The leader of the synagogue, Jairus by name, was trying to get to Jesus. The man appeared to be distraught and seemed to care little for his dignity. As he came to Jesus, he threw himself on the ground. His voice cracked with emotion. "Please, teacher. My daughter . . . my child is dying. Please, I beseech you, come, lay your hand on her. Please come and heal her so that she may live." Without a word, Jesus knelt down beside the man, helped him get to his feet, and walked with him towards his home. They all knew Jairus well, and he knew Jesus well. Jairus had been witness to a number of healings and exorcisms.

The people pushed and jostled in an attempt to get close to Jesus, some out of curiosity, others out of desperation. Hopelessness is an awful thing, Simon thought. It robs one of life . . . of joy . . . of meaning. He thought of their near-drowning experience. Hopelessness was like drowning, in one sense. One could drown in more things than water.

The disciples were trying their best to shield Jesus from the crowd as the people pushed in hard against them. Suddenly, Jesus stopped and turned to them. "Who touched the fringe of my robe?" he asked.

"Really?" Simon said. "The fringe . . . of your robe? All these people and you ask who touched the fringe of your robe? Everyone is trying their best to touch you and we are trying our best to stop them from succeeding."

But Jesus was insistent. "Someone reached out to touch me, not by accident, but deliberately. I felt healing power flow out from me."

Simon wondered how it could be that Jesus was at one moment so perceptive . . . he knew what people were thinking – not only his opponents but also his followers – and yet at other times he seemed totally unobservant, such as now. How could he be aware that healing power had gone out from him and yet at the same time not know who had received healing?

He saw Jairus's agitated expression and was about to suggest that they move on, when a woman fell down at Jesus's feet and confessed that she had deliberately reached out to touch his robe. She explained that she had been ill for twelve years . . . that she had been bleeding for twelve years. Thankfully there was too much noise for those in the crowd to hear her confession, but Simon heard it and instinctively drew back away from her. According to the law, she was unclean and anyone who touched her . . . or anyone whom she touched . . . would become unclean as well. Even if she was healed now, in order for her to be considered clean, her blood flow must have stopped for at least seven days.[3] Jesus saw Simon flinch and in response, bent down close to the prostrate, sobbing woman. Simon felt his face redden.

"My dear daughter, be reassured. Your faith in me has made you well. Your suffering is over. Go in peace." He tenderly touched her on her cheek and then took her by the arm and raised her up.

While he was speaking with her, messengers arrived from the home of Jairus. At first, they simply stood silent before the synagogue leader. He looked at them enquiringly, his desperation growing visibly. Then they blurted out, "There's no need to trouble the teacher any longer . . . your daughter has just died."

---

3. Leviticus 15:19–30.

Simon saw the colour drain from Jairus's face.

"Trouble me?" Again Jesus's voice was so kind, so filled with compassion. "Jairus, do not be fearful . . . just have faith in me."

Jairus looked up at Jesus, his eyes now overflowing with tears. He had witnessed the healing of the woman. If she could be made well, then so could his daughter.

Simon suddenly realized that Jairus had not retreated when the woman confessed her breach of the laws regarding purity, even though he had been close enough to hear every word.

Jesus stopped the crowd from following him any further and indicated that he wished to have only Simon and the two sons of Zebedee accompany him.

They could hear the sound of the professional mourners and their music long before they got to Jairus's home. As they walked in, Jesus said in a loud voice, "Why are you wailing and making such a noise? The girl is not dead . . . she needs only to be awakened."

At first, the mourners were stunned. Then they burst out into mocking laughter.

"Get them out," Jesus said to Jairus. With a motion of his hand, Jairus indicated that they must leave, and so the crowd left the compound.

Jairus's wife came out and stood weeping at the entrance to their home. Then she saw Jesus. "She started to . . . yesterday, she . . ." She looked embarrassed. "We thought it was natural . . . normal . . . she is to . . . was to come of age now.[4] But . . . it wouldn't stop . . . we did everything to make it stop, but . . ."[5]

Make what stop? Simon felt panic rising up inside him. Was this something similar to what he had just witnessed? The law says . . . but Jesus was already moving into the home and James and John were behind him. I don't understand, Simon thought. Was the law of no consequence anymore?

He stepped inside. The girl lay on a bed, stretched out in preparation for the traditional burial rites. The spices and linen cloths lay to one side. She was not breathing.

Jesus stepped closer, took her lifeless hand in his own and said, "Young girl, I tell you, rise."

---

4. "A woman came of age at twelve years and one day, and boys at thirteen years and one day." Alfred Edersheim, *The Life and Times of Jesus the Messiah*, vol. 1 (CreateSpace Independent Publishing, 2015), note 2927, 506.

5. The text does not say what the cause of death was. This is pure speculation on my part, but it is possible that Jesus's response to bleeding and ritual impurity was the reason for the combining of the two stories.

First he touches a woman with blood flow, thought Simon, and now he touches the dead body of a girl who died from . . . what? I have never defiled myself for any reason, why am I even in this room? Simon was wrestling with his thoughts when he heard the mother gasp and then cry out. He looked up. The young woman was . . . she was alive!

"I think she may be hungry, "Jesus said, smiling. "It would be good if you made her something to eat," he told her mother.

Both Jairus and his wife were overwhelmed. They were laughing and crying at the same time, holding their daughter tightly as if they would never let her go. Her mother wiped away her copious tears and went to prepare a meal for her daughter . . . a meal she had not thought she would ever prepare again. The emotion in the room had spun around from intense sadness to inexpressible joy.

Then Simon heard Jesus tell Jairus to make sure he told no one what had just happened. It only took a few days for them to realize that the parents weren't able to follow that request. Who could blame them?

* * *

As they were leaving Jairus's home, two blind men came down the side street calling out, "Jesus, son of David, have mercy on us!"

How did they know where we were? Simon wondered.

It was not far to Simon's home and the blind men followed them right into the compound. Jesus turned and asked them, "Do you believe that I am able to make you see?"

Without hesitation they said in unison, "Yes, Lord! We believe!"

He simply touched their eyes and told them that it would be done according to their faith in him. They opened their eyes, blinked, and then joyously shouted, "We can see!" Jesus firmly told them not to tell anyone, but that was like trying to stop a flood with a finger. They spread the news far and wide throughout the region.

As they were preparing to leave, a demon-possessed mute was led in. Crowds gathered in the doorway to watch.

Are we never to be left alone? Simon wondered. He thought back to the time before he met Jesus. No one other than close friends and family came to his compound then. Jesus doesn't seem to be disturbed although he has to be tired. He had said that he felt power leave him when the woman touched the fringe of his garment.

Jesus simply rebuked the demon and the man began to speak. The crowd went wild. "Nothing like this has ever happened in Israel," they shouted. Their voices echoed down the streets of Capernaum.

Later, they heard that some of the Pharisees dismissed this exorcism by saying, yet again, that Jesus cast out demons by the power of the prince of demons. Simon wondered if they had really thought that through. Even he could see the contradiction in that statement.

* * *

But the leaders were threatened by Jesus. That became even more apparent when they went with Jesus to his hometown of Nazareth. The people who gathered together that Sabbath in the synagogue were amazed by his teaching. They had heard so much about him and especially about his power to heal and to cast out demons. They had even heard that he could raise the dead. But the amazement soon gave way to puzzlement. After all, Jesus had grown up around many of them and as a child he had not exhibited any special qualities as far as they could remember. He was simply the son of an ordinary labourer, skilled though Joseph had been. They knew his mother and his siblings well. Who did he think he was to put on airs and to pretend to be a rabbi? They felt offended and refused to believe in him.

Jesus stared at the disgruntled group before him. Simon could see pain in his eyes. Then he said simply, "A prophet is honoured everywhere except in his own hometown among his friends and relations."

Unbelief is a powerful thing, Simon thought. It is also a thief disguised as wisdom . . . it robs people from receiving a blessing while causing them to think they are intelligent. How very sad.

Jesus too was stunned by their unbelief. Only a few were healed that day.

* * *

But Jesus was not disheartened. He knew his mission and he pressed on, regardless of the hostility and constant criticism. It was his example of persistence in spite of resistance that would serve the disciples well as they, in turn, went out to do what Jesus instructed them to do.

As they travelled through all the villages and towns of that area, Jesus continued to teach in the synagogues and to heal all sicknesses and diseases. He impressed upon those who heard him speak that the kingdom of God was imminent.

The crowds were relentless. While Simon found them to be a never-ending source of weariness and fatigue, Jesus appeared to be driven and energized by immense compassion. He once described them as sheep without a shepherd ... confused and helpless and vulnerable.

One day, as they looked out on the sea of humanity before them, Jesus said, "The harvest is extensive ... but those who reap are scarce." He turned to look at his disciples. There was a sense of urgency in his voice, as if what he had to say was a matter of life and death. "You must pray ... earnestly pray to the Lord of the harvest ... plead with him to send more labourers into his fields."

Simon did not know then that his obedience to Jesus's grave request would thrust him beyond the borders of everything he had ever known or thought possible.

11

Of Lambs and Wolves

The disciples had been with Jesus for quite a while at this point in time. At first, he had done every part of the ministry himself, while they observed and learned his methods. But gradually he began to involve them more and more, allowing them to assist him with various tasks while he watched and assessed them. On several occasions when they did not succeed, he explained to them what they had done wrong. This change was also evident in his teaching. In the beginning, he had taught them in a large group, sitting together with the crowds, but after he had chosen the twelve to be his close followers, he spent more time explaining the Scriptures and their proper interpretation and application to them as a smaller group. The women were always present on these occasions too, learning at the feet of the Master just like their male counterparts.

Then one day, Jesus announced that it was time for them to go out, two by two, to practice what they had learned thus far.

"I'm glad he's not sending us out alone," Simon mumbled to his brother. "At least we will have company."

"Yes, but I think the reason he is sending us out in pairs is because the law requires at least two witnesses to authenticate a testimony.[1] If only one of us tells people about Jesus's power over nature, over demons, and over death itself, they may not believe us. Besides, the great king Solomon once wisely said that if one of us is in trouble, the other can help."[2]

Simon marvelled at his brother's ability to apply Scripture passages whenever he needed to give a reason for why they did things a certain way.

---

1. Genesis 41:32; Deuteronomy 17:6; 19:15.
2. Ecclesiastes 4:9–13.

He believed this was the reason why Andrew was so godly. He had hidden the word of God in his heart, and so was always careful how he behaved.[3]

The disciples were very excited about this new ministry opportunity, even though they were a bit apprehensive. They had never gone out on their own before . . . Jesus had always been right there to help them out of sticky situations or to lift their spirits when their inabilities made them wonder if they would ever live up to his expectations.

But Jesus set their minds at ease. He told them that he was giving them *his* authority to do what he expected of them . . . so in a sense they felt that he would be with them after all. He also told them to stay within the boundaries of their own nation and not to cross over to Gentile or Samaritan territory. This would make it easier for the disciples as they could assume that most of the people they would encounter would have a tentative grasp of the Scriptures and of the messianic expectations. At least, that is how Simon encouraged himself.

Jesus told them to preach the same message they had heard him preach on several occasions . . . the nearness of the kingdom of heaven. They were to heal the sick, cleanse those who had leprosy, perform exorcisms . . . whatever Jesus had freely shared with them, they were to give back freely for the benefit of others. It was forbidden to charge for teaching the Scriptures,[4] so the disciples were surprised when Jesus told them not to take provisions with them, but to live off the generosity of the recipients of their ministry. They were to board with those who received them favourably and to let their peace remain with them, but to shake the dust off their feet when they left the homes or towns where they were not well received.

"The rabbis usually do that when they leave Gentile or Samaritan territory . . . but Jesus is applying it to fellow Jews," Simon whispered to Andrew.

"Not quite 'fellow' Jews, brother. He is talking about unbelieving Jews."

Simon nodded, but the thought still bothered him. Were not all Jews part of the covenant people of God? At that moment, the words of John the Baptizer came flooding back. He had called some of those who came to be baptized a "brood of vipers" . . . indicating that they might not be true children of Abraham.

"I am sending you out like sheep among wolves," Simon heard Jesus saying.

Really? Our own people? Simon thought. Looking back later, he realized how naïve he had been at that time.

---

3. Psalm 119:11.
4. https://ourrabbijesus.com/a-question-about-disciples-rabbis/.

Jesus went on to warn them that a time would come when they would be arrested and tried before local councils and flogged in the synagogues . . . that they would be brought before governors and kings on account of their witness to Jesus. But he told them not to be worried about how to defend themselves. In a supernatural, divine way, they would be told what to say at the appropriate moment.

The disciples looked at each other. God had often told the sages of old that their message would be met with hostility. Many of the prophets had been threatened, arrested, even executed by stoning or other frightful methods like being sawn in two.[5] But these were stories they had heard, not their personal experience. They had not been persecuted themselves, so it was hard to grasp the gravity of what Jesus was telling them.

Jesus began to quote from the prophet Micah.[6] On the one hand, this was alarming . . . according to the words of the prophet, which Jesus was now directly applying to them, no one was to be trusted – even unbelieving family members might betray them. Yet on the other hand, Micah's prophecy predicted the victory of God over their enemies. Perhaps that was why Jesus was telling them not to be afraid . . . all things would be exposed for what they were in the end. They were to fear God, rather than humanity, as he alone holds eternity in his hands.

Simon's attention was caught once again by Jesus's words about the sparrows . . . he told them that not one sparrow fell to the ground unnoticed by the Father. For that reason, they were not to fear . . . they were of far greater value to God than sparrows. Value. He was of value to God! He had never seen himself in this light before meeting Jesus, and the idea that the Almighty Creator of all things valued him as an individual encouraged him greatly.

"Whoever acknowledges me publicly on earth, I will acknowledge before my Father in heaven. But whoever does not acknowledge me on earth, I will not acknowledge before my Father in heaven," Jesus continued.

Who could ever deny him? Simon wondered.

Jesus taught them that the bond between his followers and him was to be absolute, complete, and primary. Nothing and no one was to come before him . . . not even father or mother . . . not even life itself. Ultimately, the relationship was to be so close that they could be considered one with him . . . so that whoever received a disciple, would, in a sense, receive him.

---

5. Hebrews 11:35–38.
6. Micah 7:5–7.

When he had finished giving them these and other instructions, Jesus sent them out. And so they went, preaching and teaching, casting out demons, and healing the sick . . . everything that they had seen and learned from Jesus. Some would later call them little Christs . . . copies of their master.[7]

* * *

It was while the small bands of disciples were crisscrossing the region that Herod Antipas added to his list of atrocities by beheading John the Baptizer. He had arrested John earlier for exposing his unlawful marriage to his brother Aristobulus's daughter, Herodius,[8] the former wife of his brother Philip.[9] Herod Antipas had been married to the daughter of Aretas, the Nabatean Arabian king of Petra, when he had fallen in love with Herodius while visiting his brother Philip. He not only divorced his own wife, but insisted that Philip divorce Herodius so that he could marry her instead.[10]

In a strange way, Herod revered John. He often spoke with him, protecting him from his wife's dangerous displeasure. But after drinking too much at one of his extravagant parties, Herod boastfully promised to give the daughter of Herodius whatever she desired after she had performed a lewd dance to please him and his guests. Having received instructions from her mother, the daughter asked for the head of John the Baptizer.

John's disciples came and claimed his body for burial, but his head remained with Herodius. Shortly after the beheading, reports of Jesus's activity reached Herod's ears. In his guilt-ridden, superstitious mind, the king feared that Jesus was John returned from the dead.

Jesus received the news of the unstable actions and thoughts of the king just as the disciples were busy with their debriefing sessions. He was clearly moved by the account of his cousin's murder, but he was also concerned for the safety of his disciples. He wanted to be alone to grieve, but also, Simon reasoned, to consult with the Father, as he so often did.

"Let us go off by ourselves to rest a while," Jesus simply said. But the crowds pressed in from every side . . . they too were disturbed by the news of Herod's violence. There were so many people that Jesus and his disciples did not even have time to eat, let alone process the tragedy. So they left by boat for a quiet place where they could be by themselves.

---

7. Acts 11:26.

8. Flavius Josephus, *Antiquities*, 18.5.1.

9. Matthew 14:3.

10. Josephus, *Ant.* 18.5.1–4.

＊ ＊ ＊

Winter was no more than a memory now. The area all around the Sea of Galilee was filled with a profusion of colour. The green grass made the yellow, white, and red wildflowers seem brighter . . . and the water was so blue it almost matched the sky. The barley harvest was in and farmers were preparing the soil for new crops. Passover was a few weeks away and people were enjoying the warm weather. It was so tranquil that despite the monotonous, yet hard work of rowing and steering the boat, the disciples relaxed. It was good to be alive and they cherished every moment . . . enjoying each ray of sunshine . . . every splash of the fresh, cool water on their skin. For the most part, they were all silent, thinking about John the Baptizer's tragic death. They were also well aware of the fact that this was a dangerous time for them all . . . if Herod Antipas could murder a man hailed as a prophet by so many, he could easily turn against Jesus and his followers. It was safer for them to be outside his area of jurisdiction for a time.

And they all needed the rest. There was so much they wanted to discuss with Jesus about their ministry trips. And so, they rowed north-northeast in the direction of Bethsaida to a wilderness area west of that village. They had not had time to pack much, and because Jesus had instructed them not to take extra provisions on their respective journeys, they would have to find a local farmer or marketplace to purchase food. But they would bother about that later. For the moment, they enjoyed the relative solitude.

However, as they were drawing closer to land, Simon noticed masses of people running along the shore. Oh no, he thought. They followed us. We might escape Antipas, but we do not seem able to escape the crowds!

Crowds on foot from Capernaum had arrived well ahead of Jesus . . . they stood, row upon row, anxiously waiting for him to get off the boat. How desperate can they be? Simon wondered with some annoyance. The least the people could have done was to give them a day or two to rest.

But if Jesus was put out, he did not show it at all. Even though he had not had time to grieve the death of his cousin . . . even though he needed to have time with his Father . . . time to rest and reflect and be rejuvenated . . . his mercy and compassion shone through. He led the crowd up to the gently sloping hillside and taught them and healed them.

But it appeared that in their haste to follow Jesus, the people had not thought of packing food for themselves. This reminds me of the story of the Exodus, Simon thought. It was quite natural to make these kinds of connections, as Passover was so close. Our forefathers had to leave in such haste that there wasn't even time to let the dough rise[11] . . . they also went to a place where provisions were scarce.

Perhaps there was time for the people to go buy food before sunset. Simon did not want to take personal responsibility for the crowds at that moment. They needed to leave. And so, he and the disciples approached Jesus and encouraged him to send everyone away.

Jesus looked at each one of them. Oh no, Simon thought. It is his long, lingering look . . . what is Jesus thinking? We have just returned from a journey during which others had to provide for our needs . . . is he wondering if we learned anything?

Jesus then turned to Philip and simply asked, "Where can we buy bread to feed all these people?"

Simon thought Philip was about to choke or laugh out loud. The best Philip could do was state the obvious. To feed such a large crowd they would need at least 200 denarii worth of food. It could not be done . . . and the disciples all agreed with his logic.

Smiling, Jesus simply said, "Well, why don't you all give them something to eat?"

This is a training moment, Simon realized. Jesus is about to involve us in something he already knows he's going to do. Did he bring something along that we have not seen? No, that's not possible. We carried everything from the boat to here.

The other disciples were not thinking about training. They just stood and stared at Jesus, absolutely aghast at the thought of feeding five thousand men and their families.

Simon heard Andrew tell Jesus about a boy with five barley loaves and two pieces of dried, pickled fish. But Andrew's voice trailed off into a whimper. What use was such a meagre, peasant lunch with such a huge crowd?

The disciples, exhausted of all ideas, waited for further instructions. That much they had learned. Jesus would often involve them in his ministry . . . but for the most part they were simply passive participants. They had learned that none of them could accomplish anything of consequence on their own. They needed Jesus.

"Tell everyone to sit down in groups of fifty and one hundred," Jesus told them.[12]

---

11. Exodus 12:34.
12. Cf. Exodus 18:21.

Jesus then simply prayed a customary prayer of thanks to God for what was about to happen. Later, Simon would recall this event and wonder how he could have missed so much when it was so obvious. The wilderness, the people, the seating in groups of fifty and one hundred, the miraculous and abundant provision of bread . . . all this pointed to the fulfilment of God's promise that one day a prophet like Moses would come to whom they ought to pledge allegiance.[13] Why had he been so slow to see it? His mind had been filled with earthly matters . . . liberty . . . the restoration of Israel as a kingdom . . . freedom from oppression. These ideas were uppermost in his mind most of the time and had prevented him from seeing Jesus for who he really was.

He watched Jesus take the bread, bless it, break it, and give it to the disciples to distribute. Later he would see Jesus do this again, but at this time he was blinded by the miracle taking place right before his eyes. It was as if there was no end to the bread . . . like the oil and the flour of the widows[14] . . . like the bread of Elisha.[15]

Each time the disciples ran out of food, they returned to Jesus who kept on giving them more until everyone had had their fill. He did the same with the dried fish. In retrospect, the disciples learned that returning to Jesus to be filled again was the correct order of things . . . only in Jesus were they able to re-enact his life and ministry. The power was with him, not with them, but in obedient response to his directing, they could do what he did.

After every man, woman, and child had had enough to eat, Jesus instructed his disciples to gather any bread that was left over. They gathered twelve baskets full . . . bread enough for each one of them.

"And I thought we would have to find a farmer or a marketplace," Simon said to his brother. When no response was forthcoming, he looked over at Andrew. His brother was preoccupied with other thoughts. "What is it, Andrew? Tell me what you are thinking about."

"In the wilderness, when God fed our forefathers with manna, bread from heaven . . .," Andrew began.

"It was a miracle," Simon said simply.

"Yes, but do you remember that God commanded them only to gather what was enough for the day, except on the day before the Sabbath?"

Simon was now confused. What did that have to do with picking up the left-over fragments?

---

13. Deuteronomy 18:15–19.
14. 1 Kings 17:16; 2 Kings 4:1–7.
15. 2 Kings 4:42–44.

"Simon, brother, nothing was to be kept until morning! The people had to believe that God would provide enough for each day. It was a lesson in trust."

"Well, we certainly have enough bread for tonight," Simon said, still not quite getting the point.

"Yes, if we are an obedient people, we will always have what we need. But there's more. Think, brother! After all these years . . . after all the prophets . . . after all the judgments, the exile, the oppression . . . we . . . our people are still wandering in the wilderness."

"Don't you think you're reading too much into this event, little brother?" Simon asked sucking the saltiness of the dried fish off his fingers. "I understand, really I do. It is nearly Passover . . . our deliverance from Egypt is in the forefront of your mind, but . . ."

Andrew was about to go on when they heard Jesus call them.

"The people are saying I am a prophet like Moses," Jesus said quietly.

"Well, aren't you?" Andrew simply could not help himself. He thought he had it all figured out.

Jesus did not answer him directly, but said, "They want to make me their king."

"That's wonderful!" Simon exclaimed, now very excited.

"My time has not yet come," Jesus stated flatly. "This is merely due to their full stomachs and an overreaction to the recent atrocities of Herod. You all need to get back in the boat and go over to the village of Bethsaida. Wait for me there. I will join you later and then we can return to Capernaum."

With that Jesus turned away from them, dismissing the crowd before slowly heading further up into the hills, no doubt to commune with his Father. The disciples had learned not to question his reasoning, so they dutifully returned to the boat and sailed to Bethsaida, where they waited.

* * *

But Jesus did not return, and it was getting late. Thinking that he may have gone home some other way without them, they set sail for Capernaum.[16] They were quite far from land when suddenly a strong wind came up that whipped the waves into a frenzy. They were used to storms such as these, but they were struggling, mainly because they were tired after a long day. They had not rested as planned because of the crowds . . . and while the miraculous provision of food had exhilarated them, they had missed the opportunity to

---

16. Cf. G. R. Osborne, *Matthew: Exegetical Commentary on the New Testament* (Grand Rapids, MI: Zondervan, 2010), 573 fn 3.

debrief properly. Spending time alone with Jesus had become very important to them, but it seemed as if the many needs of the people always encroached on their time.

They were still floundering in the middle of the lake in the early hours of the next morning when they saw what appeared to be an apparition of some kind, walking on the water. They were gripped with an intense fear. It was one thing to face the wind and the waves, but quite another to face some other-worldly being. Was this the spirit of someone who had drowned? Was it an omen of doom? Would they soon be following it to a watery fate?

Then they heard the voice of Jesus, over the thunderous noise of the gale. "Take heart! I AM here. Do not be afraid."

"The psalm, brother," Andrew yelled into Simon's ear.

"What psalm?" Simon yelled back, still staring at the figure on the water. "This isn't the time to quote Scripture!"

"It is always the right time to quote Scripture, brother," Andrew shouted. "The psalmist says, 'Your path led through the sea, your way through the mighty waters, though your footprints were not seen.'"[17]

"That is referring to God!" Simon shouted back. Then it suddenly struck him . . . if this was Jesus, then . . . "Lord," he shouted out to the figure, "if it is you, command me to come to you on the water!"

The disciples looked at their colleague in total disbelief. Had he gone mad?

While Simon certainly had not fully understood what he later came to believe about Jesus, the events of the past few weeks flooded into his consciousness. Jesus had calmed the storm, cast out a legion of demons, healed a woman with a chronic health condition, raised a dead girl, fed over five thousand people with five loaves and two fishes . . . if Jesus could do these things . . . and if he was now standing on the waters among the waves . . . then surely, he was more than human! This was Simon's way of putting his thoughts to the test. Everything he had witnessed up till that point was second-hand. He knew these waters well . . . he knew what he was asking was impossible, but that is why he was willing to take the risk.

When Jesus commanded him to come, Simon was ready. He catapulted out of the boat and began to walk toward Jesus. Looking back, Simon would be the first to admit that it was foolhardy . . . yet it was a brave act of faith on his part. His only regret was that it was so brief. As long as he had kept his eyes fixed on the figure of Jesus before him, he had been fine . . . but the waves,

---

17. Psalm 77:19.

and the realization that what he was doing was impossible, proved to be too much of a distraction.

He had walked some distance before the reality of his surroundings overcame his bravado. He began to go under. The sudden sensation of sinking brought fear barrelling back into his heart and he cried out, "Lord, save me! Do not let the floodwaters engulf me!"[18]

In an instant, the strong grip of a labourer's hand grabbed him and drew him close. The wind still howled about them, but Simon felt safe in Jesus's embrace. "Why did you doubt me, Simon? Do you have so little faith in me?"

When they got into the boat, the winds ceased. The disciples remembered the previous calming of the storm . . . this time they had no questions. They simply fell at Jesus's feet and worshipped him. "Assuredly, you are the Son of God." Much later, as they reflected on their statement that day, they realized how far short they fell of really understanding the full truth of what they had said.

* * *

The storm had blown the boat off course. Instead of landing in Capernaum, they landed in Gennesaret, a few miles further south. Jesus's fame had preceded him and once again they were swamped by the crowds needing healing or merely wanting to touch the fringe of his garment. All who touched him were healed. Then, they sailed on to Capernaum.

The crowd that had remained in the Bethsaida area had seen only one boat leave, without Jesus. When they realized that he was no longer there, they sailed over to Capernaum in search of him in boats that had come from Tiberias. Having found him, they asked how he got there.

Jesus ignored their question and bluntly asked them why they were looking for him. When no one ventured to reply, he said, "I'll tell you why you have been searching for me. It is not because you have grasped the truth with regard to the miracles. It is because you want more bread. You must not seek after earthly things . . . like food that rots . . . but rather you must seek after heavenly things . . . food that lasts for eternity. I can give you that food if you really want it. God has given the Son of Man that authority."

It was debatable whether they actually understood his reference to the Son of Man . . . nevertheless, they did ask what it was that they should do in order to seek after heavenly things.

---

18. Cf. Psalm 69:15–16.

"To seek after heavenly things," Jesus replied, "you must believe in the one God has sent."

Simon could not believe his ears when they responded by asking Jesus for a sign. He knew that he was slow to grasp things more often than not, but their request was way beyond comprehension. They even dared to ask if Jesus would provide for them as Moses did for their ancestors!

Without hesitation Jesus replied, "Listen carefully to what I am about to say. It was not Moses who gave you bread from heaven . . . it was my Father. And now . . . now he has given you true bread from heaven, because the true heavenly bread God gives is the one who has come from him to give life to the world."

"Then give us this bread from now on," they said unashamedly, clearly missing the metaphor.

"Just like that woman," Andrew said to Simon.

"What woman?" Simon asked.

"Remember the story I told you about the Samaritan woman? She too misunderstood when Jesus offered her living water. She expected him to give her real physical water . . . she didn't know he was talking about himself as spiritual water."

"I AM the bread of life," Jesus told them. "If you come to me, you will never go hungry and if you believe in me you will never be thirsty."

Andrew continued speaking excitedly to Simon, "It is the word of God. Jesus is alluding to what Moses said in the law! Remember? God caused our ancestors to go hungry in the wilderness so that they would learn that man does not live by bread alone . . . rather man should live by the decrees of the Lord.[19] Moses warned them not to forget that it was God that had preserved them!"

"What are you talking about?" Simon asked, both intrigued and irritated.

"In the second giving of the law, Moses told the people to be careful not to forget the Lord.[20] They were not to forget, once they had eaten their fill and were satisfied, that it was God who had sustained them in the wilderness and that it was God who had given them a land filled with good things – streams and springs and fountains. You see, I think Jesus is comparing this crowd to our disobedient ancestors. Yesterday, brother, everyone had eaten their fill and was satisfied, yet they are so fixated on material things that they missed the point entirely. Don't you see? Jesus is saying that, in many ways, our people are still in the wilderness."

---

19. Deuteronomy 8:2–3.
20. Deuteronomy 8:6–18.

"But, little brother, Jesus is saying he *is* the bread . . ."

"More than that," Andrew interrupted. "He is equating himself with the bread that we are *meant* to live by . . . the very decrees of God!"

"That just doesn't make sense."

"Think about it, brother. Moses told us to believe and obey the decrees of God. And that if we did, we would live by them. So now Jesus is saying that we must believe and obey *him* . . . and he is using the image of bread to explain this truth. He is contrasting physical bread that satisfies for a short while, with spiritual bread that satisfies for eternity. In that sense Jesus *is* the bread . . . *he* is the fountain of living water that Jeremiah spoke of . . . the fountain our ancestors rejected long ago.[21] The words he speaks, his teaching, the way he lives his life, everything about him is the way to life . . . eternal life."

"You are saying that the words Jesus speaks are God's words . . ."

"Yes, brother, and if we believe him, we will live. Through him we receive eternal life. Physical bread sustains physical life for the moment . . . spiritual bread, in this case, Jesus himself, sustains spiritual life forever."

Then why does he not simply say that? Simon wondered. Why does he speak in riddles like all the other rabbis?

Jesus continued, "You have all seen me . . . you have all been with me . . . you have all heard my words . . . and yet many of you still struggle to believe me."

I believe in him, Simon told himself, I just don't always understand.

Jesus turned and looked at Simon. He was smiling as if he knew his disciple was wrestling with his thoughts.

"Those whom the Father gives me will come to me and I will never drive them away, because I have come to do his will, not mine . . . and his will is that I will not lose a single one that he has given me. I will raise every one of them up on the last day, simply because it is the will of the Father that whoever believes in the Son will have eternal life."

That's meant to reassure me . . . to reassure us all, Simon thought. Most of the Jews believed in a future resurrection of all people. The prophets had developed a hope in a paradise-like existence for all believers that would take place at the end of time . . . all believers would be resurrected to a glorious and peaceful eternal existence. But the idea of the Messiah being the agent of such a resurrection was foreign to Simon. He decided he would have to think about that later.

The crowd was growing restless. Like Simon, they were struggling to understand, but unlike Simon, they began to grumble about Jesus.

---

21. Jeremiah 17:13.

"Who does he think he is?" they were saying to each other. "We know his parents . . . peasant labourers like us . . . how can he say he has come down from heaven?"

"If only you would stop your grumbling and listen carefully!" Jesus said. "Only those whom the Father draws to me will come to me. Nothing can happen if the Father does not will it. He draws, and those whom he draws come to me, and those who come to me, I will raise up on the last day. As the prophets said, 'All of them shall be taught by God.'"[22]

"The prophets Isaiah and Jeremiah both spoke about a new covenant where God promises to put his law inside us to become part of us[23] . . . like bread and water get inside us and become part of us," Andrew said, trying to help Simon follow the imagery.

"Yes, I remember – 'All your children will be disciples of the Lord . . . from the least to the greatest, they will all heed him.'"[24] Simon had heard the leaders quote from these prophecies when speaking about the messianic era. Although he understood what the words meant, he was having a hard time connecting the images of bread and water with the internalized, eternal word of God. And what was this talk about the last day? What last day?

Jesus was saying that everyone who heard the words of the Father and grasped their meaning would come to him. But then Jesus added, "But no one has seen the Father except me . . . only I have seen the Father."

There he goes again, Simon thought, but said nothing. He was tired of hearing Andrew's explanations. They just made him feel even more slow-witted . . . so he kept his thoughts to himself. The first part I understand. If we believe the Scriptures – the words of the Father – we will believe Jesus because he is the Messiah, the one the Scriptures speak of. But how has no one other than Jesus seen the Father? No one can see God and live.

"Are you listening?" Jesus asked the crowds. "Listen carefully because this is very important. Those who believe have eternal life. Are you listening?"

The murmurs died down.

"I AM the bread of life. Your ancestors enjoyed the miraculous provision of bread . . . manna . . . in the wilderness. But are they still alive? No, of course not. They all died."

"He is making a comparison, brother," Andrew knew he was getting on his brother's nerves, but he could not help himself. "Jesus is comparing himself

---

22. Isaiah 54:13; Jeremiah 31:33–34.
23. Isaiah 59:21; Jeremiah 31:33.
24. Isaiah 54:13.

with the manna God gave to our ancestors in the wilderness. The bread in the Exodus and the bread yesterday both came from God. They were miracles. But in both cases, it was just bread . . . physical bread that only sustains physical life. Now Jesus is saying that he is the bread that gives eternal life . . . that he is the word by which we must live. He is saying . . ."

". . . that he is God," Simon finished his brother's sentence. "Only God can give eternal life. But how can that be? We know him as a man . . . just like you and me."

Jesus continued teaching. "Standing before you is bread that comes from heaven . . . if you eat of this bread, you will never die. Do you understand what I am saying? I AM the living bread that has been sent from heaven so that all who eat of this bread will live eternally. The bread which I now offer for the life of the world . . . is me . . . my flesh."

"So, Jesus is saying he is the embodiment of God's word . . . the word we need to keep if we are to have eternal life. So believing in him is like eating the word that gives life," Simon said, vocalizing his thoughts.

"Yes, brother," Andrew said grinning from ear to ear. "You are right. That is exactly what he is saying."

But the crowds misunderstood, and they were highly offended. Their minds were so fixed on the earthly bread that they missed the spiritual significance of what Jesus was trying to explain. "How can he give us his flesh to eat?"

But their offense was about to get worse. "I want you all to listen very carefully!" Jesus shouted above the loud protestations. "Unless you eat of the flesh of the Son of Man and drink his blood, you have no life in you!"

"Drinking blood is forbidden in the law!"[25] someone shouted.

"They are taking his word literally," Andrew said alarmed. "This is not good. Just like with Nicodemus . . . they misunderstand because they try to interpret his teaching in terms of earthly things, not heavenly things. His flesh is the bread of life . . . and the life of the flesh is in the blood."

Simon looked at his brother, confused. "That statement comes from the law . . . it is about the sacrifice of atonement."[26]

"Yes, I know," Andrew replied. "I know that has to do with atonement . . . with sacrifice . . . but somehow Jesus is that atonement. Somehow his life . . . his blood . . . gives an accounting to God for us. Somehow those who believe in him become one body with him."

---

25. Leviticus 17:10–14.
26. Leviticus 17:11.

Jesus then tried to explain, by using the Scriptural images of bread[27] and blood[28] as sources of eternal life, that believing in him would produce true life. But the people were too dull spiritually to make the connection. They thought he was advocating cannibalism.

Finally, knowing that the same followers who had wanted to crown him king the day before were turning against him, he said, "If you are offended by what I have just told you, what will you do when you see the Son of Man ascend to where he was before? You are trying to understand what I have said with your limited earthly understanding . . . you can only truly understand through the Spirit. There are those among you who do not believe me."

Later the disciples realized that, even then, Jesus knew who believed in him, as well as who would betray him. Knowing the will of the Father at that moment was crucial for him. It was the only thing standing between him and the abandonment of his mission. This was a lesson they would come to learn later when they set out to duplicate the method of ministry that they had observed first-hand from the one who modelled a daily dependence and reliance on God. No one could respond to the message of the gospel unless it was revealed to them by the Father. Unless he drew them, they would not come to Jesus.

Many of Jesus's followers walked away that day. Simon watched them go with a sinking heart. Would the movement ever gain momentum? The twelve stood in a huddle on the steps of the synagogue as the crowd dispersed.

"You compared them to the Samaritan woman earlier," Simon said to Andrew. "But she believed and brought her neighbours to him."

"Yes, how tragic," Andrew replied. "She, a foreigner, had more faith than our fellow countrymen."

"He came to his own," John said, "but his own did not receive him."[29]

They fell silent as Jesus joined them. "Are you all going to leave me now as well?" he asked the twelve as they walked home together.

As hard as it was for him to process the teaching of Jesus, Simon understood enough to know that there was no other way. "Where would we go, Lord?" he asked, speaking for the twelve. "You have the words of eternal life. That much we believe . . . we believe that you are the holy one of God." Simon suddenly felt a sensation akin to patriotic pride as he spoke. He knew he was taking a

27. Deuteronomy 8:3.
28. Genesis 9:4–6; Leviticus 17:11.
29. John 1:11.

stand for the one he had come to accept as the long-awaited Messiah, in spite of the fact that there was still much he did not fully understand.

Simon had often felt like he was walking up a steep, muddy slope . . . just when he thought he was making headway he slid back down to his original starting point. But at that moment, he felt as if he crested the hill.

Jesus nodded slowly, looking at each one of his disciples . . . or, as Simon thought to himself, looking *into* each one of them. "Yes, I was directed by the Father to choose each one of you." They remembered that day well. Jesus had spent all night in prayer, and then, in the morning, he had chosen them, one by one, to be his sent ones.

"But one of you belongs to the evil one," Jesus added, almost as an afterthought. It became apparent later that he had been speaking about Judas Iscariot, one of the twelve, who would betray him . . . but the sense of camaraderie was so strong then, that this statement went unnoticed.

* * *

They had just finished eating when the attack came. Apparently, they had been watched for quite some time . . . their every move was being scrutinized. Looking back much later, Simon thought that on one hand this was wise. All too often, people did not think things through and simply plunged into difficult or dangerous situations. But, on the other hand, if someone was to scrutinize or evaluate something, they needed a proper plumb line[30] . . . something sound against which the evaluation could be measured. Starting off from a shaky foundation only resulted in some form of misunderstanding.

This was true of the Pharisees. In their zeal to ensure that the people never broke the law of God, for fear of further punishment and exile, they had created numerous extra rules and regulations. These were not written . . . but they were debated endlessly by the rabbis and others and were passed down by word of mouth. The purpose of these painfully detailed stipulations was to help the Jews keep the law in a mixed cultural setting. In one sense, at least in their day-to-day cultural life, the oral law was more binding than the written law. There was a right way and a wrong way for everything in life . . . how to sleep, how to eat, how to work, how to rest, how to wear clothes . . . But these were the precepts of men that all too often obscured the real intent of the scriptural command. The oral rules were crafted to control the external behaviour of people but largely left the internal motivation untouched . . .

---

30. A plumb line is a weighted string that is used to ensure that a wall is straight, usually during the building process.

which very often created tension in the people and bred resentment. Rarely did they inspire deeper devotion to God or encourage the worship of God. The sheer number of these extra laws tended to eclipse the Lawgiver and his love for the recipients of his law.

Simon had just licked the last grains of salt from his fingers after having eaten some dried fish, when some Pharisees and teachers of the law from Jerusalem burst through the crowds. It was highly unusual for such an important delegation to come to Galilee. Clearly, they had been sent to test Jesus . . . to see if he adhered to the teaching of the law or, more likely, their traditional interpretations of the law. And that was exactly where they found fault.

"Teacher!" they bellowed. "Why do you allow your disciples to break the tradition of the elders? They have been in the marketplace with Gentiles and have touched the unclean. So why did they not wash their hands before they had their meal?"

Was Jesus really purposefully licking his fingers right now? Slowly, he turned to face them and said, "Tell me, why do you choose to set aside the commandment of God in favour of your man-made traditions?"

The group was clearly not expecting Jesus to go on the offensive.

"Doesn't God himself command us to honour our mothers and our fathers, and doesn't he instruct us to apply the death penalty to those who curse their parents?"

A hush fell over all . . . it was an uncomfortable silence and the tension was palpable. While it was usual for rabbis to engage in animated debates, the accusations levelled at them were serious indeed.

"But you teach," Jesus continued, "that if someone dedicates their money to God, they don't need to take care of their parents. So by your deceptive reasoning, you enable children to get around the plain teaching of God's law. In this manner, you have legally invalidated the word of God by your tradition. And there are many more things like this that you do."

"The one who robs from his father and mother and says, 'There is no offense,' is a companion to thieves,"[31] Andrew whispered to his brother.

"What?"

"It is a proverb of King Solomon. Jesus is showing them that they know their traditions better than they know the Scriptures."

At this point Jesus stood up and moved to stand right in front of the Judean delegation. "You are nothing more than play-actors . . . pious pretenders, the

---

31. Proverbs 28:24.

lot of you! Isaiah described people like you: 'These people draw near to me with their mouths and honour me with their lips, but they keep their hearts far from me, and their worship of me involves nothing but commandments made up by men and learned by rote.'"[32]

Jesus did not need to quote any further, Simon thought to himself. It was apparent that everyone knew what the text said next. "I will further confuse these people . . . the wisdom of their wise will fail, and the prudence of their prudent will be dispelled."[33]

"You are people who claim to be teachers of God's law, but your actions prove you to be the exact opposite," Jesus said, still facing them.

This is the heart of what it means to follow Jesus, Simon thought. By his actions, he has shown us that we must be careful to know and to follow the will of the Father, not just do what is expedient for us. Simon remembered Jesus telling them to lay up treasures in heaven rather than on earth . . . man-made rules and regulations had no value to God.

The members of the delegation were highly offended . . . especially because they felt he had humiliated them before people they regarded as rabble. They turned and left muttering among themselves, gesticulating wildly as they went.

At first Simon wondered why Jesus had not made more of an effort to win over these apparently important people. Surely their influence would be helpful for the cause. Later he came to realize that no amount of explanation would have changed their minds. Seed that fell on hard soil simply could not grow. Only God could break up the fallow ground of their leaders' hearts.

Up until that moment, the people in the crowd gathered around them had been passive participants. But Jesus saw this as a teaching opportunity, so he called them to come closer in order to teach them a lesson from the unpleasant confrontation.

"Listen to me, everyone, and listen well. Understand what I am about to tell you. There is much at stake here and it has nothing to do with outward purity. Rather, it has to do with inner purity. Eating with unwashed hands does not defile you . . . it is not what goes into your mouth and stomach that makes you unclean! It is what comes out of you that defiles you."

"The heart . . . didn't Jesus teach us that what the heart was full of would be seen in our behaviour and heard in our speech?" Simon asked no one in particular.

---

32. Isaiah 29:13.
33. Isaiah 29:14.

"Yes," James replied. He thought for a moment and then he elaborated, "Your behaviour and your speech reveal what is inside you, and therefore your words and your actions are the true reflection of the real you. That's why Jesus always calls these leaders play actors . . . they pretend to be what they are not."

But the crowd quietly turned away and continued with their activities. All the delegation from Jerusalem had done was provide a bit of colour in their otherwise mundane and drab lives.

Jesus motioned for his disciples to follow him. It was time to go home.

"The Pharisees were clearly scandalized by your reference to Isaiah," Simon ventured to say to Jesus as they walked. He wanted to test his own conclusions about why Jesus antagonized these leaders.

"Every plant not planted by my Father will be uprooted. Let them be. There is no point in debating with those who are obstinate. Being blind themselves, they are unable to guide the blind. Instead, they all end up falling in the ditch."

Simon felt confident to ask yet another question. "Will you explain this analogy to us, please?"

Jesus stopped walking and turned to look at his disciples. They were so young, but he knew it was important that they understood the true intent of the Scriptures rather than blindly following those who seemed to be educated men. In their desire to appear wise and original before people, scholars often taught according to their own limited understanding, obscuring the plain meaning of the Scriptures.

"Are you all still so dull?" Jesus said with concern, rather than irritation. "Think about it. What you put in your mouth . . . where does it go?"

Is that a trick question? Simon wondered, but said nothing. He wasn't going to risk another rebuke . . . at least, not in front of the others.

"You chew your food . . . you swallow . . . and then? It goes into the stomach, right? And then you eliminate it. How can that defile you? But whatever comes out of your mouth comes from inside you . . . and reveals what is in your heart. That is what renders you unclean."

Jesus looked at their vacant faces. "Evil thoughts, murder, adultery, sexual immorality, theft, false testimony, slander . . . when these things are manifest in your lives, they expose an inner impurity. But eating with unwashed hands does not."

When no one said anything, Jesus simply turned around and walked on.

We must exasperate him, Simon thought. But it is not easy to shift our thought patterns after we have been taught incorrectly for years.

12

Challenging Prejudice

So, where are we going?" Simon asked his brother as they packed the last few items his wife had lovingly provided for the journey. Simon had wanted her to go with them, but she felt she needed to stay to help Zebedee with the cleaning and drying of the fish. The business had to continue with or without the fishermen.

"I don't know," Andrew replied. "Jesus said something about the northwest, but we'll know soon enough."

They followed Jesus along the well-worn trade route towards Phoenicia. The Phoenicians had established themselves as fine artisans and merchants, their wares ranging from lumber to gold, and their expertise ranging from a thriving purple dye industry to ship building. They were descendants of the Canaanites and their religion had proved to be a stumbling block for Israel in times past. They had promoted the horrific practice of child-sacrifice in their various colonies. The area of Sidon had been allotted to the tribe of Asher by Joshua, but they had never succeeded in conquering the people. King Ahab of Israel had married one of their most infamous princesses, a wicked woman named Jezebel. The prophets pronounced judgment against Sidon on numerous occasions . . . part of the city had been struck by an earthquake and had sunk into the Mediterranean.

The disciples couldn't help wondering why Jesus was taking them to this Gentile area. Simon reasoned that it might be an attempt to get the rest that had been denied them before . . . a chance to escape the crowds and the constant hostility of the leaders . . . to go to a place where no one knew Jesus's name.

But Jesus's fame had spread beyond the borders of Galilee and Judah, and in spite of his attempt to keep their presence a secret, a Gentile woman from the region came begging Jesus to drive a demon out of her daughter. Surprisingly, she correctly identified him as the Son of David, calling him Lord and begging him to have mercy on her. But Jesus appeared to ignore her, simply walking on as if he saw and heard nothing.

However, his indifference did not stop her from following them . . . crying, pleading, hounding them. The disciples became annoyed and wondered why Jesus did nothing. Eventually, James and John – the "sons of thunder" as Jesus had nicknamed them – could take the intrusion no longer. "Lord, please tell her to leave us alone. She's making such a nuisance of herself!"

Simon knew they meant well. They knew Jesus needed to rest and that he had tried to bring them to a place where they would not be swamped by the crowds and their many needs. But there was also a darker side to their request. They found her repugnant – she represented everything that was odious to the Jews. Jesus's earlier conversation with the Samaritan woman had shocked them, but at least the Samaritans had some Jewishness about them. This woman was a descendent of the Canaanites and therefore, in their minds, not worthy of any form of mercy.

Without looking at the woman, Jesus said, "I have not been sent to anyone except the lost sheep of Israel."

The brothers looked smug . . . not only was Jesus going along with their request, but he was confirming their evaluation of the woman.

However, she was not about to take no for an answer. Instead, she rushed forward and threw herself down in the dirt before Jesus's feet, begging him to help her. Once more, she called him Lord.

This piteous plea apparently had no effect on Jesus. "It is not right to take the children's bread and throw it to the dogs," he said.

This brutal statement took Simon by surprise. This was a side of Jesus he had never seen before. The statement revealed extreme ethnocentrism, and even though the term "dog" was often used colloquially by Jews to refer to non-Jews, Simon had never heard Jesus use an insult as shocking as this when speaking to a fellow human being. And what alarmed him even more was that it seemed the sentiment was shared by the rest of the disciples. He had never witnessed such bigoted sectarianism within the group before. He knew that the other Simon was a zealot and that Judas came from the more purist folk in Judea, but most of the Galileans lived among Gentiles . . . and even though they maintained a strict cultural distance from them, there was always a certain level of respectful tolerance.

But then Simon saw Jesus's face and suddenly he realized this was a test. Jesus wanted to see their reaction as he echoed what was in their hearts. He was using the woman to teach them something . . . but what was he trying to teach them?

Then the incident took an unexpected turn, at least as far as the disciples were concerned. Instead of taking offence and leaving, the woman confirmed the extreme Jewish view of her as a Gentile "dog," and willingly placed herself under the Jewish table, asking only for the unused scraps that fell from it. Her humility and her faith in Jesus were like coals of fire on the disciples' heads.[1] Jesus's radical and risky object lesson had taught them something they would never forget. In many ways, this was a turning point for the disciples . . . a major shift in their thinking . . . Jesus was not only for the Jews, but for all nations.

Jesus turned to the woman and stooped down until his eyes met hers. Her face was tear-stained. There were dark rings under her eyes and the strain caused by her daughter's condition had etched deep lines into her forehead. But as she saw the tenderness in his eyes, the look on her face began to change. It was as if she realized that she had been part of an object lesson . . . that this Jew was different from the others . . . that there was mercy and it was hers to receive.

"Dear woman," Jesus said as he held her chin up and looked deep into her eyes. "Great is your faith." He then looked up at his disciples.

Simon suddenly remembered Jesus's statement about the Roman centurion. "I have not found such faith in all Israel," he had said. The perceptive faith of the centurion and this woman, both Gentiles, were an exemplary showpiece of trust . . . a model of true discipleship. Total humility . . . total surrender . . . total dependence. Simon felt deeply ashamed. In spite of the vulgarity of Jesus's rebuke, the persistence of this woman had revealed to the disciples a faith that appeared to be stronger than their own.

Jesus looked back at the woman. "It is done as you have requested. Go home. The demon has left your daughter."

Without hesitation . . . once again demonstrating her faith in Jesus . . . the woman jumped up and ran home. Soon they all heard her shriek for joy.

Graciously, Jesus said nothing. He simply indicated that their time in Phoenicia had come to an end, and they made preparations to leave.

* * *

They left the area and at first travelled north toward Sidon, but later they turned east, following the old grain routes towards the ancient city of Dan. There, Jeroboam, the first ruler of the northern kingdom of Israel, had set up an altar and two golden calves to ensure that the people's need for religious ritual was satisfied, in order to prevent them from returning to the temple in Jerusalem.

---

1. Proverbs 25:22.

It was high summer, so they were able to sleep under the array of stars that twinkled brightly in the clear, ink-black sky. Every evening, as they sat around the campfire, Jesus opened the Scriptures to them, encouraging them to hide the word in their hearts. That was the only way they would keep themselves from being led astray by the misinterpretation of others as well as the thoughts and philosophies of the pagan nations.[2]

The scenery they travelled through was magnificent. As they crested the western mountains and looked to the east, it seemed as if they could see into the future. Snow-capped Mount Hermon lay before them like a gigantic, glistening jewel. Myrtle and wild olives trees provided shade during the warm hours of the day, while a gentle, easterly breeze cooled the nights. Even though most of the grass and wildflowers had withered under the relentless sun by that time, there was still enough vegetation to provide a soft spot on which to sleep. They even caught a glimpse of a lone, wild goat on one of the ridges close to where they were walking.

The disciples then descended steeply into the valley basin where they crossed over the rivers that flowed into Lake Hula, the pooled source of the River Jordan. Later, after turning south, they intersected the main route to Damascus. From that point on, the landscape began to change dramatically. They walked through rich farmland, famed from antiquity for its oak trees and excellent cattle.[3] For the disciples, this was a sumptuous spiritual and aesthetic feast. They were reluctant for it to end.

Their route took them down into the Decapolis on the eastern shore of the Sea of Galilee, the area where Jesus had freed the two men from demon possession. The people had rejected him at that time, but now, more than likely due to the effective witness of the two former demoniacs, crowds flocked to see him, bringing their sick and laying them at his feet. Without a trace of racial prejudice, Jesus healed them all and, in response, these pagan people, some descended from the ancient Canaanites, praised the God of Israel.

Three days later, with food supplies running low, Jesus called to his disciples. "These people have used what they brought with them and now they are hungry. If they have to return to their respective cities without being fed, they will collapse on the way."

It seemed that the compassion Jesus had for others had not yet taken root in his disciples. And worse than that, they once again exhibited a lack of faith

---

2. Psalm 119:11.

3. The prophet Amos once referred to the lazy, pampered women of Samaria as the "fat cows of Bashan." Amos 4:1–3.

in their response. "This is a remote place. There are no marketplaces close by where we can buy enough bread to feed such a large multitude. There are about four thousand men here with their women and children."

Simon wanted to remind them of the miraculous feeding of the five thousand, but he held his peace. Although he was the oldest of the group, he was reluctant to exert any form of authority. In many ways, he still lacked confidence. He felt more like a fisherman than a follower of a rabbi. In spite of the fact that Jesus was teaching them the Scriptures, helping them to memorize large portions at a time, teaching them how to interpret what they learned correctly, he felt that he still had so much to learn.

He and Andrew had often discussed the similarities between catching fish and catching people. They had spoken about the prophecy of Jeremiah where fishermen and hunters were sent by God to bring back the lapsed and dispersed people of God.[4] Perhaps Jesus had specifically chosen them because they knew that the only way to catch anything involved patience and a lot of hard work.

Jesus looked at his disciples. Was it possible that they had forgotten? Or was it because this was Gentile territory? Then he simply asked, "How many loaves do you have?"

"Seven," they replied, "and a few salted fish."

Jesus rose slowly, still looking at them to see if there was any visible spark of faith. Then he told the crowd to be seated on the ground. Taking the seven loaves and the fish, he gave thanks, broke them, and began to distribute the pieces to the disciples who, in turn, gave the food to the people. Once again, everyone had enough to eat and seven baskets full of left-over fragments were collected by the disciples.

Simon felt ashamed. Maybe he should have spoken up. What must Jesus think of him? He must think him very dull and hard-hearted indeed. Thankfully, Jesus said nothing about the incident. He simply dismissed the crowd and, having found a boat sailing to the western shore, he indicated that it was time for them to go home.

* * *

"I don't believe it," Simon said. They could hear the Pharisees approach as they shouted at the people to get out of their way, fearful of being made unclean by physical contact. The Pharisees' distinctive clothing made them stand out in the crowds, like ebony and ivory towers. Their voluminous shawls flapped as

---

4. Jeremiah 16:16.

they walked . . . sails in the wind. In their zeal to appear holy, they lengthened the fringes of their garments and wore oversized phylacteries.[5]

They came demanding a sign from Jesus. Clearly, they had not forgotten their humiliation in the matter of ritual purity. They had, no doubt, been discussing how to regain their dignity and this was their attempt to expose Jesus as one who did not meet the biblical criteria of the sages with regard to the Messiah.

How many more signs do they need? Simon wondered. The grateful recipients of Jesus's many miracles had not been silent. In fact, in their unbridled exuberance, they had made it virtually impossible for Jesus to go anywhere without being swamped by crowds demanding healing, exorcism, or provision of some kind.

"Some people ask questions because they seek answers. Others ask questions because they want to appear wise," Andrew said under his breath.

"Or to trap others," James added. "This request for a sign is not to discern truth. They have already rejected the validity of his words and his works. They only want evidence to use against him."

"Why this constant opposition?" Simon wondered out loud. "What is the point? Their repeated contention is tiresome and not edifying at all. Even if they have been offended by what Jesus has said, didn't the wise king Solomon say that a man shows intelligence by his forbearance . . . that it is his glory to overlook an offense?"[6]

"King Solomon also said, 'Do not answer a fool according to his folly,'"[7] Matthew chimed in. "Those who loathe correction prove themselves to be fools. They are not here to learn . . . the fact that they have not yet renounced their misapplication of the Scriptures reveals that."

"A sign," Jesus responded. "You want a sign. Tell me, what do you say when the sky is red in the evening?"

The Pharisees shifted from foot to foot. When Jesus began his answers with riddles, they knew that things would not go well for them. But pride made them stand their ground.

"You say it is going to be good weather, don't you?" Jesus paused for effect. "But when the sky is red and dark in the morning you say it will be stormy weather? How is it possible that you are able to correctly interpret the signs

---

5. A phylactery is a small leather box containing biblical texts written on tanned calfskin, worn by Jewish men as a reminder to obey the Torah.

6. Proverbs 19:11.

7. Proverbs 26:4.

of change in the weather, but you are unable to correctly interpret the signs of change in the times?"

Exactly, Simon thought. These leaders are totally unable to see that the prophetic words concerning the Messiah are being fulfilled in the words and works of Jesus . . . simply because he is not what they were expecting . . . and what they have been teaching others to expect. As I see it, they only have two options here . . . to admit that they are wrong . . . or to reject Jesus. There is no other choice.

Jesus turned to face the crowds that had gathered around them. "A wicked and spiritually unfaithful generation insists on signs. But there is only one sign they will be given . . . the sign of Jonah."

"Again, the sign of Jonah, without any explanation," Simon murmured.

There was sudden buzz in the crowd. "What did this mean?" they wondered.

The Pharisees were bewildered. If they let slip that they did not understand Jesus's reference to the "sign of Jonah," they would appear foolish. Once again, they were utterly perplexed. But before they could regroup and attack from a different angle, Jesus withdrew, walked down to the harbour with his disciples, and got into the boat to cross over once again.

As they neared the harbour of Bethsaida, Jesus suddenly said, "Be very wary of the yeast of the Pharisees, the Sadducees, and of Herod."

Simon looked at Andrew. In their haste, they had neglected to buy bread. Andrew turned to James and John. "Do you have any bread left?" he asked. They shook their heads. The others indicated that they, too, had none. They were so concerned about the absence of provisions that they failed to understand the real intent of Jesus's statement.

"Why are you talking about bread?" Jesus asked, with a hint of irritation in his voice. "How is it possible that you still do not understand? Look into your hearts. Are they hard? You have eyes. Why do you fail to see? You have ears. Why do you fail to hear? You are unable to remember what I have done in the past, so now you falter in the present. Don't you remember? When I broke the five loaves for the five thousand . . . how many baskets of fragments did you collect afterwards?"

Simon swallowed hard. Earlier, he had asked the very same questions of the Pharisees. Now the tables were turned. How many signs did they . . . did he . . . need?

"We filled twelve baskets," the disciples replied.

"And when I fed the four thousand with seven loaves? How many baskets did you fill then?"

"Seven," they answered.

"Then why are you talking about the need for bread? I'm not talking about bread. I am warning you not to allow even a tiny amount of the teaching of the Pharisees, the Sadducees, and Herod himself to infiltrate your minds. Do you still not understand?"

They understood. A little yeast had the ability to ferment a large piece of dough . . . in the same way, the misguided teachings of the leaders had the power to muddy the waters of their understanding. Simon determined to be more vigilant in the future. Scripture was the plumb line against which the teaching of others could be measured. When challenged, Jesus always referred to what was written . . . so Simon resolved that day to be more diligent in his memorization so that he might safeguard his heart and mind in the future.

13

Progressive Sight

As they walked through the streets of Bethsaida, the ever-expanding capital of Philip's district, Simon knew he had been wise to take Andrew and leave the city after their parents' early death. Bethsaida's inhabitants had embraced so much of the Greek and Roman cultures that it had largely lost its Jewish character. As the disciples hastily bought provisions in the marketplace, they were careful not to touch the stalls selling food prohibited in Scripture.

As they were leaving the village, some people brought a blind man to Jesus, begging him to heal him.

What a contrast, Simon thought. In other cities and towns, we can hardly move because of the crowds. But here, it was clearly not for lack of need that no one approached Jesus, but rather for lack of faith.

Jesus took the blind man by the hand and led him outside the village. The disciples thought that it was unusual that Jesus was isolating them from the townsfolk, but they were reluctant to ask any questions after the misunderstanding in the boat. Then Jesus simply spat in his hand and rubbed the saliva on the man's eyes.

Just like my mother would wipe the sleep out of my eyes in the morning, Simon thought, smiling.

"Do you see anything?" Jesus asked the man.

"I see people . . . but indistinctly. They look like trees walking around."

"He obviously was not born blind," Matthew said to Simon.

"Why do you say that?" Simon asked.

"He knows what he ought to be seeing . . . and that what he is seeing now is not correct."

That is very perceptive, Simon said, wondering why he had not seen that himself.

Once more, Jesus placed his hands on the man's eyes. "And now?" he asked.

"Yes! Yes, I can see!" the man exclaimed gleefully.

"Go home," Jesus said. "Do not return to the village." And he turned away and led his disciples further north along a well-worn trade route.

Simon was confused. Why the progressive healing? Why was the man not healed immediately? Was this a lesson Jesus was trying to teach them? Perhaps that faith grew gradually and with difficulty? He knew that he would have to unlearn a lot of what he had been taught as a child and later as a young person. Jesus had made it clear that the leaders misinterpreted the Scriptures and led people astray . . . even a little incorrect teaching could ferment in the heart, like yeast in dough, and corrupt a person. But that meant that he had to relearn everything and that was hard . . . and it took time.

Recently his wife made him discard his favourite piece of old clothing, replacing it with a new garment she had bought for him. The old one smelled like fish, she had said . . . the follower of an important rabbi should not smell like fish. At first, he was reluctant. His old clothes were comfortable and reminded him of the sea he loved so much. He had to get used to his new clothes, gradually . . . just like he had to get used to this new and radical teaching of Jesus, gradually. Right now, he felt more like the blind man in Bethsaida after the first touch . . . he still could not see clearly.

* * *

As they travelled north, Simon decided to imitate the habits of his rabbi. He began to rise earlier than the rest to spend time in prayer, trying hard to pray what was in his heart and on his mind rather than the rote prayers he had been taught by his Hebrew teachers. After the others had retired for the night, he also went to find a quiet spot, rehearsing the events of the day in conversation with the Father Jesus spoke about in such intimate terms.

Jesus continued to teach them the Scriptures as they walked and when they sat around the campfires at night. He had a way of making each passage come alive. When he retold the stories, he made them sound like so much more than just the history of the Israelites. It was refreshing to listen to him explain how the major themes were not confined to the past, but that they had a timeless relevance. Simon often saw himself in the biblical characters. In one sense it made him feel better about himself, since they seemed to be as slow to learn as he was.

The road became steeper and the landscape began to change. Looking back at one point, Simon gasped as he beheld the panoramic view where the upper Jordan River emerged from between the mountains, slicing through a large, fertile plain before flowing into his beloved Sea of Galilee. The group enthusiastically pointed out the villages around its northern shoreline. It was a happy time . . . even the memory of the crowds and the obnoxious leaders could not spoil the pure pleasure of learning from Jesus in such an idyllic setting. It was a retreat they would never forget.

East of the ancient city of Dan, they turned towards the region of Caesarea Philippi, the administrative centre of the area. It was named after Caesar Augustus and Herod Philip, to distinguish it from Caesarea Maritima which was along the Mediterranean coast. It was situated on the southwestern slopes of Mount Hermon and lay at the intersection of the main trade route from Phoenicia to Damascus. Jesus had skirted around it on their earlier trip to the north. Simon marvelled at the beauty all around him. It was a lush oasis of life with an abundance of water. In fact, it was the main source of the River Jordan and boasted a large waterfall.

Jesus reminded them that many years ago, there had been a war here between the Syrian, Antiochus, and the Greek-Egyptian, Ptolemy. Antiochus's victory secured Seleucid control over the area including Samaria and Judea until the Maccabean revolt. At one time, the Greeks had built a pagan temple dedicated to Pan, the goat-footed god, at the entrance to a large grotto at the base of a huge red rock cliff. Next to this was a white building dedicated to Augustus Caesar. Many niches had been carved into the rock and pillars for idols and altars, and pagan priests offered animals, incense and, on occasion, even children. The disciples felt they were standing before the very portals of Satan's kingdom.

Simon couldn't help comparing the misguided leaders of Israel with the misguided pagans. While it was hard to convince the Pharisees and Sadducees, at least there was a common reference point. But with the pagans, there was no such connection. Yet Jesus had indicated that the kingdom he proclaimed was for the whole world. Indeed, Simon believed that one of the reasons Jesus had begun to take them into predominantly Gentile territories was to make them realize that the kingdom of God was to expand into every people group, not just the Jews. The lesson they learned when the Gentile woman's daughter had been released from demonic possession in Phoenicia had burned that into his mind. But surely those who worshipped idols would resist a message like this? Besides, would the evil one even allow them to enter through his gates to plunder his kingdom?

They walked along the gurgling river leaving behind them the disturbing sounds of the idol worshippers. Simon marvelled at the clearness of the water which was cold and sweet to the taste. They set up camp close to one of the villages in the area. That evening, once all the disciples had turned in and Jesus had gone to find a place to pray, Simon strolled down to the banks of the river to talk to the Father about the things he had witnessed that day, as well as his growing desire to see things more clearly.

The progressive healing of the blind man in Bethsaida bothered him. In a spiritual sense, he viewed himself as one who saw dimly. He had now witnessed the errors of both his own people as well as those of the pagans. What would prevent him from deviating from the right way?

"Let me know your paths, O Lord," he prayed. "Help me to see clearly . . . help me to understand . . . help me to learn your word . . . to hide it in my heart, so that I might be protected from straying from the truth. Teach me . . . guide me . . . lead me in your true way. Do not let the sins of my youth and the limitations of my learning be stumbling blocks. Please do not let me be disappointed or dismayed or misdirected. You know my heart. You know that I am slow to learn . . . but you are good and kind and compassionate and merciful . . . please show me your way."[1]

A sense of peace flooded over him. He felt that his prayer had been heard and that the Father was pleased with his petition. He thought about his life up until that point . . . from his youth he had always given his best, but he still felt that he had never been much more than mediocre. There had been no time to better himself . . . he had mouths to feed and a business to build. One thing Simon had feared all his life, more than anything else, was mediocrity. He was not frightened of failure as much as simply being a total nonentity.

But then Jesus came, and things began to change. It was as if he had finally found purpose in his life. For the first time life seemed to make sense. Things were not merely haphazard . . . there was direction and meaning. And yet there was still so much he had to learn . . . so many things were still blurred. Like the blind man, his time with Jesus had given him partial sight. Now he desired more . . . he desired vivid clarity.

* * *

It soon became apparent to Simon that Jesus had deliberately chosen an area where they would be free from outside interference. He wanted to be alone with his disciples so that they could rest, but also so that he could take them deeper, strategically preparing the foundation upon which a community would be built. They had understood from the start that by following Jesus they would become a distinct fellowship . . . the same as those who followed the teachings of other rabbis. But Jesus's popularity had made it virtually impossible

---

1. This prayer echoes themes found in the Psalms.

for them to grow into a close-knit, integrated body of like-minded people. There was hardly time to eat, let alone time to rest and reflect or to learn from the Scriptures.

But since arriving in the area, every day, almost from the moment they opened their eyes to the time they curled up for the night, Jesus drilled them in the Scriptures. He began with the Law, but later moved on to the writings and the prophets. He asked them questions, helping them to see when what they had learned was a misinterpretation of what had been written. He gave them time to meditate and reflect on what they had learned, and he showed them how to apply the historical meaning of various texts to their situations in the present. He taught them that the Law was not the goal of Scripture, rather it was a means of helping them to live life as God intended. The Law revealed the heart of God . . . its purpose was to bring them to a place of harmony with their Creator. They learned that it was not mere external rule-keeping that was important . . . but it was an inner motivation that revealed the reality of the relationship outwardly. The goal was to reflect the person of God in and through their everyday lives.

At first, the memorization of Scripture proved to be a tedious drudgery for Simon . . . but as he learned the value of internalizing God's word, it became a joy. Jesus modelled what he taught. He never expected them to do anything he had not shown them in his own life before. Simon watched Jesus closely and even tried to copy his mannerisms. Every morning and every evening Simon reiterated his prayer for understanding, and he believed God was answering his requests. His confidence was growing.

One day, after a rather vigorous, animated discussion on the role of Israel among the nations, Jesus went to pray on his own. On his return, he unexpectedly asked them what they had heard other people say about him.

"Most people say you are a herald . . . that you are continuing the work of John the Baptizer," Thomas offered.

"Others think you are the prophet Elijah who is to come before the day of the Lord,"[2] Matthew added.

"I've even heard people say that you are one of the prophets, like Jeremiah, and that you will pronounce judgment over Israel if they refuse to repent," Philip said. "All in all, everyone thinks you are not an ordinary man . . . they see you as extraordinary . . . but they do not know exactly who you are."

---

2. Malachi 4:5. This is not an indication of a belief in reincarnation. Elijah had been taken up into heaven alive, so some of the Jews believed he would return to usher in the messianic era.

At this Jesus smiled. "They do not know how to classify me . . . where I fit in?"

Jesus was in a playful mood. Over the past few days, he too had relaxed as the strain of demand and confrontation was no longer present. Time purposefully set aside for contemplation and relaxation helped to bring balance to an otherwise intense time of study.

But then he became serious. "So, what about you?" he asked them directly. "Who do you think I am?"

Without hesitation Simon exclaimed, "You are the anointed one, the Messiah, the son of the living God." He had come to this conclusion the previous evening while mulling things over as he prayed. There were just too many things Jesus said and did to think otherwise. On later reflection, Simon realized that his confession fell short of all they eventually came to learn about Jesus.

Jesus sighed. It seemed to Simon as if a weight had dropped from his shoulders. "You are divinely favoured, Simon son of John. You could not have come to this conclusion on your own. Only my heavenly Father could have revealed this to you. This tells me that you are open to hearing the voice of God."

Simon was relieved to hear this. For months he had seen himself as the slow-witted one, but his determination to follow the example of Jesus in prayer and scriptural study had given him a spiritual sensitivity he had not had before.

But Jesus was still speaking to him. "Remember the first time we met, Simon?"

How could Simon ever forget that day . . . the day when he felt that Jesus was looking into the inner recesses of his soul.

"Do you remember, Simon?"

"Yes, Lord, I remember."

"I told you that day that you were named Simon by your parents, but that one day you would be called Cephas . . . a rock . . . do you remember?"

"Yes, Lord, I remember."

"Well, what you have confessed today is the rock . . . the bedrock foundation upon which I will build my community. The very gates of the evil one's domain will not be able to stand against my community, because this confession is the key that unlocks the kingdom of heaven. All who show the same faith in me which you have just expressed will gain access to it. And as my community, you will have the responsibility to set free those who are held captive. If you neglect this responsibility, they will remain bound."

Simon felt this was far too much to process at one time. He thought about Jesus's teaching about the wise man who built his house upon the rock. In that story, the rock represented hearing and applying the words of Jesus. The future community would be founded and built upon the declaration and understanding that Jesus was the Messiah. That made sense to him. Jesus had also indicated that this community would be given the ability to endure even in times of opposition, adversity and resistance. Jesus had added that the very gates of hell would not be able to resist their advance. That image presupposed movement . . . this community was not meant to remain static. They were to gain ground, not hold ground. Their recent trips made it abundantly clear that Jesus intended this community to include both Jews and Gentiles. His community had to grow and expand beyond the borders of Israel into the whole world.

Simon thought of what he had recently seen at the pagan temples and shrines. If he understood correctly, the domain of Satan would be plundered when Jesus was declared to be the Messiah, because that declaration was the key to unlocking the door to the kingdom of heaven. But Simon wondered how the truth about a Jewish Messiah would be understood in a world dominated by an abundance of gods, all demanding things that were forbidden in Scripture?

Jesus said that they would have heavenly authority to release these captives from Satan's grip. Simon saw that as a great *responsibility* not a privilege. As the nation of Israel, they were meant to be God's light to the nations, but they had failed because they had not understood this principle. Now he realized that in the same way, if the followers of Jesus failed to be his representatives . . . his light . . . people would be left imprisoned in darkness and ignorance.

Simon recalled Jesus's recent teaching about the vice-regency given to Adam and Eve at creation. They had been created to be God's representatives on earth. Under God they were meant to bring his rule on all of creation. But they had chosen to disobey, like the foolish man who built his house on the sand. Was Jesus now saying that the ruin of their failure was about to be reversed? Was the ruler of this world about to be stripped of his power? Would the expansion of the community of Jesus mean that the God of heaven would take back what was rightfully his? Was it that simple? Allegiance and obedience to Jesus? But was obedience ever really simple?

Simon was about to say that he was ready to take on this responsibility when he heard Jesus tell them that they were to say nothing about his identity as the Messiah. Simon wanted to protest, but his mind was already too full, so he chose to remain silent . . . for the time being.

Part III

Ripening and Reaping

*"... unless a kernel of wheat falls into the ground and dies,
it will remain only one seed."*
John 12:24

14

Paradigm Shift

Cephas." Andrew had recently taken to calling his brother by the nickname Jesus had given him.

"Perhaps we ought to call him Peter when we are in Gentile territory," James said. "They will understand the meaning of that name more easily. I don't think many of them speak Aramaic."

"Or Hebrew, for that matter," John chirped. When would his voice finally break?

"Stop it, you lot," Simon chided playfully. "What do you want, little brother?"

"I just wanted to say that I'm proud of you. We all are."

"Thank you, Andrew, but as Jesus said, I didn't figure that out on my own. It came to me while I was praying . . . well, at least during my way of praying. I was thinking about things Jesus had said and done in the past and reflecting on what I had learned, and I was telling God . . . I was telling the Father, about my assessments when it just came to me. All the evidence pointed to one inescapable conclusion. Jesus must be the Messiah. So, it was just as Jesus said – the Father somehow revealed the truth."

"I noticed you sneaking off the other evening," Andrew said, smiling.

"I wasn't sneaking . . . I just wanted to be alone."

"Well . . . I followed you."

"You what?"

"I followed you. I realized a few days ago that there was something different about you. At first, I just thought you were benefitting from Jesus's intensive teaching . . . but then I wondered if it had anything to do with you disappearing before dawn and after we drift off for the night . . . so I followed you. I'm sorry. I just had to see what you were up to."

"Well, did you learn anything from what you saw and heard?" Simon was trying to remember if he had said anything silly or personal.

"What I learned was that you have begun to do what we have all seen Jesus do . . . and I was so moved that I decided to do the same."

"So that's where you were this morning!"

"Yes. That's where I was. Brother, I feel invigorated. I did not hear God's voice or experience anything extraordinary . . . nor can I say that I have any revelation about anything in particular. But I possess a sense of peace and refreshment. Now I understand why Jesus is able to be so calm in the presence of the crowds and with the pressures of those who oppose him."

"That's precisely how I feel! It is as if the burdens of the day . . . and of the previous days . . . have been taken away. It is as if by bringing them to the Father in prayer, I am in actual fact giving them over to him. Oh, I know that sounds strange, but it is the only way I can explain my experience."

"I could not have explained it better myself, brother. Mum and Dad would have been so proud of you."

"Yes, I often wish they could see us now . . ." Simon's voice trailed off. Then he added, "Remember when Jesus spoke about putting new wine into new wineskins?"

"Yes, I do remember. That image went right over my head."

"Well, it went over mine too back then . . . but now I think I am beginning to understand what he meant. The more I pray and the more I review things in the presence of the Father, handing them over to him in a manner of speaking . . . the more I feel I understand Jesus. At first his teaching was so new and so radical that my mind felt like an old wineskin which would burst if he poured anything more into it. But now . . . now I feel like my mind is becoming new too. Not that I understand everything, but that I understand more. Does that make sense at all?"

Andrew was beaming. "Cephas! Peter! My brother, the rock!"

"Stop it," Simon said giving his brother a gentle push. "In my heart, I am still very much a simple fisherman."

"Humility with greatness . . . a very good combination," John said, teasingly.

"That's enough!" Simon said, laughing with them. "It is time for the lessons. Come."

* * *

But Simon's statement of faith could not have prepared him for the lesson that Jesus was going to teach that morning. Indeed, there was a pervasive, profound misunderstanding among the disciples regarding the mission of Jesus as the Messiah. Everything they had previously been taught about the Messiah indicated that he would be a conquering hero . . . a king like David . . .

coming to restore the kingdom of Israel. They had no way of knowing how Jesus would fulfil his role as Israel's Messiah. So, for Jesus, it was critical that they did not continue to hold their own misguided hopes and dreams for the future Messiah.

"We have spent a lot of time studying the Scriptures this week," Jesus said, "and I know it has been rather intense. But I need to lay the groundwork for what I will teach you today. I must prepare you for what is to come."

Jesus looked at each one of his disciples in turn. It seemed to Simon that he did not know where to begin.

"I have so scandalized the elders, the chief priests, and the teachers of the law, that they ascribe my ministry to the devil," he said. "My association with people they call 'sinners,' and my perceived disregard for their traditions, especially those concerning piety and purity, have turned them against me. You have seen how they have tried to trap me into saying something that will open the way for them to accuse me of heresy or blasphemy. Their ultimate aim is to execute me."

Simon drew in his breath. This is serious, he thought. Self-proclaimed messiahs before Jesus had been executed along with their followers. That was what had troubled him more than anything else when Andrew had first begun to speak about Jesus as the Messiah. But none of those so-called messiahs had done any works like those of Jesus . . . none of them had taught their followers to love their enemies . . . in fact they had all spoken openly against their oppressors, advocating violent conflict and liberation at all costs.

Jesus then began to speak about his suffering and death in Jerusalem as if it were a foregone conclusion. He tried to explain to them that this was the will of the Father . . . that he had come into the world for this one purpose – to die for the world. But then he added that on the third day after his death, he would be raised to life.

Simon was so distraught that he hardly heard the final sentence. All he knew was that this was not what he had signed up for . . . passive surrender was not an option. Jesus was the only hope for Israel. There was no turning back . . . they had come too far.

Before he knew what he was doing, Simon pulled Jesus aside and began to berate him for such defeatist talk. "May that never come to pass, Lord! I will not allow this to happen to you!"

Jesus turned and looked deep into Simon's eyes. It was one of his long penetrating stares that made Simon feel as though the very core of his being lay open for scrutiny. Simon was breathing heavily . . . he could feel his pulse beating in his temples. Jesus on the other hand, while remaining calm on the surface, seemed deeply disturbed in his soul. Once again, his ancient archenemy was making his diabolical presence known. But to use one of his loyal followers as the vehicle for temptation . . . especially one who had only recently been spiritually able to receive divine revelation . . . was distressing. But that was one of the adversary's most lethal instruments . . . using a dear friend who cared more for the wellbeing of his companion than for God's will to be done.

"Satan! Begone! I know you only too well. Once more you seek to make me stumble away from the path set before me!"

Simon was stunned. Just yesterday Jesus had said that he was hearing the voice of God. Now he was indicating that Simon was equally open to hearing the voice of Satan. It was a crushing rebuke.

But then, Jesus put his arm around Simon's shoulder and his voice became kinder. "Simon, your mind is not yet fixed on the things of God. You are thinking as a mere man."

The other disciples stood still, silently watching. While it was Simon who had done the talking, he had simply voiced what they all were thinking. They were horrified by Jesus's pronouncement of his death. Only yesterday they had envisaged their Lord being crowned king. They could not wrap their minds round this talk of death . . . the talk of resurrection was totally beyond their comprehension.

Jesus returned to the group with Simon, anxious to show that he bore his misled disciple no ill will. But for a moment he said nothing. It was clear to them all that he was profoundly troubled.

Then he said slowly, weighing each word before he spoke it, "Whoever wishes to come after me, must follow me in self-denial, even to the point of giving up everything in life, and model their lives on mine. Choosing compromise in order to preserve your life will ultimately lead to a loss of everything . . . but if you remain true in your devotion to me, you will discover the fulness of life. What benefit is it to you if you obtain everything you wish for in this life, but in the process, you forfeit eternity? Is anything more valuable than your soul?"

The disciples looked at Jesus blankly. They could not piece everything together. First he had spoken of his death at the hands of the leaders and now he was exhorting them to follow him to the point of total self-sacrifice. What did the one have to do with the other? Was Jesus telling them that they would all meet with the same fate as he would? Would their movement be cruelly crushed as the others had been? Was this inevitable? If so, what was the point of it all?

And yet, Jesus had also indicated that his death was not the end, claiming that after three days he would be raised from the dead. In his initial distress, Simon had dismissed this statement. But as Jesus went on to speak about the Son of Man coming with the hosts of heaven to judge all people, saying that some of them would witness the coming of the kingdom, Simon wondered if somehow Jesus's death was the event that would usher in his reign as king. None of this made any sense to him, but that was the only way he could make sense out of what he had heard. Perhaps it was a metaphor? But he dared not speak again.

* * *

"What are you doing here, Simon?"

Simon started. He had not heard Matthew approaching. Indeed, it was hard to hear anything over the loud gurgling of the river . . . which was why he had chosen to sit there on the riverbank. He wanted to be on his own for a while so that he could regain his composure.

"I came here to be by myself," he replied. "I just need to be alone to think about the past few months and . . . well . . . to think about yesterday. I thought I'd learned something by now . . . that I had made some progress. But perhaps I've learned nothing at all."

"That's why I came to ask you what you are doing here?"

"I just told you what I was doing here," Simon said, slightly irritated.

"You have been avoiding us . . . and you have been avoiding Jesus."

Simon nodded, but said nothing.

"May I . . .?" Matthew indicated that he wanted to sit down next to Simon on the grassy embankment.

Simon wanted Matthew to go away, but he did not wish to appear rude. He had come to appreciate Matthew over the past few months and thought of him as a good friend . . . not just a fellow disciple. He did not want to offend him. "Go ahead," he said simply.

Matthew sat down and then said, "Do you remember the story about Elijah and the prophets of Baal?"[1]

Simon snorted. Of course he remembered the story.

"Forgive me. I did not mean to . . ."

But Simon motioned with his hand for his friend to continue.

"Elijah won the day, didn't he? It was a great triumph for him, and it was a turning point for many in the crowd. His words and his actions showed them

---

1. See 1 Kings 18 and 19.

the truth and helped them to make the right choices . . . just like your words and actions showed us the truth the other day."

Simon swallowed hard. "Thank you," he said.

"But what happened shortly after his great triumph?" Matthew continued. Simon remained silent.

"Not that I'm suggesting Jesus is like Jezebel . . . heaven forbid . . . but I do think that there is a similarity between Elijah's reaction to the threats of a wicked queen and your reaction to the righteous rebuke of Jesus. I think in both cases there was an overreaction . . . a loss of perspective, perhaps? Maybe a paralyzing sense of self-pity mixed with a good measure of self-doubt? A desire to give up? Am I right?"

Simon stared at the rushing water but said nothing. He knew that Matthew was right.

Matthew was silent for a while. He wasn't sure how to continue. The last thing he wanted was to add insult to injury.

"Do you remember how the story ends? God asks, 'What are you doing here, Elijah?' So, I repeat my initial question to you. What are you doing here, Simon?"

"You don't understand," Simon said slowly. "You don't know what it's like . . . I feel so ashamed."

"You don't think I know what it's like to feel ashamed?"

Matthew had carried a burden of shame concerning his past for a long time after joining the band of disciples. "You know that tax collectors are despised in Israel as people view them as collaborators with the Romans. But the past is the past. There is nothing I can do to change it. It is impossible to go back and undo the things I shouldn't have done, the words I shouldn't have said. But since Jesus called me to join our community, I have discovered that I am not trapped by my past. When he looked at me, he did not see what I was at the time . . . he saw what I could be . . . what he would make of me. So now, when my feelings of shame return, I remind myself that Jesus is still at work and that I have a better future lying ahead of me. I am not who I once was."

Simon looked up at his friend and smiled. Yes, Matthew understood.

"I've been there on that mountain with Elijah, too," Matthew continued. "I've stood at the mouth of the cave and heard the rush of the winds of shame . . . experienced the earthquake of humiliation . . . felt the fire of self-reproach. But these emotions were all of my own making and as long as I let them rage, I could not hear the voice of God speaking to me through Jesus. I had to still the noise of my failures . . . my bad choices and decisions . . . the many statements I made that I once thought were irrevocable. I had to consciously move into a place of silence where I could hear the positive again and regain some perspective."

"Maybe that's why I'm here, Matthew, . . . to hear God's voice in the silence."

"That river is not silent," Matthew said.

They both burst out laughing.

"Come, let's go back. We all miss you, Peter."

"Oh, stop," Simon said. But he appreciated the reminder. Jesus's positive evaluation transcended Simon's negative attitude towards himself. He had made a mistake . . . but that did not mean all was lost. It just meant he had more to learn.

* * *

A few days later, as evening was drawing near, Jesus approached Simon and asked him to accompany him up the mountain to pray. Simon looked at snow-capped Mount Hermon looming before him. It is a very high mountain, he thought. Will these fisherman legs of mine be up to the task?

"Don't worry, Simon. We will not go all the way to the top . . . just about halfway."

Halfway? Simon thought. That is still quite a bit of climbing.

Jesus simply smiled. The earlier confrontation was forgotten. The lesson learned.

"Go, get James and John as well," Jesus said. Simon felt guilty leaving his brother behind, but Andrew reminded him that it was not the first time Jesus had chosen the three to be his closer companions and that Jesus no doubt had good reason to do so.

They set out on the well-worn path as the light around them began to change. The air was cool and crisp. At first, they walked through vineyards planted in the rocky soil of the foothills, with fig and apricot trees growing alongside. Then they walked through cornfields . . . pear trees replaced the figs. Later, after they passed the last patches of tilled soil, they came to a point where there was nothing to obstruct their view. Then they turned to look back over northern Galilee.

The view was overwhelming. The Sea of Galilee shone like a jewel in the deepening rose-red hue of the setting sun. It had a colour Simon had never seen before . . . the colour of a ripe yellow-green pear. The surface looked calm and absolutely flat. The sun took on a rich gold colour as it sank in the west, resembling a gigantic dome slowly diminishing in size. They watched until it disappeared completely. In the twilight, they began to see the first stars and then, out of the dark shadows cast by the mountain to the east, the moon began to rise.

"I now know what Moses must have been thinking as he stood on Mount Nebo looking out over the promised land,"[2] Simon said. Then he turned to look up at the dull dusky crown of Hermon. "Just as long as we don't die on this mountain," he muttered under his breath.

"Come," Jesus urged them. "There are some grassy banks just a little further up. We can pray there."

Simon was tired and thought that the gravelly slopes looked perfectly fine for prayer, but he said nothing.

The path became steeper and the climbers moved slower than they had before. They were getting tired. Although they had done nothing particularly strenuous that day, the climb and the altitude were having an effect on them. Simon comforted himself with the thought of a bit of a nap before he prayed that evening.

As they crossed over the first ridge of snow, Jesus turned off the path and led them along a narrow crease in the mountain until they came to a fairly large area of flattened grass, glowing pale yellow in the moonlight. Jesus indicated that this was where they would pray. Simon found a cosy spot and curled up in his cloak for a short nap first. Apparently, James and John had the same idea.

Simon woke with a fright. He heard voices. All sorts of scenarios ran through his head, ranging from bandits to Roman soldiers, but nothing could have prepared him for what he saw when he peeked out from under his cloak.

Standing before him, as radiant as the sun in its noontime brilliance, stood Jesus flanked by two men, equally glorious in appearance. Simon did not know how he knew, but he was convinced that the men were none other than Moses and Elijah. Was it because they, like the disciples, had been on mountains in the stories that made him think that?[3] He wasn't sure. But he was certain these two spiritual giants from Israel's past were standing with Jesus.

When he heard what they were talking about, his hair stood on end. His heart began to pound in his chest and his mouth became dry. They were talking about Jesus dying in Jerusalem. Why this sudden preoccupation with death? Were they encouraging him to follow this path to self-destruction? Or were they comforting him? He couldn't tell. But in his mind, it didn't matter. Jesus was in danger . . . they were all in danger.

---

2. Deuteronomy 32:48–52.
3. Exodus 19:16–20; 24:1–18; 1 Kings 18:1–40; 19:8–18.

He was aware that the others were now awake as well, both staring in wide-eyed disbelief at the otherworldly scene unfolding before them. The last time he had felt so afraid was during that awful storm on the Sea of Galilee. His breathing was rapid . . . short bursts of vapor clouded his vision as he exhaled. For some inexplicable reason, a psalm suddenly came to mind. "The Lord is my light and my help – of whom then shall I be afraid? In the day of trouble, he will keep me safe in his tent . . . he will raise me out of reach on a high rock."[4] Suddenly he had a crazy idea. If he could somehow keep Jesus here on the mountain . . . stop him from going to Jerusalem . . .

At that moment, Simon realized Moses and Elijah were about to leave. "Wait!" he yelled before he could stop himself. "Wait! Please wait." He stumbled to his feet. Fear and grief had given birth to a plan bordering on lunacy. "Lord, Master. It is good that you are not alone tonight . . . that we are here with you. We can build you a tent right here on this high rock . . . I mean, on this mountain. We can build three tents . . . one for you, one for Moses and one for Elijah . . . so you can be safe from your enemies! You can hide here until the troubles have passed."

He heard John's high-pitched voice, "Simon! Look!" A thick, yet almost luminous, cloud suddenly descended on them. Simon fell to the ground in terror, cringing with fear in the grass. He heard a voice coming from within the cloud. "This is my well-loved Son, whom I have chosen. Listen to him!"

Simon was still breathing hard. He could taste blood in his mouth and knew he must have bitten his lip when he fell to the ground. He could hear John whimpering. But the voice was no longer speaking, and the cloud lifted. He dared to look up. Jesus was standing alone. He was no longer dazzling. It was as if nothing unusual had just happened.

"Get up," Jesus said. "You don't need to be afraid."

The three disciples rose slowly to their feet. What had they just witnessed? Everything looked so normal now. No glory, no otherworldly beings, no voice, no terrifying cloud. All was peaceful and calm, their surroundings bathed in the pale light of the moon. The only sound was that of the gentle breeze whispering through the grass.

---

4. Psalm 27. As I meditated on this event as recorded in the synoptic Gospels, reading the various commentaries on why Simon Peter made such a nonsensical remark, it came to me that the word "shelter" or "tabernacle" or "tent" is often used in the Old Testament to indicate a place of safety. In keeping with Simon's earlier protestation, this might have been what he had in mind that night.

Jesus said nothing more. He simply wrapped his outer garment around himself and lay down to sleep. Apparently, they would talk about it in the morning.

* * *

Simon did not sleep well that night. He kept thinking he was hearing voices, and when he peeped out from under his cloak, he thought he saw shapes moving in the shadows. Why had Jesus brought them here? What was it that they needed to learn? Why Moses and Elijah? Were they there as representatives of holy Scripture? That was how the rabbis often referred to the collection of scrolls . . . as the Law and the Prophets. And why was Jesus talking about his death in Jerusalem yet again?

All these thoughts and more troubled Simon throughout the long night and when the sun peeked out over the ridges, his mind was still racing. At one point he had been aware of Jesus pacing a short distance away, praying, as was his custom, to the Father. In order to stay warm, Simon spoke to the Father as best he could from under his cloak – an act he was ashamed of later. Had he known then what he came to understand as events unfolded, he would have been more supportive of Jesus. How alone Jesus must have felt!

After the usual morning greetings between themselves, and a short blessing spoken over their meagre meal, they shared some food, rubbing their hands together to keep warm. Thankfully, they had not forgotten to bring provisions along this time.

Jesus seemed anxious to leave . . . as if he knew he was needed below. As they carefully picked their way down the mountain, Simon thought of Moses descending Mount Sinai. What was he thinking about after he had met with God face to face? Was that very different to what they had experienced the night before? The cloud . . . the voice . . . was Moses just as terrified? Simon could not remember any hint of that in the stories he had been told . . . and yet, hadn't Moses been scared when he first met God at the burning bush? Perhaps Moses had become so familiar with God's voice that he was no longer afraid by the time he met God on Mount Sinai.

"Don't tell anyone what you saw last night until after the Son of Man has been raised from the dead," Jesus said suddenly.

The disciples looked at each other. How would they keep such an experience to themselves?

I wonder why we must keep this secret? Simon thought. Surely, I can share this with Andrew . . . what if he asks me? Should I lie to him? He's my brother . . . he knows me better than anyone else . . . he will surely know something dramatic has happened the moment he sees my face.

But Simon kept his thoughts to himself. A little further along he made a mental note to ask Jesus about the Son of Man term when he was alone with him.

As Jesus walked ahead of them, John whispered to his two fellow disciples, "What is this talk of rising from the dead? Does he mean like the widow of Nain's son . . . or like the daughter of Jairus? Or is this what will happen to all of us at the end of the age? I've heard the rabbis talk about it. 'Man lies down, never to rise,' they quote from the sage, 'he will awaken only when the heavens are no more.'[5] Is that what Jesus means?"

"I have no idea," Simon replied. "All I know is that I don't want him to die in the first place. Surely that can be prevented?!"

"But if Jesus is the Messiah, why then does he say that . . ." James began and then decided to ask Jesus instead. "Why is it that the teachers say that Elijah must come first?" Apparently, this had been bothering him all morning. He had opened his mouth several times to say something. But now that the subject had been broached, and since they would not be able to discuss the night's event in front of the others, he overcame his usual shyness and simply blurted out what was on his mind.

"That's a good question, James," replied Jesus. "The teachers of the law are correct in saying so. He must come first and reconcile all things."

Jesus suddenly stopped. They gazed out over the view before them. The sea was sparkling like millions of jewels in the morning sun. Simon could see some minute fishing boats returning from the night's long toil. The morning mist still clung between a few crevices and ravines, softening the ruggedness of the rocky mountainside. The usual sounds of morning activity came drifting up to them from below.

Jesus turned and looked at his disciples. "What you are really asking, James, is if Elijah is to reconcile all things, then why do I say it is written that the Son of Man must suffer and die and be raised from the dead? Am I right?"

James turned bright red. He should have known better than to ask a leading question. With Jesus it was always best just to say what was on your mind . . . to ask direct questions . . . as he always seemed to be able to discern the underlying issue anyway. It was as if he could read their hearts.

---

5. Job 14:12.

"Listen carefully to what I say now. Elijah has come, but they rejected him and his efforts . . . just as it was written. Since they have rejected the messenger, will they receive the Son of Man?"

He turned and continued their descent. He had answered, yet not answered. It was a technique of his they had come to know and appreciate. Rather than giving them a clear answer, he left them with a question to wrestle through themselves.

* * *

They heard the commotion before they saw its origin. There was a loud disagreement below where they had left the other disciples. Simon had been making comparisons between their ascent up Mount Hermon and Moses's ascent up Mount Sinai and consequently, when he heard the noise, he quite naturally thought about the first time Moses came down from Mount Sinai. He too heard the noise of the people below. Joshua said that it sounded like war in the camp, but Moses knew that it was the sound of depraved revelry. Aaron had not managed to keep the people true to the faith, and at their insistence, he had made a golden calf. The worship of the one true God had been compromised.[6]

But neither a golden calf nor wild idolatry greeted them. Instead, they saw the other disciples beset by the teachers of the law. Around them a large crowd had gathered. The disciples were so preoccupied that at first they did not notice Jesus and the three disciples' arrival.

So, they follow us even to the ends of the earth, Simon thought. At first, they only attacked Jesus, but now they are attacking us, too. Did they purposefully wait until Jesus left before challenging and embarrassing his followers?

A man in the crowd saw Jesus approaching and alerted the others. They all turned and ran toward him, as noisy as an offended gaggle of geese. The scribes sauntered up in the rear, aloof and smirking.

"What is the trouble?" Jesus asked them.

A man from the crowd replied. "Teacher, I brought my son. He is possessed with a dumb spirit. When the spirit takes over him, it casts him to the ground . . . thrashing about, he foams at the mouth all the while grinding his teeth until he is utterly exhausted. Since you were not here, I asked your disciples to cast out the spirit, but they were not able to do so."

"How long will you waver between belief and unbelief?" Jesus asked. Simon saw the colour drain from Andrew's face as he realized Jesus was addressing them. "Are you still part of this warped and crooked generation? How much

6. Exodus 32.

longer do I need to be with you? How much longer will it be before you embrace and embody my teaching?"

This sounds like the Song of Moses, Simon thought. Jesus is comparing us to our faithless ancestors in the wilderness. Moses called them a stiff-necked people. Are we any different? We are slow to learn . . . slow to apply all that he has taught us. If we are going to be his followers, we must begin to follow . . . really follow . . . everything he does, everything he says, everything he is. We must possess his mind and his heart. We must walk like him, talk like him, think like him. Otherwise we will simply continue to repeat the faithless generations of the past.

Jesus turned to the father of the young man and said, "Bring him to me."

As they did so, the demon manifested itself, and the young man fell to the ground, rolling about and foaming at the mouth.

Clearly moved with deep compassion, Jesus asked the father how long his son had suffered from this condition.

"Ever since he was a child," the father replied in anguish. "It has thrown him into the fire and into the water, trying to destroy him." The father began to weep and to implore Jesus, "Please, if you are able, have mercy and help us!"

"*If* I am able?" Jesus repeated the words as if to indicate to the father his need to free himself from doubt in order to embrace faith instead.

Simon couldn't help but think that such prolonged anguish and anxiety would drive out even the strongest faith.

Jesus looked deep into the father's eyes.

Simon knew that look. The look that lays bare the deepest recesses of the soul . . . a look that reveals the very heart of God.

"For those who believe, all things are possible," Jesus said.

The father dropped to his knees. "I do believe! I do! Please, help me. Disregard my unbelief!"

The commotion had begun to attract an even larger crowd of curious onlookers. Jesus was no showman and did not play to the crowds, so he addressed the deaf and dumb spirit directly and, with a voice of absolute authority, commanded it to leave the young man and never return. With an ear-shattering shriek, the spirit ripped itself out of the young man, leaving him motionless on the ground. Some in the crowd thought he was dead, but Jesus reached out, raised him to his feet, and gave him to his father.

With that, Jesus left and returned to where they had been staying. The disciples followed, bewildered with all that had taken place. Simon was thrilled that they were so preoccupied with what had just happened that none of them thought to ask about what had happened on the mountain.

"Why weren't we able to drive out the demon?" Andrew asked Jesus.

Simon went to stand at his brother's side. Andrew was clearly upset by their inability to perform the exorcism, not necessarily out of a sense of pride, but out of a sense of failure. Perhaps he was hurt by what Jesus had said to them as well. Whatever the reason, Simon thought his brother needed a bit of emotional support.

"When dealing with the demonic," Jesus said, "you must be armed with the unlimited power of God. Authority is not an independent gift exercised apart from God . . . the ability to drive out demons comes from a daily reliance on him alone. It is faith in his authority and faith in his power that enables you to confront the dark forces of evil. And that faith only comes when you are in a vibrant and dependent relationship with God."

Simon knew Jesus was referring to the need for unceasing prayer. When Jesus prayed, it was not a mere recitation of words, but a real and vital expression of his dependence on his Father. He never did anything before receiving direction from God. Simon had been trying to learn this lesson, but he knew that he still had a long way to go before he could claim that level of reliance so evident in Jesus's life.

"If you have faith in God," Jesus was saying, "even if it is as small as a mustard seed . . . if it is faith founded upon God . . . faith directed by God . . . nothing will be impossible. You will be able to overcome any and every obstacle. Not even a mountain like this will stop you."

Simon looked up at Mount Hermon. That is a very big mountain, he thought. But our God is even bigger. May that confidence be mine always, even in my darkest hours, he prayed.

"Come," Jesus said, "we must return to Galilee. There is little point in us prolonging our retreat here since they have found us." Jesus had half a smile on his face.

Pity, Simon thought. He had enjoyed both the time of relaxation as well as the time of intense teaching. He took one last look at the mountain where he had witnessed the glory of Jesus. Then he turned and thought about the return journey. They must remember to get provisions before they leave.

15

The Measure of Greatness

They crossed over the upper Jordan River north of where it runs into the Sea of Galilee. In many ways, Simon found the journey invigorating . . . there were so many new and beautiful things to see. At first, he wondered why they had not crossed back over by boat from Bethsaida as they had come, but as they walked, he reasoned that Jesus may have wanted to avoid being noticed by the crowds. It was as if he was preparing himself for something different . . . something new.

As they passed Chorazin, Jesus suddenly stopped and stared out at nothing in particular. Since leaving Caesarea Philippi, the conversation had been strained because the disciples were still smarting from their failure. Now they stood silent, waiting for him to speak.

After what felt like an age, Jesus turned to them and said, "The Son of Man is about to be delivered into human hands. They will put him to death, but he will be raised again on the third day."

The grief Simon felt was complex. On one level, it was genuine grief. None of them wanted the Lord they had come to respect and love so much to die. But on another level, every one of them wanted to see the kingdom restored to Israel. The talk of betrayal and death eclipsed the idea of resurrection, for in their minds, the resurrection was only to take place at the end of time. But they said nothing, confident that Jesus would explain himself when he thought the time was right.

* * *

They had just got back to Capernaum when the collectors of the temple tax confronted Simon. He was returning from the harbour where he had gone to check on his boat and to discuss the state of the business with Zebedee.

There was quite a lively debate over this half-shekel tax. Some said the payment should be collected only once in a lifetime for those twenty years old or over as outlined in the law.[1] Others argued that it should be a yearly tax as agreed by the returnees during the time of Nehemiah.[2] Then there were those who believed it should just be voluntary. But the practice now was to collect the tax just before Passover to pay for the expenses of the festival. Simon had heard that these collectors had already taken in so much money that the temple authorities did not know what to do with it all and they were wasting it on frivolous decorations.[3]

Simon wondered if these collectors might be hoping to catch Jesus in breach of his tax obligation since he was well known for his non-traditional stance. When the collectors asked if he and Jesus regularly paid the required tax, Simon answered in the affirmative. Thankfully, the rest of the disciples were still below the age of twenty, so he did not have to answer for them.

After returning home, Jesus asked Simon what he thought about taxes. "From whom do the Gentile kings demand customs and taxes? From their own children or from others?"

Simon looked at Jesus. Was this a riddle or a trick question? What king would demand money from his own children? But Jesus seemed serious, even though he was smiling, so Simon simply replied, "From others."

"Exactly!" Jesus said. "So the members of the royal family are exempt, correct? However, to avoid unnecessary offense, let's pay the tax."

Simon looked embarrassed. Since giving up his fishing trade to follow Jesus, ready money was a problem. To be sure, the business had continued under the watchful eye of his wife, with the help of Zebedee and his wife, but Simon's own purse was empty. He would have to ask them for the half-shekel.

Jesus noticed his disciple's hesitation. Smiling he said, "Simon, go to the sea and cast a line. Open the mouth of the first fish you catch, and you will find the exact amount that both of us owe. Use it to pay the collectors."

Looking back later, Simon couldn't help but chuckle to himself. The incident was a great reminder that the one who could provide so many fish that a boat threatened to capsize, was the one who could also provide a single fish to pay the temple tax. The Lord could and would provide for his children.

* * *

As is common with all of broken humanity, the disciples often disputed among themselves as to who would be the greatest in the coming kingdom. The only

---

1. Exodus 30:11–16.
2. Nehemiah 10:32–33.
3. Josephus, *Wars of the Jews* 5.210.

example they had in their hierarchical culture was that of the Pharisees, Sadducees, scribes, and Herodians and there was little to commend them in terms of humility. The disciples' failure to cast out the deaf and dumb spirit in Capernaum was all too quickly forgotten, and soon they were vying for position once again. Looking back later, Simon would realize how little they understood at that time about life in the kingdom. But Jesus's repeated remarks concerning his imminent death did make them wonder what would happen if they were suddenly left leaderless. Who would assume the position of master or rabbi? Would it be Simon? Some of them were already calling him "Cephas," the rock. Or would it be John or James? Jesus often singled them out together with Simon.

If they thought their whispered conversations were unknown to Jesus, they were in for a surprise. One day, without warning, he asked them what it was they were discussing. Simon looked at James and John, the two who had been most vocal. Their faces turned a dark crimson colour, and they said nothing.

"Do you remember when I spoke to you about self-denial?" There was not so much as a nod from any disciple. "Well . . . do you?" Jesus prodded. This time there was an embarrassed murmur of agreement from one or two. "Well, you ought to know by now that the kingdom of God does not function in the same way as human kingdoms. If you want to know who is the greatest in the kingdom, I'll tell you. The greatest in the kingdom is the one who is servant of all."

Simon smiled when he noticed the reaction of the younger members of the group to the use of the word servant. A servant held no position in society. The Roman centurion who had come to Jesus was unique in his concern for his servant . . . that was unusual . . . most masters wouldn't even know the names of their servants. And yet, Simon thought, if they applied Jesus's words to their relationships, then that would remove all strife and arguments. If every follower of Jesus seriously sought to serve the other, none would seek their own advancement. All would be equal in their service of love.

A little child was peeking through the door from the alleyway, idly twirling a twig in her fingers as she and her friends listened to Jesus speaking to his disciples. She blushed when Jesus indicated for her to come closer, but she came shyly and stood before him. Her friends were giggling behind their cupped hands at her apparent misfortune, secretly wishing Jesus had called them.

After a few words of comfort and reassurance, Jesus turned the little girl to face the disciples. "A little child has no position of note in our society. Children are dependent on the goodwill of their parents, relatives, and others. They are defenceless and vulnerable and, if completely abandoned, they will not survive long. You all need to become like children. You need to recognize your vulnerability, your complete dependence on God, if you are to be a part of the kingdom community."

This requires a complete shift in our understanding, Simon thought to himself. It reverses the standard practice of every sphere of life we have ever known, even within our fishing trade. But I understand the principle . . . there is but one Lord . . . the rest of us are all his servants. In serving each other we are serving him."

Jesus gave the girl a fond pat on her cheek and let her return to her friends. They scampered down the street squealing with laughter.

"Anyone who welcomes even the littlest one in my name, welcomes me. And whoever welcomes me, welcomes the one who sent me," Jesus said.

"Teacher," John squeaked. His voice had finally broken, but in unguarded moments, especially when he was excited about something, the old high pitch would break through once more. He cleared his throat and then continued. "We saw . . . that is, James and I saw . . . a man driving out demons in your name and we told him to stop, because he was not part of our community."

"No, John," Jesus said, rather sharply. "Do not stop him. Anyone who does a good work in my name will not speak ill of me afterwards. You must understand. Those who are not against us are for us. Believe me, anyone who serves another with something as simple as a cup of water, will not forfeit their reward."

"I really like this teaching," Simon whispered to Andrew. "It speaks not just of the equality among us as his community but also of a unity between each individual member of his community and the Lord. Even though we are his servants, whoever receives us, receives him. Whoever serves us, serves him. In a sense we are more than just simple representatives if we bear his name. It is as if we *are* him to others. Does that make sense?"

Andrew nodded, but said nothing. He had become increasingly quiet since the incident in Caesarea Philippi. Unlike his older brother, Andrew was not prone to quiet pondering. Perhaps he too was trying to process this very new way of thinking, so Simon let him be.

"In time, there will be those who will seek to mislead these little ones," Jesus continued. "You know those large millstones turned by donkeys? Well, it would be better for those who mislead little ones to have one of those large millstones tied around their necks and to be drowned in the sea."

What a vivid and awful image, Simon thought. The Romans do that to people they wish to punish . . . is Jesus saying that punishment would be preferable to God's punishment?"

But Jesus went on to paint an even more disturbing picture. He spoke about the inevitability of spiritual stumbling blocks in life. There would be people who would lead the naïve astray . . . then he added that it would be better for one of those persons to undergo physical mutilation to prevent such misdirection than it would be to incur God's wrath.

Then we ought to deal with such people swiftly, Simon thought, before they can wreak havoc in our community. We must especially protect the vulnerable in our midst. But how can we identify such a person? he wondered.

"Be exceptionally careful not to despise even the littlest ones of mine. Do not hold them in contempt, regardless of their status in the community. Angelic beings who live in the very presence of almighty God have been assigned to watch over them because even the least of them is of great value to him."

"Value!" Simon said under his breath. Jesus has taught on this before. Every one of us is valuable to God and therefore there is no room for prejudice or disdain.

"Think about shepherds," Jesus continued. "Let's say one of them owns a hundred sheep . . . if one goes missing, what do you think he will do?"

"He'll go to look for it," the disciples said in unison.

"Yes, he will leave the ninety-nine and go in search of the lost one."

Simon remembered a prophecy against the shepherds of Israel. They did not take care of the flock and they did not bring back those who strayed, nor did they search for the lost. God spoke against those shepherds and vowed to remove them. Then he promised that he would be the shepherd of Israel.[4]

"And if the shepherd finds the lost sheep," Jesus continued, "he rejoices greatly. You see, every single little one . . . those whom the world may reckon as lowly or insignificant . . . they are all precious to your Father. It is not his will that even one perishes."

Then Jesus added what seemed to Simon to be a disconnected statement. "Salt is good, isn't it? But salt that has lost its saltiness can't be made salty again. So have salt in yourselves and be at peace with one another."

Then Simon noticed the look on little brother's face. Something was clearly bothering him. Perhaps it was time for him to show concern and see if he could help.

* * *

Simon took Andrew aside and together they walked down to the sea. When he was certain they were alone, he asked what was bothering him. "You have

---

4. Ezekiel 34.

not been yourself, brother. I know something is bothering you and I want to help. Was it what happened at Caesarea Philippi?"

Andrew said nothing. They continued to walk along the shoreline in silence for a while.

Then Simon added, "All of us have made mistakes, Andrew. Remember my mistake? I rebuked Jesus! And he took me to task! I felt so stupid for days after that."

"It's not about what happened at Caesarea Philippi," Andrew blurted out.

Simon stopped and placed his hands on his brother's shoulders. "Then tell me what is bothering you. Is it me?" He suddenly wondered if Andrew felt that he had excluded him by not sharing what had happened on the mountain. He was about to say something when Andrew began to pour his heart out like a torrential rainstorm.

The problem centred around James and John. It had started several months before when Jesus had first begun to include three of the original four fishing partners to be in his close inner circle. At first it had not bothered Andrew in the slightest because he was thrilled to see his brother favoured. But then James and John began to tease him about being the one left out, and their behaviour towards Andrew began to change. At first they ignored him . . . but recently, the two brothers had begun to correct Andrew or instruct him as if he were somehow less competent. And this superior attitude was not restricted to Andrew. John's remark earlier that day was just one of many examples which proved that they viewed themselves as better than the others.

"Brother, I must confess, it gave me great pleasure to hear Jesus correct him so harshly," Andrew said, shedding angry tears as he spoke. "It is high time that they get taken down from the lofty perch they have created for themselves."

Simon burned inside. Why had he not noticed this before? Andrew wasn't the sensitive type, so the offence had to be real. But Simon also knew that this kind of disharmony could potentially rip the community apart . . . they would have to find a solution as soon as possible. Jesus had said that his community would be one founded on love, and love assumed a forgiving attitude when one member wronged another. But were there limits as to how often someone should be forgiven? Andrew had been the brunt of the two brothers' dreams of grandeur for some time now. How long could such a thing be overlooked?

"Andrew," Simon said once his brother had fallen silent, "forgive me for not being a better brother to you these past few months. I have been so preoccupied with my own lack of understanding, that I have not been there for you. I am going to be more attentive in the future . . . I promise. I will be a . . . I will be a better shepherd to you."

At this, Andrew spun around and glared at his brother, furious at the condescending remark. His eyes were like coals of fire, his breath short and quick. "I'm no lost sheep, brother," he spat out as hot tears spilled over his cheeks. "And you . . .," his bottom lip began to quiver violently, "you are not my father!" With that he stormed back to Capernaum.

"What . . . ? What did I say?" Simon called after him. He resolved to deal with this matter as tactfully as he could.

* * *

Later that day, as if he had been eavesdropping on the disastrous conversation on the shoreline, Jesus began to teach them about forgiveness. He told them that the offence should initially be contained strictly between the parties involved so as to prevent further problems and division in the community.

Simon glanced up nervously and silently mouthed to Andrew that he had not betrayed his confidence. From the scowl on Andrew's face, it did not appear that he believed him. Andrew refused to make any further eye contact.

"Should your brother or sister refuse to listen after you have shown them their fault, then take one or two witnesses with you and lay the case before them all, because a matter must be determined by the testimony of two or three witnesses.[5] Then . . . and only then . . ." Jesus paused as if to let the disciples realize the gravity of what he was about to say, "if the offender still refuses to listen, you may bring the matter before the whole community. And if they disregard the will of the community, they are to be removed from it and treated as an outsider, just like you would treat a tax-collector or a pagan."

In other words, we must do our utmost to win them back, Simon thought. Tax-collectors, pagans, and other outcasts had often been the object of Jesus's ministry . . . so, they are to be viewed as sheep to be found! O Father," he silently prayed, "help me to restore the relationship between my brother and our former fishing partners and to bring them back together once more."

"Remember what I told you in Caesarea Philippi," Jesus continued. "As my community, you will have the responsibility of setting at liberty those who are held captive. If you neglect this responsibility, they will remain bound. Now I say again, your earthly concerns have heavenly consequences. So bring your concerns before my Father in heaven in order that he might grant you wisdom and guidance in your decision making. And always remember that when you assemble in my name, I will be there."

---

5. Numbers 35:30; Deuteronomy 17:6; 19:15.

Yes, Simon thought. I am in need of wisdom and guidance. Somehow, I need to talk with . . .

At that moment Simon saw Jesus rise and leave the compound, so he quickly followed.

* * *

"Lord!" Simon called after Jesus. Coming alongside him, at first Simon said nothing as they walked through the narrow streets of Capernaum. He often wondered how many ears behind the walls of black basalt on either side of them would hear him, so he held his peace until they emerged into the wider market area.

Jesus had not said a word since Simon joined him, but now he stopped and looked at his disciple as if to say, "Yes? What is it you wanted to ask me?" There was a faint hint of a smile on his face that made Simon wonder if Jesus knew what was coming.

"Lord, about forgiveness . . . the rabbis say that we should offer forgiveness three times[6] . . . this demonstrates a forgiving spirit, right? As the sage said, 'God does all these things to a man two or three times to bring him back from the pit so that he might bask in the light of life.'"[7]

Jesus smiled at Simon. He had really come a long way from the cynical man he had once been.

"Is there a question for me in this, Simon?" Jesus enquired.

"Yes, Lord. I want to know if there is a limit as to how many times I should forgive the members of our community when they sin against me. Would seven times be enough?"

"No, Simon," Jesus replied, placing his hand on Simon's shoulder. "Not seven times . . . more like seventy-seven times."

A verse flashed through Simon's mind. "If Cain is avenged seven times, then Lamech is avenged seventy-seven times."[8] Did that mean that the forgiveness offered in Jesus's community ought to be as extensive as the vengeful spirit of one of the most wicked men on earth?

"Simon, allow me to speak to you in a parable."

Jesus went on to tell a story about a king who wanted to settle his accounts with his servants. One who was brought before him owed a vast amount. The king sentenced him and his entire family to be sold into slavery to repay the

---

6. This is apparently based on Job 33:2–30 and Amos 1:3; 2:4, 6.
7. Job 33:29–30.
8. Genesis 4:24.

debt. But when the servant begged for mercy, the king relented and forgave him all he owed. However, this same servant then refused to forgive a fellow servant who owed him an insignificant amount. Instead, he had him thrown into debtor's prison. The other servants were deeply distressed and reported this to the king. So the king had the ungrateful servant brought back to him.

"'You evil servant!' the king shouted. 'I forgave you all you owed me because you begged for mercy. Shouldn't you have done the same to your fellow servant?' The angry king," Jesus went on, "then had this servant handed over to the tormentors until his debt was paid completely. Simon, hear me well . . . my heavenly Father will do just as the king did if you refuse to forgive your brothers and sisters with all sincerity instead of merely out of legalistic obligation."

"We need to forgive as we have been forgiven because we have been forgiven the greater amount." Simon summed up what he understood from what Jesus had said.

"That is correct, Simon," Jesus affirmed. "Seventy-seven times. Was there anything else you wanted to ask me?"

"There is much I want to ask, but this is sufficient for now. I have something I must do first."

"Tell him to be patient. Thunder lasts only for a short time." Jesus smiled and went on his way, leaving Simon wondering, once again, how he knew.

* * *

Jesus had avoided Jerusalem ever since the controversy regarding the man healed on the Sabbath at the Pool of Bethesda. Instead, they had travelled all around Galilee, the Decapolis, Phoenicia, and Gaulantus. But the popular festival of Tabernacles was drawing close and many pilgrims were preparing for the feast. This festival was one of three major, annual celebrations all men were expected to attend – the Feast of Unleavened Bread, the Feast of Weeks, and the Feast of Tabernacles.[9]

While all these festivals celebrated Israel's unique relationship with God, the Feast of Tabernacles followed on the heels of the Day of Atonement on which the High Priest made atonement for his own sins as well as for the sins of the entire population of Israel. For eight days, while living in temporary structures made out of leafy branches, the Jews gave thanks for God's kindness in granting them a good harvest. They symbolically recalled their journey from being slaves in Egypt, to being nomads in the wilderness, to becoming

---

9. Leviticus 23; Numbers 29; Deuteronomy 16.

conquerors of Canaan, the promised land. Some even said the festival spoke prophetically of the coming of the Messiah.[10]

Jesus's brothers had seen and heard much of what the disciples had seen and heard . . . exorcised demons proclaiming Jesus to be the Son of the Most High God . . . the healed people calling him a prophet . . . others even daring to speculate that Jesus was the long-awaited Messiah. But his brothers had not come to the same conclusion as the disciples.

Mockingly, they questioned Jesus about attending the feast. Surely if he was who the people seemed to think he was or, as they put it, if he was who he seemed to think he was, why not go and declare himself to be the one to fulfil the prophecy? It was a crude challenge that revealed the hardness of their hearts.

I cannot stand in judgment over them, Simon thought. There was a time when I was also sceptical . . . when I too questioned and doubted. But I'm surprised that they do not pay heed to the convictions of their parents.

However, Jesus simply dismissed their disrespectful taunting by stating that he would do things according to his set agenda. While they were free to do as they pleased, Jesus had a strict schedule provided, it seemed to the disciples, on a daily basis, as he met with his Father. And so, Jesus's brothers left in great merriment . . . later, they would come to regret their idle prattle.

* * *

A little while after his brothers had left, Jesus and his disciples also went to Jerusalem to attend the feast. In order to avoid the packed roads taken by the other pilgrims, Jesus decided to go through Samaria. He sent messengers ahead to find accommodation for them in a particular Samaritan village, but the Samaritans there refused to grant his request for lodging for the night. It was not unusual for pilgrims to pass through Samaria,[11] so the refusal to offer hospitality struck Simon as odd. He wondered if the hostility was a result of the attitude of the messengers . . . would the Samaritans have refused Jesus if he had gone in person?

James and John wanted to call down fire upon the village in the same way Elijah had when he challenged the prophets of Baal on Mount Carmel.[12] Simon glanced at Andrew to see his reaction to this latest arrogant outburst from their former fishing partners. If their attitude remained unchecked, this kind of

---

10. Zechariah 14:16–17.

11. Josephus, *Ant.* 20.4.1.

12. 1 Kings 18:38.

spiritual superiority could sour others in the group. In fact, Simon wondered if this was not already the case, which might account for the Samaritan's response. Andrew had become quite disillusioned in spite of his brother's valiant attempts to remind him that they all made mistakes and were therefore all equally in need of forgiveness . . . especially one to the other.

For a while, Jesus said nothing. He simply stood there looking at James and John with a pained expression on his face, as if the heartlessness of their desire was a personal affront to him. Jesus's silence was often more difficult to deal with than his verbal correction, Simon thought. It had a way of dismantling one's defences prior to the actual discipline.

"Your spirit indicates a complete misunderstanding of the very reason I have come to the earth," Jesus finally said. His tone was quiet but sharp. "You have been with me this long, and still you lack understanding. I have not come to destroy but to save. Examine your hearts and mend your ways."

The brothers were visibly shaken. Simon could see tears welling up in John's eyes. It was time, he thought. Perhaps this rebuke would serve to check their downward spiral into authoritarianism. He looked over at Andrew . . . was that a look of pity on Andrew's face? Perhaps they could work at forgiveness and reconciliation after all.

"Come, let us go on to a different village," Jesus said.

Simon watched Jesus as they walked. There was a purposefulness about him, as if he was determined to go to Jerusalem . . . as if there was something specific he knew he had to accomplish there. Did his resoluteness have anything to do with his predictions concerning his betrayal and execution? Simon fingered his fishing knife in his belt, wondering if he was prepared for a life-threatening crisis? In his mind, he resolved to protect Jesus, no matter what might happen.

* * *

As they walked toward Jerusalem, a fellow pilgrim, who happened to be a teacher of the law, worked his way through the crowd until he was walking alongside Jesus. "I will follow you wherever you lead," he said. The fact that this teacher of the law had not gone up to the feast early with the rest of the pilgrims from Galilee, but had waited to go with Jesus, showed his willingness to sacrifice his own reputation in the eyes of his peers.

But did this man realize what it meant to truly follow Jesus? Simon wondered. Following Jesus was not something easy to be engaged in casually. It was like exchanging one's birth family for a foreign one where rules and customs were the complete opposite of all one had known before.

"Wherever I may lead, you say?" Jesus asked. "You must consider where I may lead before you commit yourself to such an undefined undertaking." Jesus was smiling as he said this, but Simon understood the challenge. "Wherever" was such an open-ended word.

"Let me ask you this," Jesus continued. "Are you willing to forfeit all your rights to ownership and to your possessions? Animals and birds have dens and nests, but the Son of Man lays his head on a borrowed pillow."

"Jesus means that there can be no divided allegiance when we decide to follow him," Simon said to the two fellow pilgrims walking next to him. He began to tell them about his own struggle with regard to security. "When Jesus first invited me to follow him, my primary concern was my fishing business and my family," he confessed.

He proceeded to relate what had happened after that night of fruitless fishing and how all his defences and objections had fallen away when he witnessed the authority and power of Jesus. "And I've been learning to relinquish my ideas, my dreams, and my ambitions bit by bit ever since. I'm still not sure of *where* he may lead me, and I have recently been tripped up by my old ways of thinking, but every day is an adventure in learning a new way of living."

One of the men suddenly addressed Jesus. "Lord, I will follow you, but first I need to fulfil funeral obligations for my family."[13]

This was not an unreasonable request, Simon thought. After all, honouring your parents in life and in death was required by the law.[14] But then, it dawned on him that while the first would-be follower had set no parameters, this man had very clear boundaries as to what he was prepared to sacrifice in order to follow Jesus. It was, in essence, an indefinite request for postponement.

"Do not use family obligations as an excuse to delay your total commitment to me," Jesus said. "Let those who do not follow me fulfil these earthly duties. There is no time to lose . . . go and proclaim the present reality of the kingdom."

The other man then asked, "Surely you cannot object to me bidding my family farewell prior to a lifelong commitment? Even Elisha was granted permission to first greet his family."

---

13. The burial custom at the time was rather involved and complex. The body was first wrapped in spices and strips of linen (but not embalmed) and then laid in a tomb to decompose. A year later, the family would reenter the tomb, remove the bones of the deceased person, and place them a small stone box, known as an ossuary. So this request may have been for the man to wait until this process was complete.

14. Exodus 20:12; Deuteronomy 5:16; Genesis 25:9; 35:29; 50:5–6, 13.

"But," said Jesus, "do you remember what Elisha did after Elijah called him? He burned his plough and sacrificed his oxen. For Elisha, there was no turning back. So it should be with you. Those who plough the fields will tell you that you must have a single focus while ploughing . . . you cannot be distracted by any other matter. It is the same with service in my kingdom. You cannot waver in your decision to follow me."

This sounds so harsh, Simon thought. But I know that one cannot be a double-minded person when following Jesus. If I hadn't decided to leave my livelihood . . . to leave my wife and my house and my friends behind . . . I might have been very tempted to abandon the community several times now. These men may be sincere, but they need to weigh the options . . . they need to count the cost . . . they need to be prepared to surrender everything. I need to be prepared to surrender everything.

Simon suddenly stopped walking. Andrew slammed into him from behind. "Brother, you can't just stop with no warning."

"Forgive me, Andrew, but I was just wondering . . . what is my level of commitment? Am I prepared to give up everything? I was just thinking of what Azariah said to King Asa . . . that if the king turned his back on God, God would turn his back on him.[15] There are so many things in life that are potential distractions, and it is so easy to be led astray by things that look good at the time, but that can ultimately consume you like a disease from inside. What if there is still something that I am nurturing in my innermost being . . . something that will lead me astray in spite of what I have said before with regard to following Jesus?"

"Brother, you have already shown your level of commitment. Besides, I am sure this is something we have to revisit often to make sure our focus is still fixed, right?"

"Yes," Simon said, starting to walk again. "You are right . . . at least, I hope you are right." The brothers laughed. Andrew's mood seemed to be lighter. Simon hoped that he had made peace with James and John, but he said nothing.

* * *

The first glimpse of Jerusalem as they crested the Mount of Olives never ceased to stun Simon. Ever since he had first come to the city as a child, the sight of the monumental walls that shaped the platform on which the temple stood always left him breathless. The gold of the temple cast a warm glow on all the surrounding structures so that it seemed as if the entire city was illuminated.

---

15. 2 Chronicles 15:2.

And at this time of year, the gold was echoed in the changing colour of the foliage in the valleys.

Jesus began to teach publicly about halfway through the festival. Under the shadow of the imposing southern wall, he sat on the steps and addressed the crowds in the plaza below. Many ritual baths were situated in this large open area, and pilgrims from all over Israel and from the dispersion gathered there throughout the day. They came to witness the procession of priests drawing water from the Pool of Siloam with a golden vessel – the water was then poured out as an offering on the altar.

Some would sing the song of praise from the prophet Isaiah: "We give thanks to you, O Lord! Though you were angry with your people, you have turned aside from your anger and have comforted us. You are the God who grants us victory and therefore in you we will be confident and unafraid. You are our strength and song and you have become our deliverance. With joy we draw water from the fountains of your salvation. We praise you Lord; we glorify your name! We proclaim your deeds among the people and declare that your name is great! We sing to you, Lord, because you have done marvellous things. We want this to be known in all the world! O you inhabitants of Zion, shout for joy for the Holy One of Israel is in your midst."[16]

By this time great numbers had swelled the ranks of the pilgrims. Many heard the words of Jesus and marvelled at his teaching, especially since, as far as they knew, he did not have the educational credentials of the other rabbis who had studied at the feet of famous men.

But Jesus presented them with his own credentials. He told them that his teaching came from the One who had sent him . . . that he was seated at the feet of the greatest teacher of them all, God himself. Those who sought to know the will of God more clearly, would recognize that the one reflected the other.

Simon thought about the hours Jesus spent in prayer with the Father, every morning, every evening, every moment of every day. It was as if he was in constant communion with the Father, and that he spoke only what he heard, and did only what he saw. That was what Simon wanted more than anything else . . . a deep, meaningful, life-dictating relationship with the Creator. Only then, he believed, would he find contentment and fulfilment and true joy.

As he had done so many times before, Jesus quickly shifted from the defensive to the offensive as he replied to his detractors. "You received God's law through the mediation of Moses. Why then do you not obey the law? You are actively plotting to kill me."

16. Isaiah 12.

"Are you out of you mind?" someone shouted from the midst of the crowd. "No one is plotting to kill you!"

But Jesus was not to be interrupted. "One miracle," he shouted back. "I performed one miracle . . . and you were all put out. Tell me, when must a child be circumcised? What does the law say? On the eighth day, right? So, what do you do when the eighth day just happens to be the Sabbath day?"

Simon could see the amazed expression of those in the crowd. They seemed to understand where Jesus was going with this questioning. Normally, Simon mused, because they were not encouraged to think things through, they blindly accepted the teachings of the leaders and were quite content to be led by the nose like oxen, rather than to think critically for themselves.

"So," Jesus continued, "if it is permissible to circumcise your sons on the Sabbath to avoid breaking the law, why is it forbidden to restore an entire human being on the Sabbath. Your thinking is far too shallow, and your judgment is superficial. You need to think things through carefully and prayerfully in order to come to the right conclusions!"

At this point it dawned on the people in Jerusalem that Jesus might indeed be the man the authorities were seeking to arrest. Why then, some wondered, was nothing being done about his very public appearance? Was it possible that their rulers had come to the conclusion that Jesus was the Messiah? "That is not possible," others argued. "The teachers have told us that the Christ will appear suddenly and unexpectedly . . . and yet we know exactly where this man comes from."[17]

"Really?" Jesus asked. "You know me, and you know where I am from?"

Yes, Simon thought, they know him, but only on one level. There is so much more to Jesus's identity than his geographical hometown. I was also led astray at first by surface matters until I got to know him better.

"To assume you know me based on what you can observe is a mistake," Jesus continued. "To know me apart from the one who sent me is insufficient. You may think you know where I am from, but as you do not know the One who sent me, you ultimately do not know anything about me at all. But I know him because I am from him and have been sent by him."

These statements frustrated some, and for a moment they contemplated seizing Jesus themselves to deliver him to the authorities, but they held back because they feared those in the crowd who were persuaded by his teachings. Simon could hear some in the crowd whispering . . . didn't the miraculous

---

17. This belief is not found in any biblical text and is more than likely a reference to an apocryphal writing such as 4 Ezra 7:28; 13:32; Baruch 13:32.

works of Jesus prove that he was the Messiah? But Simon was not the only one who heard what was being said . . . a number of Pharisees were moving among the crowd as well and they immediately sent for the temple guard to arrest Jesus.

Is this what Jesus was talking about? Simon wondered nervously. This hostility could lead to Jesus's death . . . but would they dare kill him when so many believe in him?

As the guards approached, Simon began to look around for possible escape routes, but Jesus's calm demeanour set his mind at ease. Jesus was in control of his time . . . he had said so many times.

Looking at the guards and then at the crowd, Jesus said, "I will only be with you for a little while longer, and then I will return to the one who sent me. There will be a time when you will seek after me, but then it will be too late . . . you will be unable to find me because you will be unable to come to where I am."

But this statement by Jesus only confused the crowd even more. A few wondered if he was going to leave Israel altogether to live among the dispersed Jews in other countries. Others speculated on whether he would teach the Greeks. Much later, when Simon reflected back, he realized that although these statements were uttered in ignorance at the time, they were almost prophetic, anticipating the spread of Jesus's message among the nations.

* * *

"Our leaders think they are so pure, but inwardly they are not cleansed of their own personal filth," Simon said to Andrew as they watched the temple guards hovering at the edge of the crowds. "They like people to think that they are so righteous and yet they are underhanded in their dealings with people who do not agree with them. Behind their smiles their teeth are like swords and their tongues are like daggers. They will ultimately bring a curse on us all."

"At least the guards are being exposed to Jesus's teaching," Andrew replied.

"Yes, Andrew," Simon sighed. "As always, you see the light in the darkness. Thank you for once again helping me look beyond my negative self."

It was the last great day of the feast . . . the guards had doggedly followed Jesus and his disciples wherever they went in Jerusalem. On this eighth and final day, the Jews celebrated the historical end of their wilderness wanderings by dismantling their temporary shelters and returning to their permanent homes. For seven days, the priests had filed past them as they stood on the temple steps, down to the pool of Siloam to draw water to pour on the altar. On this final day, they would do the same, but they would circle around the altar seven times instead of once before pouring the water on it.

Some said this ritual was to commemorate the water supplied from the rock in the desert.[18] Others said that it was to remind them that they had been given a land with streams and springs of water.[19] Still others wondered if it was not some form of prophetic anticipation of the fulfilment of Ezekiel's vision of water flowing from under the threshold of the temple down where the southern steps now were, into the valley below and then eastward toward the Dead Sea.[20] Other's remembered Zechariah's prophecy that water would flow out of Jerusalem on the great day of the Lord, half flowing to the eastern sea and the other half to the western sea.[21] The rabbis taught that Jerusalem was the navel of the world, so any water flowing out from the city would eventually cover the earth.

As the priests began to ascend the steps on their return from Siloam, the jubilant crowd waved leafy branches in the air, singing songs of praise. Suddenly, above the singing, a voice boomed out: "Those who are thirsty, ought to come to me and drink, for if you believe in me, know this: I am the one out of whom rivers of living waters will flow."[22]

The priest carrying the golden pitcher had such a fright that he very nearly tripped over one of the uneven steps. For a moment he stood still, with a startled look on his face, trying to find the source of the interruption. Then he saw Jesus standing on the steps. He shook his head and grumbled something under his breath, before continuing up the stairs, trembling as he went. But apart from a few murmurs here and there, the crowd was largely silent, their branches motionless. The rays of the sun fell on Jesus in such a way that, to many, he appeared to be shining. Simon thought he looked regal, the very image of a king.

"But what on earth does he mean?" Simon asked Andrew. Even he was rather taken aback by Jesus's sudden outburst.

"Well, according to the prophets," Andrew said, "rivers of living water are meant to flow out of the temple and out of Jerusalem. Perhaps he is saying that, as the Messiah, he is the embodiment of the city and the temple? I don't know, Simon . . . this is prophetic speech. As with most of Jesus's hard sayings, I am sure we will understand some day in the future."

---

18. Exodus 17:6; Numbers 20:8.

19. Deuteronomy 8:7.

20. Ezekiel 47:1–12.

21. Zechariah 14:8.

22. I have chosen to translate this statement of Jesus in this manner based on John's editorial comment in verse 39 and his own vision recorded in Revelation 21:6, 22, and 22:1–2.

Suddenly and simultaneously, the people in the crowd regained their composure. Some shouted out that Jesus was a great prophet. Others dared to say he was the Messiah. This started the argument about the origins of Jesus all over again, and once again, there were some who wanted to have him arrested. However, the guards returned to the chief priests and Pharisees empty handed, claiming that they had not arrested Jesus because they had never heard a man speak as he did.

Later, Nicodemus told the disciples that the leaders were enraged . . . none of the Pharisees believed in Jesus and they thought the crowd was simply ignorant and cursed because of their ignorance. Nicodemus said that he had tried to temper their negative attitude toward Jesus, arguing that the law required a proper trial before a verdict was pronounced. But they simply dismissed his statement in light of Jesus's Galilean origin. When he heard this, Simon couldn't help thinking that the crowd was not quite as ignorant or cursed as the leaders seemed to think, because they had used the exact same argument. What a pity the leaders were not honest enough to delve deeper. If they had simply consulted the census records, they would have discovered that Jesus was indeed born in Bethlehem, because he was of the line of David. The curse, it seemed, was on them too.

16

Light in the Darkness

Early the next morning, long before dawn, Simon sat looking out across the Kidron valley at the Holy City. The temple had shone like a sparkling jewel throughout the night as the golden oil lamps were kept burning during the feast. Some said the lamps represented the pillar of fire that had led their ancestors out of slavery to freedom.

Simon was meditating on what Jesus had announced as the procession of priests moved past them up the southern steps of the temple. This was not the first time Jesus had referred to himself as "living water." Was Andrew correct in thinking the statement had something to do with the prophecies of Ezekiel and Zechariah? If so, what exactly did that mean? They spoke about a stream flowing from the temple and the city, not from the Messiah. Jesus indicated that the streams would flow from the very midst of his being . . . from his belly, as it were. Was he saying that as the Messiah, he was the navel of humanity? . . . that from him humanity would be reborn? Simon repeated his questions to the Father in the form of a prayer, asking for wisdom to understand.

And then there was the talk of betrayal and execution and rising from the dead that hovered at the back of his mind all the time. Jesus had become a real threat to the establishment. His repeated correction of their faulty teachings made them look foolish . . . they did not take kindly to the sniggering of those they looked down on as the common folk. Thankfully, the guards had not acted on the instructions of the chief priest and Pharisees, but how long would it be before they launched another attack? So far, the presence of the crowds had kept them from arresting Jesus openly, but the leaders were so underhanded in many of their dealings, what would prevent them from disposing of him when no one was around to raise an objection?

Simon's thoughts were interrupted by Jesus who indicated that he wanted to be in the temple courts at dawn before the crowds set out on their journeys back to their towns and villages. In the pinkish glow of the rising sun, Jesus and his disciples made their way down into the valley, up the other side, and up the steps into the temple precinct. There Jesus sat down to teach those who gathered around him.

Suddenly the peacefulness was shattered by a pleading scream. Scribes and Pharisees poured into the temple courts, dragging with them a woman who was desperately trying to keep her cloak about her otherwise naked body.

For shame! Simon thought. Whatever she has done does not warrant such brutal, public humiliation. Surely they could have kept her in private custody until a trial could be arranged.

Trembling, the pathetic figure stood before Jesus, her feet bare and bleeding, her hair dishevelled, her face streaked with copious tears. There was an angry red mark on one cheek. The stunned crowd looked on as her accusers gathered around. Surprisingly, Jesus had not moved at all. He simply sat there as if the chaos unfolding before him had been expected.

"Teacher," one of the Pharisees bellowed out. "This woman has been seized for adultery . . . we caught her in the very act!"

"Where, then, is the man?" someone shouted out. "She could not have committed adultery on her own!"

A murmur of agreement rippled through the crowd, but one of the scribes yelled back that the offending man had escaped and could not be identified because it had been dark at the time.

"More than likely they allowed him to escape," Simon said to Andrew.

"Or he was no longer present," he replied.

"In that case, there are no witnesses! If they had caught her in the 'very act,' the man would have been apprehended too," Philip ventured.

"Whatever the truth," Simon replied, "this is a travesty of justice."

"Teacher," one of scribes stepped forward, "in the law, Moses commanded us to stone such a woman."

"She must be betrothed,"[1] Andrew said. "Otherwise they would have demanded death by strangulation according to their tradition. But the law is clear. Both parties ought to be put to death![2] It has happened in the past that young people who love someone other than the person chosen for them by their parents, get together secretly and . . ." Andrew suddenly blushed beet red and fell silent.

---

1. Deuteronomy 22:23–24.
2. Leviticus 20:10; Deuteronomy 22:22.

"But Jesus, we want to hear if this is how you understand the law," the scribe continued. "What do you say?" By the smug look on his face, the scribe quite clearly thought he had a watertight case. Regardless of his reply, Jesus would either be guilty of not upholding biblical law or of contradicting Roman law that said the Roman government alone was allowed to issue a death sentence.

But Jesus remained silent. He simply bent down and began to write something on the ground with his finger.

"What is he doing?" Simon whispered to Andrew. "Is he not going to set them straight?"

By this time a number of the scribes and Pharisees were making themselves heard. They were not about to let this go by without some word from Jesus.

When Jesus looked up, he gazed on each one of them until even the most belligerent had fallen silent. "Let the one who is faultless, cast the first stone." Then he continued to write on the ground with his finger.

"Brother!" Andrew said, "brother, I know what he just did! Remember the story of Daniel and Belshazzar?"

"Do you mean the writing on the wall?"

"Yes," Andrew continued. "Remember that human fingers appeared and wrote that God had numbered the king's days and that his reign would be brought to an end?"

"And his reign would be given to the Medes and Persians, but what has that got to do with . . ."

"You skipped the middle part," Andrew said excitedly. "The middle part said that he had been weighed in the balances and had been found wanting."[3]

"Yes," Simon said, "yes, I see what you are saying. So, Jesus has turned the judgment on them. They have been weighed in the balance of the very law they seek to uphold, and by their own guilt, they are not fit to execute the verdict of stoning! Jesus didn't say that she shouldn't be stoned . . . he just said that whoever casts the first stone has to be guiltless. That's brilliant!"

Crestfallen, the woman's accusers left one by one, until the woman was left alone, sobbing before Jesus. "Woman," Jesus said, standing up in front of her, "where are your accusers? Has no one condemned you? Has no man judged himself blameless and therefore worthy to put another human being to death?"

"No one, Lord" she said, between sobs.

Jesus walked up to her and gently lifted her torn cloak to cover her exposed shoulder. She looked up and he met her eyes.

---

3. Daniel 5:27.

Simon suddenly felt a wave of emotion sweep over him. Those eyes, he thought. She is looking into those deep pools of immeasurable grace and forgiveness. Like so many others, she will see her fault reflected in his eyes . . . but she will also feel that gaze penetrate the very depths of her innermost being, revealing not what she was, or is, but what she can become if she leaves her life of sin and follows him.

"Well then, neither do I condemn you," Jesus said gently. "You are free to go, but . . . you are also free to choose to live a life without sin."

For a moment it looked as if she would crumble at his feet, but then she gathered her courage, and slowly left the place of her humiliation. This was surely a day she would remember all her life, Simon thought.

Jesus then turned to those who had witnessed the entire event. He motioned for them to follow him into the treasury which was located in the court of the women. The sun had risen by this time and the golden oil lamps had been extinguished. He walked up to one of the huge stands that held the bowls and said, "I am the light of the world. Follow me and you will never walk in darkness . . . by my light you will be led into life."

"Solomon wrote something like that," Andrew said. "'The path of them who seek after righteousness is like the rising of the sun at dawn that grows brighter and brighter until it gains full strength,'[4] he quoted. "As our ancestors followed the pillar of fire in the wilderness until they came to the promised land, so we too must follow Jesus until he leads us into his kingdom. Well, at least, that's what I think he means."

"I think you are right, brother. But I also think that Jesus is saying he is what Israel was meant to be," Simon replied.

"How so?" Philip asked.

"The prophet Isaiah repeatedly spoke of Israel as a servant destined to be a 'light for the nations.'[5] Jesus taught us those passages while we were in Caesarea Philippi. The servant was to bring the message of salvation to the ends of the world."[6]

"Yes, and do you recall what Jesus's mother, Mary, told us about the time she and Joseph took Jesus to the temple for the purification ceremony when he was a baby?" Philip asked. "Didn't that righteous man . . . what was his name . . . ?"

"Simeon," Simon said with a slight smile.

---

4. Proverbs 4:18.

5. Isaiah 42:6.

6. Isaiah 49:6.

"Right! Simeon. Well, he said that Jesus was the light that would bring light to the nations."[7]

"True, but Jesus also told us that we are the light of the world,"[8] Andrew countered.

"Perhaps it is in following him closely that we reflect his light, brother. But here come those Pharisees again! What now?"

"So, you bear witness to yourself, do you?" the Pharisees asked Jesus. "Then your witness is not valid."

"These must be the same men who objected to the healing of the man at the Pool of Bethesda," Andrew said. "If I remember correctly, they made a similar objection to Jesus bearing witness to himself on that occasion."

What happened next happened so quickly. One moment, Jesus was defending his position to bear witness to himself because his Father validated his testimony. The next moment, the leaders were wanting to stone him for blasphemy, believing he claimed to be God. The argument had gone back and forth. Jesus claimed that if they truly knew God, they would know him. The leaders claimed that they knew Abraham as their earthly father and God as their heavenly Father. Jesus said the reason they were not able to understand him was because their father was the devil, and this was the reason they wanted to kill him. They responded by calling him a demon-possessed heretic. Things totally got out of hand when Jesus indicated that Abraham had rejoiced at the thought of his coming. The leaders seemed to understand him to say that he had seen Abraham and they mocked him for it . . . he was only thirty-three years old. But then Jesus claimed to have existed before Abraham as the great I AM. That was when they picked up stones to kill him, but Jesus managed to disappear into the crowd where the leaders did not dare lay a hand on him.

* * *

That Sabbath as they were walking past the temple gate, they saw a well-known beggar who had been born blind. The disciples had previously been taught that sickness, if not a direct result of the person's own sin, could be traced back to the sin of the parents, grandparents, or even the great-grandparents.[9] And so they asked Jesus whose sin had caused the man's blindness.

"No one's," Jesus replied.

---

7. Luke 2:32.
8. Matthew 5:14.
9. This was based on Exodus 34:7.

They were not prepared for this answer. Who was to blame for his predicament?

"His blindness is for the glory of God," Jesus explained, "so that the greatness of God might be displayed through him."

It was clear that they did not understand.

"As long as it is day, we must perform the works of the one who sent me," Jesus said, preparing them for what he was about to do. He knew that after the altercation of the other day, the disciples wanted him to keep a low profile. "The night is fast approaching when we will not be able to do any work . . . while I am here, I must shine out the light."

With this he spat on the ground, made a small ball of mud with his saliva, and applied the mixture to the man's eyelids. "Go," Jesus said, "wash your eyes in the Pool of Siloam."

Oh, Jesus, Simon thought. It is the Sabbath. You just made clay . . . they will accuse you of working . . .

Later that day, word came to Jesus that the healed man had been excommunicated from the synagogue. Apparently, on returning home there had been quite a debate as to his identity. People simply could not believe that he had been healed. In an attempt to settle the matter, they had taken the man to the Pharisees, who, on hearing the man's account of the healing, concluded that Jesus could not possibly be from God as he had once again broken the Sabbath. This was just what Simon had feared. But the Pharisees could not dismiss the fact that a miracle had taken place . . . if Jesus were not from God, then how did he possess the ability to heal this blind man? The man's parents were summoned and questioned, but they refused to testify because they were afraid of being excommunicated as well. So, in the end, the Pharisees refused to accept the man's statement, declaring that his defect was a result of his sin.

When Jesus heard what had taken place, he immediately went to look for the man. When he had found him, he asked if he believed in the Son of Man. Recognizing Jesus's voice, the man replied, "If you will identify him, I will believe in him."

"You have both heard him and seen him . . . in fact, you are looking at him," Jesus replied.

"Lord, I believe," the man cried. Then falling to his knees, he worshipped Jesus.

Jesus was moved with compassion as he held the sobbing man. "I came into this world to expose the inner reality of humanity," he said, "so that those who know they are blind may see, and those who obstinately claim to see may be shown to be blind."

Some Pharisees overheard him, and they scoffed. "Ha! So, we are blind, are we?"

"If you were aware of your blindness, healing would be possible for you and you would not be guilty of sin. But since you claim not to be blind, healing is not possible and so your guilt remains."

Having said this, Jesus turned toward the man, raised him up, and together they walked away with the disciples. Having been expelled from one community, the man was now accepted in another. There was much merriment on the Mount of Olives that evening.

17

The Shepherd and His Sheep

Jesus's training method was very practical, Simon decided . . . more like an apprenticeship than anything else. Everything Jesus taught the disciples was set within real-life situations. He lived out what he spoke, modelling his instructions and demonstrating the lifestyle he expected them to emulate. His teaching was radically different from anything they had ever heard before, and yet what he presented was logically consistent with the ancient writings. They had listened to Jesus demolish the contradictory arguments of the leaders as he reasoned with them, quoting what the law and the prophets really said in stark contrast to what their traditions claimed had been said.

As they travelled from village to village, Jesus exposed them to various vocations, situations, cultures, belief systems, and languages, which served to break down barriers as well as their stubborn nationalistic pride and prejudice. They learned first-hand that while other people appear to be different on the surface, underneath the physical, the traditional, the rhetorical, and the practical, people are all essentially the same, suffering with the same fears, frailties and failures. Thinking back on this much later, Simon would realize that this had prepared the disciples for their eventual global ministry . . . making disciples of all nations. They had previously believed that the nations were to come to Mount Zion so that they might submit to the sovereignty of the God of Israel. They had never thought that Mount Zion was to be uprooted and cast into the midst of the Gentiles . . . that they as the living stones of the new temple and the new Jerusalem would move out into the world, pushing back the very gates of hell as they plundered Satan's strongholds of darkness.

Often, after particularly difficult altercations with the leaders in Jerusalem, Jesus and his disciples would cross over the Jordan and stay in Bethany, where John the Baptizer had taught and baptized his followers. Once, they had travelled a bit further south so that they would pass through the hilly countryside of

Bethlehem, where Jesus had been born, and where many shepherds raised the lambs used for the daily temple sacrifices. The disciples had observed the shepherds and their wonderful ways with their flocks. They had seen the high stone walls of the enclosures, built to protect the sheep from predators such as lions, wolves, and jackals. Out of necessity, the shepherds would often have to lead their sheep far from the enclosures in order to seek out the best grazing. For this reason, there were specific watchmen who looked after the enclosures in the absence of the shepherds. These watchmen knew the shepherds well and consequently only allowed them access to their own enclosures.

Simon thought it was amazing that the sheep knew and obeyed only the voice of their own shepherd, ignoring the whistles and calls of the other shepherds. Contrary to what he had heard about these men, he witnessed their tenderness as they cared for the lambs in particular, because they had to be without blemish if they were destined for the altar. At one lambing, the disciples watched a shepherd wrap the newborn lambs in strips of linen to protect them from the harsh environment. Mary, the mother of Jesus, had once described how she had used these strips of cloth to wrap Jesus in when he was born, before she placed him in the stone feeding trough. The disciples had discussed this at length, recalling the words of John the Baptizer when he described Jesus as "the Lamb of God who would take away the sins of the world." Jesus had been wrapped in the same strips of linen as the sacrificial lambs.

What they had observed on that trip helped them understand what Jesus was saying when he compared himself to a good shepherd. At first, when Jesus began to speak about thieves and robbers seeking to gain entrance to the enclosures by climbing over the walls, and about how sheep only heeded the voice of their own shepherd, they did not follow what he was trying to teach. But then he spoke more directly, comparing himself to the gate through which the sheep could enter to find safe shelter. When he spoke about those who had come before him, people who only wanted to steal and kill and destroy, Simon recalled the prophecy levelled against the so-called shepherds of Israel who did not care for the sheep but abused them for their own gain.[1] While masquerading as shepherds, the Sadducees, Pharisees, and scribes largely sought to enrich themselves, twisting the plain meaning of the Scriptures to their advantage. In stark contrast to them, Jesus declared that he had come to give abundant life to the sheep who followed him.

He was the good shepherd, he said, who would willingly lay down his life for the sake of the sheep in his care. Those who cared little for the sheep would

---

1. Ezekiel 34.

desert them in times of peril, but not the good shepherd. He knew his sheep and his sheep knew him and they would hear and obey only his voice. Jesus spoke of other sheep that needed to be brought into the enclosure so that all his sheep might be one flock.

But then a deep, dark shadow was cast over the idyllic picture painted by Jesus, when once again he began speaking about his death. He described it as a voluntary laying down of his life for the sake of the sheep. He said that no one could *take* his life, but that he would *give* it willingly of his own accord . . . only to take it back up again later. This was the plan of the Father, he added.

Those who heard him were divided in their opinion of him, some saying he was demon-possessed or mad while others thought him eloquent and wise . . . none of them could dismiss the fact that the healing of the man born blind was yet to be satisfactorily explained.

* * *

At this time, Jesus decided to send out seventy-two disciples from his larger following to go to the villages and towns that he was about to visit himself. He issued the same instructions to them that he had given the twelve that were sent earlier, telling them that the harvest was ripe and plentiful, but that the workers were few and that they were to pray for more workers like them. They also received the same warning . . . they were being sent out as lambs amongst wolves.

Hearing Jesus speak these words once more, Simon remembered how he had struggled to comprehend why Jesus would refer to their fellow countrymen in terms of wolves. But now, having been subject to their violent opposition himself, he understood. This was another benefit of Jesus's training method, Simon realized. Jesus would often repeat himself in different places and to different people, giving his disciples further opportunities to learn what they might have missed before.[2]

When the seventy-two returned, invigorated because even demons were subject to them in Jesus's name, Simon remembered his own sense of excitement as he anticipated giving a report of what had transpired along the way on their ministry trip . . . but that had been cut short with the news of John the Baptizer's murder and the ever present needs of the crowds. This time, however, Jesus was able to listen patiently as the excited pairs related their adventures.

"Yes," Jesus said eventually, "I observed the evil one fall from heaven. You were given authority over the forces of wickedness, and consequently you have

---

2. Philippians 3:1.

returned unharmed. But your true source of joy should not be that the powers of darkness are subject to you . . . rather rejoice that your names are indelibly recorded in heaven. You are known to the Father."

Then Jesus broke into spontaneous, triumphant praise to the Father for his gracious revelation of the truth to his followers, which the Father had planned all along. He thanked the Father that what had been revealed to him, he had in turn revealed to the disciples. Then, turning to his disciples he told them that they were blessed, because what they saw and heard were things that kings and prophets had longed to see and hear, but had not.

Jesus is in a good mood, Simon thought. I can't remember when I last saw him quite as happy as he is now. Somehow I have to keep it this way. The protective, fatherly concern Simon felt for Andrew was now extended to include Jesus and the other disciples as well. Simon cared for his new family members and wanted only the best for them. But very soon, this care and concern would be tested to the limit in the near future.

* * *

Jesus was always breaking traditional moulds, especially those which caused the exclusion of others. He wanted to make people understand that in the eyes of the Father, every human being was precious. For instance, there was a teacher of the law who asked Jesus what he had to do to inherit eternal life.

That's the wrong question, Simon thought. Hasn't he learned from the very Scriptures he has studied for so many years that even the best human being fails to keep the whole law? No one can *do* anything to inherit what can only be given by a merciful, gracious, loving and forgiving God. If one could do something to earn salvation, that would mean some people were better than others, whereas the Scriptures plainly teach that all of us have sinned! As the sage said, "Who can produce something pure out of what is impure?"[3]

Jesus surprised them all with his reply. "Tell me what you understand from what is written in the law."

"Well," the man responded, "we are to love God with our entire being and to love our neighbour in the same way that we love ourselves."

"Well done," Jesus said. "That is the correct answer. If you *can* do this, you will live."

"*If* I can . . .?" The man clearly looked uncomfortable. Something Jesus had said disturbed his sense of equilibrium. "But who precisely is my neighbour?" he asked.

---

3. Job 14:4.

Ah, Simon thought. There is someone he clearly does not love in the same way he loves himself.

"Let me tell you a story," Jesus said. "A man was walking down from Jerusalem to Jericho. You know the road . . . there are quite a few rocky crags for robbers to hide. Well, the man was alone and thus quite defenceless. Some robbers attacked him, stripped him of all his possessions, beat him severely, and left him for dead on the side of the road. Not much later, along came a priest. But when he saw the man, he was afraid of being defiled by what appeared to be a dead body, so he passed by on the other side. A Levite also saw him and for the same reason he too passed by the man. Then a Samaritan came along."

A Samaritan! The hatred between Jews and Samaritans was legendary and deeply entrenched. Everyone in the crowd sucked in air as Jesus spoke the word. Simon felt that he would have reacted in the same way had he not been exposed to the Samaritans in a positive setting. In truth, he *had* reacted in the same way when Andrew first told him about Jesus speaking to the Samaritan woman.

Jesus continued. "When the Samaritan saw the man, he took pity on him. He stopped, cleaned his wounds with oil and wine, and wrapped them with strips of cloth. Then he put the man on his donkey and took him to a place where travellers could stay overnight. There he cared for him. The following day he paid the innkeeper handsomely to look after the man until he returned. He also promised to reimburse him for any extra charges incurred."

Jesus looked at his disciples. He had a smile on his face and a twinkle in his eye.

"Tell me, now . . . which one of the three men acted in a neighbourly manner to the man who had been robbed and beaten?" Jesus asked.

For a moment, the teacher of the law seemed lost for words. He could not bring himself to utter the word "Samaritan." Then he finally blurted out, "The one who demonstrated love through merciful acts of kindness."

"Well, then," Jesus said. "Off you go. Do as the Samaritan did."

A number of people in the crowd went quite pale at this point and turned away. Some were ashamed, others angry. That was not quite what they had expected. They felt Jesus had insulted them by suggesting they should be like the Samaritans.

Simon also remembered back to the time when they had stayed overnight with Mary, Martha, and Lazarus in Bethany. Once again, Jesus broke a traditional mould, this time with regard to the role of women in society. Others expected Mary to fulfil her tasks in the preparation of the evening meal, but, in flagrant disregard for the rules of the day, she chose to learn from the rabbi, sitting, as was the custom of disciples, at his feet. When Martha complained bitterly about this perceived impropriety, Jesus dismissed her complaints by telling her that Mary had made a spiritual choice that transcended the conventional role of housekeeping. Martha was flustered by his reply, but she sensed that Jesus was a man who looked beyond traditional patriarchal inequalities to the original creation order where both male and female were created in the image of God . . . complimentary in function and equal in value . . . and Martha loved him for it.

Jesus also broke with the traditional mould of prayer. When new followers asked Jesus to teach them to pray, as John the Baptizer had taught his followers, he would lay out a formula for them to follow. But the disciples knew that this was a structure, not a standard prayer to be recited, as the method of Jesus's communication with the Father was radically different from those prayers taught by their leaders.

On one particular occasion, Jesus offered a brief explanation, in the form of a parable, about how this prayer would work. In his story a man received an unexpected visitor after the marketplace had closed. Having no food to offer his guest, the man hurried to his friend's house to ask for help. Because it was late, the friend and his family had already gone to bed, and he was reluctant to disturb his children. But everyone knew that to refuse aid to any member of the community, regardless of the inconvenience, would reflect negatively on the entire community. So, because the man was determined and persistent, the friend gave him what he needed for his guest.

Jesus went on to show how this related to life in his Father's kingdom. Petitioners might feel that their request is impudent, inconvenient, or irrelevant to the Father. That was why the prayers they learned by rote were often limited to vague petitions. But the King delights in his subjects, and therefore is willing to respond to their petitions just like a good father responds positively to the requests of his children. The custom of the King is to answer prayer. This reveals the reality of the kingdom and the generosity of the Father to a watching world.

God is not some distant, uninterested, indifferent divine being, Simon thought. He is intimately interested in the lives of all his people . . . that's why Jesus teaches us to address him as Father. A good father knows how to give good gifts to his children . . . and the Father receives honour through his bountiful provision, his preservation, and his protection. His heavenly will is seen on earth through answered prayer.

God was near, not far off. This knowledge brought great comfort and peace.

* * *

For the most part, Simon was aware of his limited cognitive abilities. He knew that it took him a bit longer than many people to grasp certain things. But at times he wondered if he really was as dimwitted as he thought he was. How was it possible that those who believed themselves to be learned men, could at the same time be so foolish when it came to Jesus? They had seen the same miracles and heard the same teachings, and yet they came to very different conclusions.

Simon realised that no matter where they were or whom they were with, the same accusations were flung at them. Jesus was accused of casting out Satan by the power of Satan. Others demanded further signs to prove that he was the Messiah. Some were so focused on external ritual that they missed the true internal nature of holiness.

Simon remembered how once at a meal Jesus had taken the Pharisees and the teachers of the law to task because of their tendency to concentrate on the minuscule details of their traditions in their attempts to obey the law, while missing the more important matters of justice and mercy. He criticized them for always wanting what was best for themselves, ignoring the plight of the people and overburdening them with rules and regulations. Their focus on their many extra-biblical oral laws obscured the Lawgiver, and what was meant to grant access to the knowledge of God and his ways had instead become an insurmountable barrier of requirements.

How is it that they cannot see that they are as guilty of opposing God as our ancestors were? Simon wondered. Our ancestors dismissed God's word by killing the prophets . . . our leaders now dismiss God's word by locking it behind doors of ritual, traditions, legalism, and false piety.

Jesus often spoke openly about the hypocrisy of their leaders. He knew that by doing so he earned their bitter opposition, but he also knew that he must speak the truth and that bowing to the fear of man would incur the wrath of God. Those who heard him were left with two choices: either they could obey him wholeheartedly and risk losing friendships and relationships, or they could disobey him, or perhaps only obey him half-heartedly, and lose everything in the end.

* * *

Most people assumed that tragic suffering would only befall those who had sinned. One day, someone mentioned an incident in which Galileans had been martyred in the temple by the tyrannical Roman governor, Pilate, while offering their sacrifices.

"Why are they referring to this tragedy?" Simon whispered to the others. "Is this a veiled threat that the same fate may be ours if we continue to follow

Jesus? Do they assume that we are part of some nationalistic movement just because we are mostly Galileans?"

"Or are they nationalists themselves, hoping to justify their intentions?" John whispered back.

Jesus had no time for veiled threats, so he simply cut to the quick, pointing out their faulty theological conclusion. They believed that some suffered calamities because their sins were worse than others, as if there were degrees of sin. But he warned them that all would suffer the same fate if they refused to turn from their own sinful behaviour. Referencing another tragic event, this time involving Jerusalemites, not Galileans, in which the Tower of Siloam had collapsed on eighteen men working on Pilate's aqueduct, Jesus again emphatically denied that the calamity was caused by their sin. He ended with the same warning. All sin leads to death. If they remained unrepentant, they would all be annihilated.

"Surely he can't mean that the nation of Israel will be destroyed?" James said aghast.

"That's exactly what he means," said Simon the zealot, warming to the idea. "Haven't you been listening? Our nation is ripe for judgment because we have rejected God's law and replaced it with our own traditions. And now our leaders are rejecting Jesus as well . . . just like our ancestors rejected the prophets. That's why he is talking about his death all the time. He knows they are going to kill him."

"Simon! That really is not helpful," Philip objected.

No one knew at that time just how right Simon was.

Jesus illustrated his point with a parable once again. This time, he referred to a barren fig tree that was given a period of grace in which to bear fruit. If it did not, despite having received extra care and fertilizer, it was to be cut down.

Simon made a face that said "I told you so."

* * *

On the next Sabbath, Jesus healed a woman who had been plagued by a demonic spirit for eighteen years. The ruler of the synagogue was enraged and began to berate the people, telling them to come on days other than the Sabbath for healing.

Simon was stunned by the man's total lack of empathy. This woman had persisted in worship for eighteen years in spite of her condition . . . surely, he ought to be delighted to see her finally released from her infirmity.

"Play-actors!" Jesus thundered. "That's what you are! Your practice condemns your speech! Every one of you will release your ox or donkey on the Sabbath day so that it can drink water – your law even allows you to draw the water! Here is a daughter of Abraham . . . a member of our own faith and family. How on earth can you think that it is wrong to release her, whom Satan has kept bound for eighteen years . . . eighteen years, mark you . . . how can it possibly be wrong to release her on the very day given to us by God for restorative rest?"

Simon noted that the congregation was sharply divided between those who were humiliated and consequently infuriated, and those who were delighted with Jesus's deeds and words. They too felt they had been released from bondage that morning.

In many ways, Simon thought to himself, the bondage imposed by Satan and the bondage imposed by these leaders are very much alike. Both rob people of the joy of God's salvation and liberation.

* * *

When winter had stripped the landscape of all colour, except for various shades of dull greys and browns, Jesus and his disciples returned to Jerusalem for the Feast of Dedication.

As a child, this feast had been one of Simon's favourites because it commemorated the Maccabean conquest of the Syrian forces and the rededication of the temple. The Syrians, under the leadership of their evil ruler, Antiochus IV, had prohibited all Jewish religious observances and they had defiled the temple by erecting an altar to Zeus.[4]

As part of the celebration and for the duration of the festival, Jerusalem would sparkle at night like a star-studded sky as pious families burned oil lamps in their windows . . . each night the number of lamps was increased until the city itself appeared to be one big shining light.

But the days were gloomy, cold, and wet, therefore Jesus was walking under the shelter of the cedar roof of the porch known as Solomon's Colonnade, on his way to the Court of the Women, when he was accosted by a group of hostile leaders. They urged him to clearly reveal, once and for all, if he was the Messiah.

This is another silly trap, Simon thought. They have enough evidence already. What more do they need other than something with which they might accuse him?

"The answer to your request for clarity is self-evident," Jesus replied. "You have repeatedly witnessed my identity through the works I have done. But the fact that you are not of my flock prevents you from believing in me. As I said

---

4. 1 Maccabees 1:41–64.

before, my sheep hear my voice and they follow me and obey me. I know them and they know me, and in me they have an eternally secure life. They rest in the very palm of my hand and I will not allow anything or anyone to snatch them from my grip. My Father, who is greater than all, has given them to me. He, too, has them in the palm of his hand as he and I are one."

At this point, the leaders were so beside themselves with anger, that they contemplated stoning him, contrary to Roman law.

"They are all too quick to cast stones, these leaders of ours," Simon said to the others. "Have they forgotten their humiliation? In these very courts, Jesus exposed them for their double mindedness. Do they think they are now without sin?"

"So, you want to stone me, do you?" Jesus said, slowly and deliberately. "For which one of my works are you going to condemn me?"

"Not for your works," one shouted, "but for blasphemy! You claim to be divine, but you are a mere mortal!"

Jesus replied, "Don't our Scriptures call those who were consecrated to positions of divinely representative authority, 'gods,' to signify their new status?[5] Could we not then use that term for the one set apart by God for himself so that he might send him into the world to fulfil his own purpose? If my work is that of my Father, how can you accuse me of blasphemy for calling myself God's son? If you are not willing to believe my *words*, then believe my *works*. By the witness of those works you may believe that the Father is in me and I am in the Father."

"But they won't believe because they don't want to believe," Simon muttered under his breath. "None are so blind as those who refuse to see."

There was a sudden mad shuffling around as the leaders tried to grab Jesus so they could take him before a tribunal. But in the mayhem that ensued, he and his disciples slipped through the crowds and left Jerusalem. They returned to Bethany beyond the Jordan, where John the Baptizer had ministered at first. The place invited a comparison between the two cousins: John had never performed miraculous works, but his testimony concerning Jesus was confirmed by the wonders Jesus performed. And so, in that place, many believed in Jesus.

---

5. Psalm 82:6.

18

Counting the Cost

In spite of the fact that many believed in him, Jesus's following was dwindling. While crowds still gathered to hear him teach, the numbers who remained close to him were becoming smaller and smaller, perhaps because of fear or perhaps because of the cost involved in being a disciple of Jesus. Someone asked him if this would be the reality of his ministry . . . that only a few would be saved.

"There is a narrow door," Jesus replied, "through which compromise cannot pass. Choices have to be made and many things relinquished and left behind. Once that door closes, it will not be reopened."

Looking back, Simon was glad he had worked through most of his fears and objections prior to following Jesus. There was still much that he needed to deal with, but his initial decision to leave his old life behind in order to embrace a new life with Jesus . . . to squeeze through that restraining narrow door . . . had helped him to sort out the good from the not so good.

Jesus once again began to make plans to return to Jerusalem. A group of Galilean Pharisees came to warn him that Herod was determined to kill him. Whether this was true or not was unimportant. Even rumours carry an element of danger . . . any miscalculation, whether in an attempt to protect oneself or to retaliate, could lead to unnecessary confrontation. Simon thought it was alarming that the religious authorities and the secular authorities appeared to be uniting against Jesus, but, as usual, Jesus did not appear to be overly concerned. He knew that no human being, regardless of their station in life, had ultimate power over matters of life and death.

"Tell that crafty king that I will not be intimidated! I will complete my ministry in his jurisdiction very soon as I am pressing on to Jerusalem . . . because it is not possible for a prophet to die outside of Jerusalem."

Jesus sighed deeply. He had one of those far away looks on his face, as if his mind was somewhere else. "O Jerusalem . . ." he said, "Jerusalem, you stone and kill all those who come to draw you back to your God. Just as a mother hen gathers her chicks under her wings to keep them from harm, so I, too, wanted to protect you from the coming desolation . . . but you have refused to hear me as well. You will only see me again once you acknowledge me as your Lord."

For a while, everyone felt awkward. No one knew what to say or what to do. The Pharisees began to leave in small groups, but one of their leaders came to invite Jesus to his home for a meal.

"Not another meal on a Sabbath," Simon muttered. "Why do they always invite him on the Sabbath? Don't they know by now that he will always cause them indigestion by doing something that offends them?"

* * *

Jesus had made it clear on several occasions that the original purpose of the Sabbath was for recovery . . . recovery of land, of resources, and of people. It was God's gift of healing meant to benefit all. So, it was no surprise to the disciples when, during that meal at the prominent Pharisee's home, he healed a man suffering from oedema. To the group's credit, the Pharisees said nothing when Jesus pointed out once more that they would not hesitate to rescue children or animals from a pit on the Sabbath day.

But their silence may have been due to the fact that they were more concerned with matters of seating at the table. The guests all attempted to choose the places of honour for themselves. Jesus however pointed out that it was better to choose a lower place and be elevated later by the host, than to choose an honoured position only to be asked to move down after a more important guest had arrived.

Yes, Simon thought. Better to humble yourself than to be humbled by someone else.

But Jesus took the idea of humility even further. Turning to the host he said, "Inviting only those who will invite you back later, brings no reward. Rather invite those who are not able to repay the honour . . . the poor, the disabled, the lame, the blind . . . then you will receive a blessing at the resurrection of the just."

One of the guests overheard what Jesus had said to their host. "Those who eat at the feast in the kingdom of God are blessed indeed," he said piously.

"Indeed," Jesus replied. There was a lull in the conversation at that moment and Jesus took full advantage of it. "There once was a great feast and many guests had been invited to attend. As is our custom, once everything had been prepared, the servants went out to inform those invited that all was now ready, and that they should come. Can you imagine their surprise when, one by one, the guests began to make excuses as to why they could not attend!"

"How rude," one man said.

"Mind you, their excuses were all very respectable," Jesus said with a faint smile on his lips. "One said he was busy surveying his newly acquired farm; another said he was occupied with five yoke of oxen he had just purchased; and still another said he had to attend to his new wife."

"Ah, the problems of the wealthy," Simon whispered to Andrew.

"Yes, but who in his right mind would buy a farm or a yoke of oxen, without first checking them out thoroughly?" Andrew replied.

"Or attend to a new wife? It wasn't like he was being called to go to war!"[1] Philip added.

"But would you believe it," Jesus continued, "every one of the invited guests declined!"

"That must have been terribly humiliating," said another rather indignant guest who seemed to have had some experience with disrespectful members of the more affluent classes.

"Indeed, it was," Jesus said. "But then the master of the house told the servants to go and invite all the disadvantaged members of society . . . they were to go into the streets, down alleys, into hovels, and gather in the destitute and the disabled and the disenfranchised."

There was an uncomfortable silence at the table. No one wanted to make eye contact with Jesus or with each other. The idea was unthinkable. The master would lose the respect of his peers, or worse still, he would lose his status in good society.

"This story never gets old," Andrew said to Simon.

"Regardless of the version," Simon replied with a smile.

But Jesus was not quite finished. "After they had done what their master had ordered, there were still empty places at the table. So, the master ordered them go outside of the city to gather in all those found in the lanes and on the main roads and compel them to come to his feast."

Some of the guests thought that those found "outside of the city" represented non-Jews and they were highly offended.

As they rose to leave in protest, Jesus said, "None of the original invitees will find a place at my feast."

---

1. Deuteronomy 24:5.

The shock was so great that those who had risen to their feet remained standing where they were. They all stared at Jesus. Then Jesus rose and left the house.

*　*　*

As they were walking along, Jesus turned to those who were following and said, "If you are not willing to devote yourselves entirely to me . . . if anyone or anything prevents you from surrendering your whole life to me, be it a parent or a possession or even your own life . . . then you cannot be my follower. Following me will be costly and if your mind is not fixed on me, you will fall away. You must consider yourself dead to everything you once held dear."

The disciples looked at each other and then they looked at the perplexed faces of those around them. It was a hard saying, to be sure, but they understood what Jesus meant. Many people had stopped following him already because it demanded too much from them. Following Jesus required the forsaking of all other competing alliances, and so it was better to consider the commitment well before making the decision to follow him. That way, those things could not tempt you or trip you up along the way.

"Let me put it like this," Jesus continued. "Suppose you want to build an observation tower for your orchard. Wouldn't you first write up a proper budget to make certain you had enough money for the building costs? You would be humiliated if you were not able to complete the task, wouldn't you? Or imagine you were a king on the brink of war with a neighbouring hostile nation. Wouldn't you make sure that you had enough men and resources for a victory prior to engaging the enemy? If, after inspecting your troops and examining your treasury, you found that you were not in a position to win, you would still have time to sue for peace. So, you too have to make sure that you are not a double-minded person before you choose to become my disciple."

Simon thought back to the time when he had fallen down before Jesus's feet in the boat, confessing his inadequacies . . . telling Jesus that he did not feel that he was equal to the task . . . that he was not disciple material. There were times when those feelings came bubbling back up to the surface, and they made him doubt his decision to follow Jesus. At those times he would always cling to what Jesus had promised in reply . . . that he would make Simon the person he was meant to be.

19

Losing to Find

The Pharisees were very strict with regard to ritual cleanliness, so they limited their circle of friends to those who were like them in every way. Jesus was the exact opposite. He enjoyed the company of those who were completely unlike him . . . he knew that those were the people who needed him most.

Once again, the Pharisees criticized Jesus for eating with people they considered undesirable.

How long will they continue to attack him? Simon wondered. They won't stop until they crush him. They want to humiliate him . . . they want to see him fail. It is so amazing that out of the same mouth, they both bless and curse him.

But Jesus was not disturbed by this renewed attack, and he responded with three of his most powerful parables. "Suppose one of you had a hundred sheep," he began.

"I remember Jesus telling us this story," Andrew said to Simon, "but the Pharisees are not going to like being compared to shepherds."

"I think Jesus knows that, brother," Simon replied.

"At least they will think that the shepherd is a rich man who can afford a hundred sheep?" Matthew added.

"Maybe the flock belongs to a whole family?" John ventured.

"Like some of the sheep farmers in Bethlehem," James said to support his brother.

"Suppose one sheep goes missing," Jesus continued. "Would he just leave it to die alone in the wilderness? Or do you think he would leave the ninety-nine with the other shepherds and go to search for the lost one?"

"I think you are right, John," Simon said. "There's more than one shepherd."

Jesus continued, "I think he would search until he finds it, don't you? And when he has found it, he would be overjoyed. He would gently gather it up

171

and carry it back home on his shoulders. The whole community would rejoice with him when he returned home safely."

"Or perhaps it is the community's flock," John said. "That's why the whole village gets together to rejoice."

"Let's not forget this is a parable Jesus is telling us, not a true story," Judas grumbled.

"They will rejoice," Jesus said, "and likewise all of heaven rejoices when one lost sinner repents and returns home to God."

"That's the point of the parable," Judas said again. "Jesus eats with these so-called objectionable people with the hope of taking at least one home to God."

"You are right, Judas," Simon said, patting him on the back. "But in one sense, I think we are all like the lost sheep. We have all, at some point in our lives, gone astray.[1] We all went our own way, until Jesus came and found us."

"Or what about a poor woman," Jesus continued, "who loses one of the ten silver coins she received as her dowry?"

"Ouch! The Pharisees won't like being compared with a woman, either . . . rich or poor," Simon chuckled.

"Don't you think she will light a lamp, clean out the whole house, and search for it until she finds it? Of course she will! And when she finds it, she will be so happy that she will invite all her friends and neighbours to celebrate the fact with her. In the same way, the angels of God rejoice in heaven over one sinner who repents."

Simon looked over at the Pharisees. The hatred in their eyes shone like a blazing fire. But things were about to go from bad to worse.

"A father had two sons," Jesus began his third parable, "and the younger of them asked to receive his inheritance early."

The shocked look on the faces of those listening to Jesus showed that this request was universally unacceptable. To ask for an inheritance prior to the father's death was the same as wishing him dead.

"The father loved his son, so he divided his possessions, giving his younger son a third of all he possessed according to our law of inheritance, which was basically what he had asked for. Soon, the young man packed his belongings and left for a far-off country, where he squandered his money on loose living . . . wine, women, and endless parties. As you can imagine, he ran out of money and all his so-called friends abandoned him. He finally found a job tending pigs."

The people in the crowd gasped. Pigs were considered unclean animals and to work with them would be the ultimate humiliation for a Jewish person.

---

1. Isaiah 53:6; 1 Peter 2:25; Ezekiel 34:6; Acts 20:28.

"This parable is different from the first two," Andrew said.

"How so?" John enquired.

"Think about it. The lost sheep wandered off by accident. It didn't mean to get lost. The coin, on the other hand, was mislaid by its owner. But this son left his father wilfully."

"Not to mention the fact that he probably left his father and his brother on bad terms," Simon added.

"One day, as he was feeding the pigs," Jesus continued, "the young man thought to himself: 'The servants who work for my father eat better than I do. Maybe I could go back to him, confess that what I did was wrong . . . that I am therefore no longer worthy to be considered his son . . . and then beg for a job as one of his servants.' And that is exactly what he did," Jesus said.

"He's such a good story-teller," Simon said. "People are hanging on his words."

"But the Pharisees hate his stories," John replied. "I think they think the parables are too simplistic, and therefore beneath their dignity. They feel insulted."

"I think they would be insulted regardless of what Jesus said or did," Andrew added.

"But would you believe it?" Jesus said. "While the son was still quite a distance away from home, his father, who had been watching the road ever since his son had left, hoping for his son's return, saw him coming. He flung open the door and ran out to meet him."

"No self-respecting father would run anywhere," Judas said.

"Now you're missing the point," James said. "The Father in the story is God . . ."

"Yes, that is true," Simon jumped in, "but more importantly, this is so unlike everything we've ever been taught before about God. Our leaders made us believe that God is distant and indifferent . . . that he rejoices when those who wander away from him are destroyed. But I have learned in this short space of time in which I have known Jesus, that God is intimately interested in every one of his creatures. He longs for those who have gone astray to return to him. As Jesus has just said in the parables about the lost sheep and the lost coin . . . all heaven rejoices when even one sinner repents and returns to him."[2]

"The son fell to his knees before his father and repeated the request he had rehearsed while he was still in the pig sty," Jesus continued, "but his father would not even think of granting his request. Rather, he called his servants

---

2. Ezekiel 18:23; 2 Peter 3:9; 1 Timothy 2:3-4.

and had them clothe his son in his richest robe. He had a signet-ring placed on his son's hand and had sandals placed on his bare feet. The father even called for his other servants to slaughter the calf that had been fattened for a special occasion, so that they might celebrate the return of his son."

Jesus was silent for a moment, as if to allow those who were listening, time to process what he had just said. Then he added, "Meanwhile, the older son who had been working in the fields was on his way home when he heard the sound of festivity coming from the house. The interesting thing about this son is that he knew his father quite well . . . for this reason, he did not go into the house, but called one of the servants to find out what was going on inside. You see, he knew that his father was merciful and that he would forgive his younger brother should he ever return home . . . that was what he feared most of all."

"Just like Jonah, hey brother," Andrew said. "He refused to go to the Ninevites because he knew God would forgive them if they repented."[3]

"When the older brother heard that his worst fears had been realized," Jesus continued, "he refused to go in at all. Instead, the father went out to plead with him to come in because his brother who had been dead to them had returned . . . he was alive and well and therefore this reunion was a cause for joy and jubilation."

"That younger son was once me," said Matthew. "I know what it's like to suffer the reproach of my 'older brothers.'"

"I think that there is more to this story than that," Simon ventured. "At least you were one of us . . . but remember that woman in Phoenicia?"

"And the Samaritans," Andrew added.

"I think Jesus is trying to tell us that we ought to rejoice when the Gentiles repent and turn to God, too," Simon continued.

"But there's even more to this, Simon," Philip pointed out. "Look! The Pharisees clearly see themselves in the older son. They are offended and seem to be getting ready to leave us yet again. Some have already left."

"I wish that they would stay away and leave us in peace," Simon grumbled.

"That would be convenient to us," Andrew mused, "but who knows . . . one of them might just see themselves as lost and turn to Jesus. Just think how heaven will rejoice then, hey brother?"

"Not just heaven," Matthew added. "If only those of the Pharisees who did believe in Jesus would have the courage to say so, I would rejoice!"

"Be patient with Nicodemus, Matthew," James said. "He will find his courage some day when it matters most."

---

3. Jonah 4:2.

"I think that we are in danger of missing the point of this last parable," John said suddenly. "Think about it. The older son believed that his sonship was based on merit . . . his hard work and his external obedience. But the father loved both his sons, simply because they were his sons, not because of what they did for him."

"That's right," Simon said. "The law says something like that about us, doesn't it?"

"Yes," Andrew said. "It says that God did not love Israel because we were a great nation or because we deserved to be loved. Rather, he loves us because . . . well, just because he loves us."[4]

"And he is faithful to the promises he made to our ancestors," Simon filled in.

"We serve a great God," Thomas said. "A very great God, indeed!"

* * *

Jesus then told them another parable about a shrewd manager who worked for a very wealthy man. The manager had squandered his master's money and was about to be dismissed. In an attempt to provide for himself in the future, once he no longer had a full-time position, the manager decided to partially write off the debts of those who owed money to his master.

As a former tax collector, Matthew understood what the steward was doing. "I am ashamed to say that when some of my former colleagues exacted taxes from our own people, they would add on a cut for themselves. Please believe me when I say I never did that. But the idea was to add to their income by charging more than the Romans required. They kept the excess amount for themselves. This manager seems to have done the same . . . by writing off what he had added on, he gave the debtors the impression that he was being kind to them. But he had been robbing them all along."

"That is shrewd," Simon said. "I knew you charged less than the other tax collectors, Matthew. That's why I always tried to steer my boat your way after a catch."

"I could have been rich today, my friend," Matthew said.

"Yes, rich in money . . . but poor in conscience," Simon replied.

"That's true!" Matthew agreed.

"I'm confused," James said. "Is Jesus saying we ought to be like this shrewd manager?"

---

4. Deuteronomy 7:7–8.

"Not really . . . well, in a certain sense, yes," Matthew replied. "I don't think he is saying that we are to copy the man's dishonesty, but rather, we should copy his ability to think ahead and plan for an uncertain future. I think all too often we don't think about the future . . . we all keep on living our lives and then, when disaster strikes, we are not prepared to deal with it."

"You know, he has been talking about his betrayal and death a lot lately," Andrew said softly. "Do you think we need to be preparing ourselves for trouble?"

"Don't be ridiculous," Judas said irritated. "No one will betray him or do anything to him while the crowds are around."

"Look at them sneering at Jesus," Philip said, pointing at the Pharisees. "They are plotting something – of that I am almost certain."

"It's because they are lovers of money," Matthew added. "They love to justify themselves in their own eyes, but God knows their hearts. What Jesus says exposes what they are really like inside."

"It's funny how the things we value as humans are not valued by God," Thomas said. "Think back to the time before you met Jesus. I think everyone of us valued earthly things . . . we all wanted a better life for ourselves and our families."

"That's different, Thomas," Simon said. "There's nothing wrong with wanting the best for our families. I think God wants the best for us too . . . or, at least, that's what I think Jesus has taught us in the past. But it is the *love* of money that becomes a problem, because it gets in the way of us loving God. He's said it before – we cannot love God and money."

"Shh," Andrew said suddenly, "he's telling another story. Listen!"

"There once was a very wealthy man who lived in a very big house and he denied himself nothing," Jesus was saying. "At his gate lay a poor, diseased beggar by the name of Lazarus. The beggar had oozing sores all over his body and the street dogs used to lick his wounds. He was desperately hungry and longed for some scraps from the rich man's table, but no one took pity on him. In time, mercifully he died, and the angels came and carried him away to be with Abraham in the place of the dead. The rich man also died shortly afterwards and was buried. He too went to the place of the dead, but he went to the other side from where Abraham and Lazarus were . . . and there he was in torment as he stood in the flames. The man asked Abraham to send Lazarus to dip his finger in water to cool his tongue because he was in such pain. But Abraham pointed out that there was a deep abyss between them and no one could cross from one side to the other. He also reminded the rich man that he had led a life of ease while Lazarus had suffered and now the tables had been turned."

"Why are they getting so angry?" John asked, pointing at the highly animated Pharisees.

"I think they recognize the rich man in the story," Andrew said. "Did you notice that Jesus did not mention his name? They know who he is talking about."

"You mean this is not a parable?" John asked.

"It doesn't sound like one . . . listen."

Jesus continued. "The rich man then begged Abraham to send Lazarus to his five brothers to warn them of the fate awaiting them if they did not mend their ways. Abraham then pointed out that his brothers had the Scriptures to guide them, but the rich man persisted in his request, saying that if a ghost from the dead visited them, they would change their ways."

At this point Jesus paused. He looked at his disciples as if to alert them to something important he was about to say . . . something they needed to hear and remember for future reference.

"But once again, Abraham refused to concede to his request," Jesus said. Again he paused and looked at his disciples. "If they will not learn from the Scriptures, they will not be persuaded even if someone was to rise from the dead."

"Just like the older brother in the parable about the lost son," Simon said. "He wouldn't come into the house even though the one who had been dead was alive again. Brilliant story, don't you think?"

"Brother," Andrew said, his eyes big and round, "when Jesus speaks about being betrayed and executed, he always says that he will rise from the dead on the third day."

"Yes," Simon answered, "he does . . . but look! The Pharisees are storming off once again. You are right . . . I think they know who the rich man is, and I think they know who his five brothers are too. They are just like the older brother – they cannot rejoice at the lost being found . . . at the salvation of the repentant."

"Brother," Andrew whispered, "didn't you get what I was saying? Jesus was trying to prepare us . . . didn't you see how he looked at us? The leaders don't believe him now and they won't believe even if he were to be raised from the dead. We need to be like the shrewd manager . . . we need to be prepared."

"I think you are reading too much into this, Andrew," Simon said. "I am ready to defend Jesus against any attack. I promise you, I will not allow him to be betrayed or killed by anyone. Trust me."

"I still think we ought to be prepared," Andrew muttered, as if to himself. But the group was moving on and so he dropped the subject.

* * *

They had been walking along for a while when suddenly Jesus stopped and turned to them. "You all need to be on your guard. There are many people and things and circumstances in life that may cause you to stumble and fall. Your faith will be severely tested from time to time. But make sure you are not the one through whom the testing comes . . . it would be better for those people who cause others to fail to be thrown into the depths of the ocean with a heavy weight tied around their necks. So, check your attitude on a regular basis – if people sin against you, rebuke them privately, and if they repent, be quick to forgive them, even if they sin against you seven times in a day. Every time they ask for your forgiveness, you must give it freely."

The disciples looked at each other. If this was what was required of them, their faith was too small.

"Help us to have a stronger faith," they said.

"You don't need more faith," Jesus said. "It is not the size or strength of your faith that matters. It is your faith and trust in a great and powerful God that counts. You must always remember that. It is not your greatness . . . it is his. So don't let anything get in between you and your faith in him. You must strive to have humble thoughts and to live humble lives. Just as a servant serves his master without seeking equality or preferential treatment, so you too must serve God without wanting to be rewarded. True service to God is the result of gratitude, not merit."

"That's hard," Judas said. "Who can live up to that?"

"Yes, it is hard," Simon agreed. "But that is why he has taught us that it is in losing our lives that we find them. Don't you see, Judas? That has been the point of all his teaching. Finding life is in losing it. If we love earthly things we will lose out on spiritual things. The love of money . . ."

"Yes, I heard him too," Judas said angrily. "I heard him. But which one of us is able to deny himself completely? We live in this world. If we don't provide for ourselves, then where will we be in a few years' time?" And with that Judas stormed off.

Simon was taken aback by the sudden outburst. What was that all about? he wondered.

"Don't be offended," John said. "Judas likes nice things. This teaching is difficult for him."

"But he's the keeper of our communal purse," Simon said. "Jesus has just said that there will be things in life that could cause us to stumble . . . do you think keeping our money purse could be a problem for Judas?"

"Perhaps," John replied, "but that is something he will have to work through."

"Or lose what we are all wanting to find," Simon added. "This is not just a lesson for him . . . it is a lesson for us. Whatever gets in the way of following Jesus completely needs to go."

20

Kingdom Life

"Someone's coming!" Andrew had been rather nervous since Jesus's last confrontation with the Pharisees. The disciples gathered round to watch as a young man came running towards them.

"Andrew," Simon said, "it's just a messenger."

"There will be enough time to speak, young man," Jesus said as he stepped forward to greet the messenger. "First take some refreshment. You look thirsty and tired."

"Many thanks, teacher," the young man replied, "but the message is urgent."

John handed him a cup of cold water. How John had changed since he and his brother were rebuked by Jesus for wanting to destroy a Samaritan village. He had become so thoughtful and kind. The messenger gulped down the cup of water.

"I have come from Bethany. The sisters, Mary and Martha, sent me to tell you that their brother, Lazarus, is very sick."

"This sickness will not end in death," Jesus said. "This is for the glory of God and God's Son will be glorified through it."

The messenger appeared to be more relaxed on hearing what Jesus had to say and agreed to have some food with them. After he had left, Jesus continued to instruct the disciples in the Scriptures, asking questions, helping them to see the meaning behind the original message, and teaching them how to practically apply what they learned to their everyday lives. It did not seem odd to them that he made no effort to go to see Lazarus. They all knew it was a difficult time and that the threats of the leaders were very real. However, it did come as a surprise when, after two days, Jesus suddenly informed his disciples that they were to return to Judea.

"But rabbi," they protested, "just the other day they were threatening to stone you! Why would you want to return now?"

"As long as we walk in daylight, we will not stumble." Jesus replied. "The light clearly reveals what needs to be avoided. It is when we walk in the dark, that we are in danger."

"I think I know what he means," Simon whispered to Andrew. "He's been praying to the Father every night and every morning. Jesus never does anything spontaneous or irrational. He always checks in with the Father to make sure he is walking according to his will."

Then Jesus added, "Lazarus is sleeping, and I need to go to awaken him."

"Oh, that's good news," James said. "If he is resting well, he will get better soon."

"No, James, you misunderstand," Jesus replied. "Lazarus is dead. I realize this is hard to comprehend, but it really was good I was not there. Oh, you will see soon enough that this is for your benefit . . . it will strengthen your faith in me. Come, we must go now."

As Jesus walked away, Thomas turned to the other hesitant disciples and said, "Let's follow him. If we die, at least we all die together with him."

Little did he know that his pessimistic view of this return to Judea would soon prove to be partially correct.

* * *

As they walked down to Bethany through the barren landscape of the Jordan valley, the disciples discussed among themselves various protective strategies they could employ if they were attacked. Judas stubbornly maintained that nothing would happen to Jesus while he was surrounded by the crowds. The leaders would not make such a bold move.

"And what if they devise some scheme where they can arrest him without anyone knowing?" Andrew asked.

"Just how do you think they will be able to do that?" Judas countered. "They would need one of us to side with them against Jesus."

"One of us to betray him, you mean," Simon said.

"And Jesus did say he would be betrayed," John added, concerned.

Judas was clearly irritated. "So, which one of us do you think would do something quite so underhanded, huh?"

The disciples looked at each other. Judas was right. They all loved Jesus too much to betray him.

* * *

When they arrived in Bethany, they discovered that Lazarus had been buried four days ago. Many people had come from nearby Jerusalem to comfort the two bereaved sisters. Martha was outside the house when someone told her that Jesus and his disciples were on the outskirts of the village. She ran to meet him without thinking to tell Mary first.

"O Lord," Martha said, "thank you for coming, but I'm afraid you are too late. My brother has been in the tomb for four days already. If you had been here, I am sure he would not have died." She suddenly looked up at him and added, "But I still believe that whatever you ask, God will grant it to you."

"Martha," Jesus said tenderly, "your brother will rise to life again."

"Yes, I believe that he will be raised on the last day," she replied.

"Martha," Jesus cupped her tear-stained face in his hands, "I am not talking about the future only, but about the present. Martha, I AM the resurrection. I AM life. Apart from me there is no resurrection or life. Those who believe in me have life even though they die . . . and those who have this life and believe in me will never die. Do you understand and believe this?

"Yes," she said without hesitation. "Yes, Lord, I have always believed that you are the Messiah, the Son of God . . . the one for whom we have all been waiting."

"Where is Mary?" Jesus asked.

"She is still in the house with the other mourners. I didn't stop to tell her you were here. I'll go and call her now."

With that, Martha left to tell Mary that Jesus was asking after her. When the mourners saw Mary leaving with Martha, they supposed they were going to mourn at the tomb, so they followed.

When Mary reached Jesus she was overcome with emotion and fell at his feet crying, "Lord, if you had been here, my brother would still be alive."

The disciples could see that Jesus was deeply moved as he asked where they had laid the body. While they were leading him to the tomb, he wept unashamedly.

"He must have loved him very much," someone said. Another commented, "He opened the eyes of the blind man. Surely Jesus could have prevented this death, had he not been driven out by our leaders."

When they got to the tomb Jesus told them to remove the large round stone that had been laid across the entrance of the cave.

Martha objected. "Lord, he has been in there for four days. The body must be decomposing by now and there will be an awful stench."

"Martha," Jesus said, "did you not understand when I said that if you believe you will see the glory of God? Roll away the stone."

Martha nodded to a group of young men and they set about removing the stone. There was a stunned silence. People drew back, away from the opening, expecting foul fumes to overwhelm them. Then Jesus prayed to the Father and thanked him for always hearing his petitions. They were simple words spoken for the benefit of those standing around him.

Then he spoke with a voice like thunder, "Lazarus, come out to me!"

At first, the disciples heard nothing. Then they heard a faint rustling inside the cave . . . then a soft groaning sound like someone waking from slumber. The people in the crowd were hardly breathing. Then they saw him. Lazarus had been bound with strips of linen with spices in between . . . it was difficult for him to walk. He came shuffling slowly to the mouth of the cave. There was a cloth over his face, but no one needed to see his face to know that it was Lazarus himself . . . this was no apparition . . . this was no ghost. Lazarus was alive!

"Unwrap the grave cloths and set him free," Jesus said.

Years later, when the disciples tried to describe the scene to those who had not been present, they struggled to find words that could adequately explain the sheer joy that flooded over everyone, especially Martha and Mary, at that moment. There was such jubilation and weeping and praise. And many put their faith in Jesus and, as Jesus had said, the disciples' faith was strengthened too. Later they would need that assurance more than they could have imagined at the time.

* * *

They had been at the home of Mary, Martha, and Lazarus for two days when a messenger arrived from Jerusalem. He asked to speak to John.

John returned to the group, his face pale. "What is it, John?" Jesus asked.

"That was a messenger from Jerusalem. I know the High Priest's family . . . he was sent to warn us that the Sanhedrin is plotting to put you to death, Jesus."

The disciples all began to speak at once. "Quiet down," Jesus said. "Please, John, continue."

"It seems some of those who left here the other day when . . . when . . .," John hesitated.

"When I was raised from the dead?" Lazarus offered.

"Yes, thank you," John continued. "They went and told the Pharisees what had happened here. The Pharisees, in turn, called a meeting with the Sanhedrin. It seems they are afraid that if the Romans think you are a threat to the empire, they will lose their status and position. Some even believe the Romans might destroy Jerusalem and the temple."

"Trying to keep their lives, they are losing them," Simon said to Andrew.

"Didn't Jesus say that the brothers of the rich man would not believe even if someone was to rise from the dead? Maybe this is what he was trying to tell us," Andrew replied.

"But apparently, Caiaphas . . .," at this point John swallowed hard, "Caiaphas indicated that it would be better for them to offer you to the Romans . . . that way one person dies instead of the nation."

"How could they . . . how could they betray one of their own?" Philip was beside himself with anger.

"This is the betrayal Jesus was telling us about," Andrew said to Simon quietly.

"It could be," Simon replied, "but they will have to find us first . . . and get past us!"

"Martha, Mary, Lazarus," Jesus said calmly, "thank you for your outstanding hospitality. But I think it is time for us to move on across the Jordan once more. It is not yet my time . . . come, we must be going."

"Why?" Judas asked under his breath.

"Why what?" Simon replied as they packed their few belongings in their travel bags.

"Why always run away? Why not confront them? Think about it. Jesus didn't run away from the legion of demons. He wasn't afraid of that terrible storm. Why run away from the Sanhedrin? They are only a handful of men."

"Men with power and connections," Andrew said.

"I don't know why we are 'running away,' as you put it, Judas," Simon said straightening out. "But like king David, I too would rather fall into the hands of a gracious God than into the hands of wicked men.[1] Nevertheless, I do believe the day will come when there will be a confrontation and we must be prepared."

"That is what I told you the other day, brother," Andrew said reproachfully.

"Yes, dear brother, and you were right. I was wrong. Forgive me."

"It's time to leave," Thomas said, poking his head around the door.

Simon looked over at Judas. There was a dark cloud over his face. What was he thinking?

* * *

Jesus always led by example. Whatever he expected his followers to do, he demonstrated first by his own actions. Wherever he went, he would teach everyone about life in the kingdom, but his instruction was not limited to words only. Simon felt that sometimes the best lessons were those learned from Jesus's behaviour.

The religious leaders, and those who followed them, had strict social rules that governed the way they interacted with those who were not like them. But

---

1. 2 Samuel 24:14.

Jesus seemed to delight in the very people the leaders sought to avoid. Like the lepers.

Jesus and his disciples were travelling along the border of Samaria and Galilee when ten lepers approached them on the outskirts of a village. Standing at the distance prescribed by the cultural and ritual practice of the day, they cried out to Jesus to have compassion on them. But instead of walking up to them and laying his hands on them as he had done with people previously, Jesus simply told them to go and show themselves to the priests.

"Why must they go and show themselves to the priests?" Philip asked. "They should only do that after they have been healed."[2]

"I'm not sure, Philip, but I am sure Jesus knows what he is doing," Simon replied.

Then they heard shouts of pure joy coming from the direction in which the lepers had gone.

"Well, there you have your answer, Philip," Simon said. "They were healed when they obeyed Jesus."

Then they saw him. One of the lepers came running back over the hill, shouting out loud praises to God. When he got to Jesus, he lay prostrate before him and thanked him repeatedly.

"He's a Samaritan," James said.

"And he was a leper, but neither fact prevented Jesus from having compassion on him," Simon reminded him.

"Forgive me . . . I didn't mean . . ." James stammered, blushing at his judgmental remark.

"Where are your nine companions, since you have returned alone? Were they not healed too?" Jesus asked. Then turning to his disciples he said, "Only one has shown gratitude . . . and he is a so-called foreigner, one that is usually excluded from the commonwealth of Israel."

Simon thought James was going to burst into tears. "Forgive me . . ." was all he could say.

Then Jesus turned to the healed man and said, "Please, stand up. Your faith in me has cleansed you from your disease. You may return to your family and your friends now."

Gratitude makes one's face shine, Simon thought to himself. Godliness is so important, but without gratitude . . . without being content with what God

---

2. Leviticus 14.

graciously gives us each and every day . . . godliness is ugly and empty and of little value to anyone.

He turned to James and hugged him. "We are all still learning, James," he said. "It isn't easy to undo what we once believed."

* * *

Jesus was often asked to explain what he meant when he spoke about the kingdom of God. As Simon listened to him explain his views to yet another group of Pharisees, Simon thought about how many in Israel believed that the kingdom of God was the visible, physical, geo-political territory that was once consolidated by David and Solomon. As far as they were concerned, the Messiah would be a champion who would deliver them from foreign domination, like one of the judges of old.

But, Simon thought, Jesus believes that the kingdom of God is not of this world. It is a spiritual kingdom and therefore it is made manifest in the lives of those who are a part of it. In that sense, the kingdom of God is a lifestyle . . . an abandonment . . . a surrender to God and to his will.

As they walked along, Jesus told his disciples that a day was coming when they would long for one, single day with the Son of Man, but they would not see it. "Don't listen to those who tell you the Son of Man has returned . . . you will know when he has returned because the event will be as evident as the lightning that lights up the whole sky."

"I must confess, I really don't understand this talk of returning," Simon whispered to Andrew. "Returning from where?"

"I don't know, brother, but I am sure it will all become clear in time," Andrew replied.

Jesus's face suddenly darkened.

There's that look again, Simon thought. I wish I had the ability to set his mind at ease. Nothing will happen to him while I'm around.

"But first the Son of Man must be rejected by this generation. They will put him to death . . . you must be prepared for this."

Simon was about to say something, but then Jesus continued.

"The return of the Son of Man will be as much a surprise as the coming of the flood in the days of Noah or as the destruction of Sodom and Gomorrah in the days of Lot. Those people were simply going on with their day-to-day lives when destruction suddenly overcame them. It will be exactly the same when the Son of Man returns. That is why it is so important for you to be ready . . .

you never know when the end will come. So don't be double-minded . . . if you seek to preserve this life, you will risk losing life altogether."

How can I prepare myself for something I don't really understand? Simon thought. Maybe that is the essence of faith . . . to simply entrust yourself wholeheartedly to God and to follow him into what is otherwise unknown to you. To live according to the principles of kingdom life.

21

The Right-Side Up

They were still sitting around the morning fire when Andrew suddenly spoke. "Lord, we have been trying to follow your example by praying to the Father every evening, reviewing what we have said and done during the past day, and every morning, asking for his guidance as we begin the day . . . and, for the most part, we also pray as we go through the day as well. We know this is how you determine what you will do and what you will say . . . you have taught us that . . . and we have witnessed that and experienced it for ourselves. But, Lord, how do we know when we need to stop praying for something or about something? I suppose what I am trying to ask is, how long must we continue to pray if it seems as if our prayers are not being heard?"

Jesus smiled. Nothing seemed to delight him more than when his disciples asked questions. "Let me tell you a parable," Jesus said. "Imagine that in some town, there was an unrighteous judge who feared neither God nor people. In this same town, there lived a widow who was being hounded by an unkind person. Every day, she would come to the judge to ask for his help . . . and every day, he would ignore her. But one day he had had enough. 'I can't stand this any longer,' he said. 'Even though I fear neither God nor people, I'm going to grant this widow's request . . . otherwise she will drive me insane with her persistent nagging.'"

The disciples all laughed. When Jesus told his parables he would often liven them up with actions and change his voice to suit each character.

"Now, here's the lesson for you all. If the unrighteous judge is prepared to grant the widow's persistent petition, how much more will the righteous Judge of all grant the petitions of those who cry out to him day and night? He will not ignore them but will see that their petitions are granted when the time is right . . . and he will give what is right and good."

Jesus paused. This was a lesson they needed to learn with regard to prayer and he wanted them to understand what he was about to say. "The Father knows your petitions before you pray to him. He knows what you need, but he also knows what is best for you. You see, persistence in prayer is for your benefit . . . when God does not answer your petitions immediately it is not because he does not hear or that he does not care. No. It is because he knows that perseverance demonstrates dependence on him, and that perseverance builds strong character in you. It creates hope . . . and boosts your faith.[1] In a certain sense, God is like a farmer waiting for the harvest . . . the seed of faith must grow before it can produce a bumper crop. Nevertheless, you will not wait indefinitely, because God knows that delayed hope makes the heart weary, but yearning realized brings meaning to life."[2]

"Thank you, Lord," Andrew said. "I must be honest . . . it has been difficult for me. I have been praying about . . . something . . . well, I will continue to pray. I know that the Father will answer when the time is right, and perhaps with an answer that will be better than that for which I am asking."

"I want to tell you another parable," Jesus said. "There were once two men . . . one was a Pharisee and the other a tax-collector." Jesus made a face at Matthew.

They all laughed.

"Well, one day they both went to the temple to pray. The Pharisee prayed like this." Jesus stood up and fluffed out his robes, imitating the voluminous clothing of the Pharisees. "'God,' he prayed. 'Thank you that I am better than other people . . . thieves, sinners, sexually immoral people . . . or even this tax-collector. Twice a week I deny myself food and water and I give ten percent of everything I receive. Thank you that I am so very good.'"

Other people started to come closer, and a small crowd began to form around them. Everybody loved Jesus's stories.

"But, the other man," Jesus continued, "the tax-collector . . . he stood far away and could not even lift his face toward heaven. He beat his chest and cried out for mercy. 'Have mercy on me, dear God, I am a sinful man.'"

Simon recognized the very words he had used when he finally realized who Jesus was. "Leave me, Lord," he had said, "I am a sinful man."

"I tell you, God will hear this tax-collector rather than the other man," Jesus said as he sat down once more. "God will always graciously hear the humble . . . and he will always humble the proud."

That is a saying I must remember, Simon thought. God humbles the proud, but graciously hears the humble.[3]

---

1. Cf. Romans 5:3–5.
2. Proverbs 13:12.
3. 1 Peter 5:5; Proverbs 3:34; James 4:6.

"It is true. That man was a proud man." The disciples all looked up at the same time. A Pharisee had joined the growing crowd while Jesus had been speaking. "We obey the law because we fear breaking the law and thereby invoking the anger of God," the Pharisee continued. "Our forefathers were taken into exile because they disobeyed the law. We seek to prevent that from ever happening again."

"There is God's law and then there is your law," Simon countered.

"Yes? Well then, fisherman, let me ask you a question from the law. May a man divorce his wife because she displeases him, for whatever reason he chooses?"[4]

Simon suddenly felt as if he was sinking into the Sea of Galilee again.

"Do not be drawn into their internal arguments," Jesus said. "The school of Shumai says one thing and the school of Hillel says another." Turning to the Pharisee he said, "That is your dispute, not ours. But let me ask you this. What does Scripture say? When God created humanity, he made them male and female, didn't he? When he brought Eve to Adam, God said that because they were perfectly complementary to each other, a man would leave his parents to unite with his wife, and they would become one. In other words, they are no longer two separate beings, but one new being, because they have been made one by God himself. There is a unity of both body and spirit. No human can undo what God has done."

"Now it is you who speaks against the law!" the Pharisee shouted. "Moses clearly commanded us to give an unwanted wife a certificate of divorce and then to have her removed."

"You misunderstand and misinterpret the law," Jesus said, raising his voice slightly. "Moses permitted divorce . . . permitted, not commanded . . . he permitted divorce to protect the women from hard-hearted men like yourself. But divorce is contrary to what God intended in the beginning. Hear me and hear me well." Jesus stood to face his accuser. "If anyone divorces his wife except for sexual immorality and then marries another, that man commits adultery. That is the law."

The Pharisee's face turned deep crimson. He muttered something under his breath and then stormed off. Jesus had touched a nerve.

"But Lord," Andrew said, "if this is the case, then perhaps it is better not to marry?" Simon looked at this brother in total disbelief. "No, I don't mean to say . . . Brother, you are fortunate . . . you have a wonderful wife. But think

---

4. Deuteronomy 24:1. There was a difference of opinion on this matter between two Jewish schools of thought at the time. The school of Shumai was stricter than the school of Hillel.

of those men who are married to, well, difficult women. If they cannot divorce their wives, then they are trapped with no possibility of escape."

"Excuse me," Mary of Magdala said. "Have you ever tried to think of how we women must feel? We have to put up with your snoring and your moods and your smells."

The disciples all burst out laughing. Andrew blushed from his toes to his head. He wished he had never opened his mouth.

"I will say this to all of you, men and women alike," Jesus said, once everyone stopped laughing. "There are many reasons why people choose not to be married, perhaps because of a birth defect or a later injury. For some, the unmarried state is preferable, especially for spiritual reasons . . . so that the man or woman may be wholeheartedly focused on the kingdom." Jesus fell into that category. Unlike most Jewish men of their day, he had never married, because he had dedicated his life to the care of his family, the study of the Scriptures, and the development of the disciples. "But do not misunderstand me," Jesus continued. "God created men and women for each other. He said that it was not good for a man or a woman to be alone. Together they are better . . . they were made to fulfil each other."

Childish giggles suddenly broke in upon the uncomfortable silence. Many women had brought their children to Jesus for him to bless them.

"No," Judas stood up and began to shoo the mothers away. "Can't you see that we are busy?"

"Stop," Jesus said. "I delight in all children, so let them come to me. Believe me, the kingdom is meant for those who are like children." Having said that, he laid his hands on each and every one of the children and gave them his blessing. Looking back later, Simon wondered if it ever occurred to the mothers that at that moment of blessing, Jesus already knew what was waiting for him in Jerusalem.

* * *

The time had come for them to leave. Some of the disciples doused the fire, while others went to the marketplace to purchase provisions for the trip. As they were walking, a well-dressed young man ran up to Jesus to ask him a question. "Good teacher," he began, "what must I do to inherit eternal life?"

"We've heard this question before," Andrew said to his brother.

"Yes, but why does this man call Jesus 'good'?" Simon replied. "You know what Jesus always says . . . only God is good. Is it possible that he knows that Jesus is more than a mere man?"

"You know the commandments," Jesus said to the man. "Obey them and you will live."

The man looked as if he had been struck by lightning. "The commandments? All of them?"

"Yes," Jesus said. "Do not murder, do not commit adultery, do not take what is not yours, do not testify falsely against another, honour your parents . . . and love your neighbour in the same way as you love yourself."

The young man smiled a huge smile. "I have kept all of those ever since I was a child," he gushed. "Is there anything else I should be doing?"

Jesus stopped and looked at the young man. It was one of his deep, penetrating stares. Then he said, "Yes, there is one more thing you should do. Your possessions . . . sell them all and give the money away to the poor and destitute . . . in that way you will store up treasures in heaven. And then come and follow me."

The blood drained from the young man's face. From the way he was dressed it was clear that he was wealthy, and Jesus had just exposed his worst fault – greed. The young man regained his composure, scoffed at Jesus and walked away.

"It really is difficult for the wealthy to see the value in anything else but what is earthly and temporary. That is why it is virtually impossible for them to enter the kingdom of God," Jesus said sadly. "You might as well try leading a camel through the eye of a needle."

"I thought wealth was a sign of God's favour," Judas said. "This is like your teaching on divorce. It is impossible to follow this. If this is true, then no one can enter the kingdom."

"True," Jesus replied. "It *is* impossible for human beings. That is why you need God . . . he is the only one who can grant you access to his kingdom."

There was an awkward silence. Judas was clearly upset. Simon remembered what John had said about Judas liking things. Did this incident with the wealthy, young man uncover an underlying struggle against greed in Judas?

"Well," Simon said trying to lighten the sudden solemn mood, "we left everything to follow you!"

Jesus smiled. "Yes, Simon, you have sacrificed much. But let me tell you this . . . whoever has given up the things they once held dear . . . houses, spouses, siblings, parents, or even children for the sake of the kingdom of God . . . God will reward them many times over, both in this life as well as in the life to come."

"That is so contrary to life," Judas said softly. "It is all upside-down."

"Contrary to life? Upside down? No, Judas, this is life . . . true life, the right-side up. Sadly, many who think they are first, will find out that they are actually last, and those who think they are last . . . or those whom the world thinks are last . . . they will be first in the kingdom."

Judas snorted, but said nothing.

"I need to tell you another parable," Jesus said as he turned to continue walking. "The kingdom of heaven is like a man who owned a large piece of land. Early one morning, he went out to hire labourers to work in his vineyard. They agreed on a price and set off to work. Later, the same man found other men who had not yet been hired and he sent them into his vineyard as well, promising to pay them whatever would be fair. And he did this, three more times, each time at a later hour, hiring those whom no one else had employed. At the end of the day, he called all the labourers together and began to pay each one, starting with those he had hired last. When those who had been hired first saw that he paid the last the same amount that they had agreed upon at the beginning of the day, they assumed they would be paid more because they had worked longer and harder. But the man gave every labourer the exact same amount. Those who had been hired first began to grumble and complain saying that the man was unfair. But the man pointed out that he had paid them the amount he had promised. If he decided to pay every labourer the same, that was his choice. He could do what he pleased with his money. Who could find fault with him because he was gracious and generous?"

Jesus paused. "So, I say again . . . those who think they are first, will find out that they are actually last, and those who think they are last . . . or those whom the world thinks are last . . . will be first in the kingdom."

"This is nonsense," Judas spat out. "There's nothing right-side up about this at all!" With that, he stormed off ahead of the group.

Jesus stood, watching him as he went. Then he turned to the rest of the disciples and said, "We are on our way to Jerusalem. This time I will be betrayed into the hands of the Sanhedrin . . ." A shadow came over Jesus's face. Simon thought he saw a profound sorrow in his eyes. "I will be betrayed . . . then they will condemn me to death and hand me over to the Romans to be abused and executed."

No one said a word. No one knew what to say. Jesus had predicted his death more than once now, and it began to dawn on his disciples that perhaps he believed his death was an event he could no longer avoid. But suddenly Jesus looked up at them and they saw that a light had returned to his dark eyes.

"Yes, they will condemn me and execute me, but on the third day, I will be raised to life!"

22

In the Shadow of the Cross

They chose once again to walk the well-worn path to Jericho along the Jordan valley. Salome (the wife of Zebedee and sister of Mary the mother of Jesus)[1] was with the group together with a number of other women from Galilee. As they were walking, she came up to Jesus. She held his arm for a moment, indicating that she wanted to speak to him. When he stopped walking, she knelt down before him.

Jesus could not help but smile at her. He knew she was about to capitalize on the fact that she was a close relative. "What is your request, Dodah?"[2]

"Well, Achyan,"[3] Salome began, "remember how you said that when you come into your kingdom, your twelve disciples will sit on twelve thrones judging the tribes of Israel? I want you to grant that your two cousins sit on the right and on the left of your throne."

Jesus bent down to help his aunt stand back up again. James and John stood close by looking a little embarrassed. Jesus motioned to them to come closer. He knew them well enough to know that they had put their mother up to this.

"I'm not sure you two realize what you are asking of me," he said.

"We just thought that . . ." John started, blushing furiously as he spoke.

"We thought we would ask before anyone else did," James added, completing John's thought.

"Let me ask you this," Jesus said. "You heard what I said earlier about my suffering, didn't you?"

Now both brothers blushed. Salome could not look Jesus in the eyes.

"We did," they replied in unison.

---

1. See John 19:25; Matthew 27:55; Mark 15:40.
2. Dodah is Hebrew for aunt.
3. Achyan is Hebrew for nephew.

"Well, then let me ask you this. Are you prepared to share in my experience of suffering?"[4]

"Yes . . . yes we are," James said, trying to sound brave. "We all are willing to lay down our lives for you and your cause."

"Did they just ask for positions of honour in the kingdom?" Andrew asked Simon.

"They did," Simon said indignantly. The others were equally angry, more out of a sense of jealousy than piety.

"And there I was thinking that they had changed," Andrew said, loud enough for James and John to hear.

"I have no objection to you sharing in my sufferings," Jesus said with a tinge of sadness on his voice. "And you will share in them. But as to sitting on my right and on my left, that is another matter entirely . . . one which my Father alone can grant."

The other disciples were now murmuring loudly amongst themselves. At the time, they all wanted to sit on the right and the left of Jesus, but later, when they considered the cost associated with these positions, they wondered at their callousness.

"Come, let us go over there. I need to talk to you twelve . . . alone," Jesus said.

Salome did not appear to be offended. She had done what any mother would have done for her children.

Jesus sat down on a large boulder. At first, he said nothing. Simon disliked any period of silence because as a child it often lead to a scolding. He had always struggled with that.

"I want you to think about how worldly governments function," Jesus began. "How do the rulers of the pagan nations exercise authority?"

When no answer was forthcoming, Jesus continued. "They are in absolute control over their subjects, aren't they? Pagan rulers are despots and tyrants, and they rule by force. What you are yearning for . . .," Jesus paused and gave each disciple the same penetrating look, "what you are all yearning for is in complete contrast to the way of life in my kingdom. Your present way of thinking is pagan. In the kingdom, those who wish to rule over others must do so from a position of servanthood. As I have said before, rulers in my kingdom must be servants, and it is through selfless service that they will find their greatness."

---

4. Literally, "the cup I am about to drink." This is an Old Testament reference to suffering as a result of divine retribution. Cf. Psalm 75:8; Isaiah 51:17; Jeremiah 51:7; et al. It was fulfilled in the crucifixion. Matthew 26:39.

"There we go again," Judas mumbled under his breath. "It's all backwards . . . the last will be first . . . the first will be last . . . rulers must be servants. This is nonsense."

"If you want to follow me, you must imitate me," Jesus stated emphatically. "I did not come to exercise absolute authority over you or anyone else, for that matter. I have come to serve and to sacrifice my life for your sake and the sake of many others. I am going to give my life as a ransom for many."

Simon later wondered if it was at that moment that Judas made his decision. If this was the way of the kingdom, he would have no part of it.

* * *

Their journey continued along the Jordan valley, bordered by steep escarpments on either side . . . the mountains of Samaria to the west and the mountains of Perea to the east. The air was quite warm and humid, but still pleasant. Far below, the banks of the Jordan River were covered in luscious, deep green vegetation – the soil was rich and fertile. Older travellers told tales of encounters with lions and leopards, and at one point in their journey, a startled porcupine gave Simon such a fright he felt quite ill for a long while afterwards. But the jewel of the river was Jericho, the City of Palms, with its blazingly bright bougainvilleas, and its many fruit and palm trees.

Jericho was the oldest inhabited city in all Israel. It had been the first fortified city captured by Joshua. Rahab, the Canaanite prostitute, who had helped the spies escape from certain capture, had found her place in the nation of Israel through her faith in their God. The first sin of the new nation in the promised land had taken place in Jericho, when a man by the name of Achan had disobeyed the command to destroy everything and had kept some of the spoil for himself. His sin had cost Israel dearly as, despite their victory at Jericho, they were immediately defeated by the much smaller city of Ai because God would not go out with their troops.[5] Joshua had cursed Jericho that day, stating that whoever rebuilt the city would lay its foundations at the cost of the life of his oldest son and would restore its gates with the life of his youngest son.[6] The curse remained unfulfilled for more than five hundred years until the wicked king Ahab rebuilt it – his firstborn son and his youngest son both died in the process.[7] Since then, many palaces and fortresses had been built there. The Roman, Mark Anthony, gave his balsam plantations in Jericho to

---

5. Joshua 7.
6. Joshua 6:26.
7. 1 Kings 16:34.

his Egyptian lover, Cleopatra, as a gift. She, in turn, had leased them to the infamous King Herod for a very generous fee. For Simon, it was a city of mysteries and intrigue.

Large cities like Jericho attracted different people for different reasons. Some, out of desperation, came looking for a better life, but fell on hard times and became beggars. Others, like tax-collectors, were opportunists whose main aim was to exploit the larger population. These two groups were on opposite ends of the spectrum of society, yet both tended to live on the margins . . . discarded, excluded, disliked, and avoided.

As Jesus approached Jericho, many came out to meet him. They wondered if he would be like Joshua of old . . . the conqueror and liberator they all longed for. On the outskirts of the city, two blind beggars sat listening, hoping that some passer-by might bless them with a coin or some food. One of them, a man by the name of Bartimaeus, perked up as he heard the approaching crowd. Something was happening and he needed to capitalize on whatever it was.

"What is going on?" he yelled out at no one in particular.

"Jesus the Nazarene is passing through our city," someone shouted back.

"Jesus!" Bartimaeus cried. He turned to his fellow blind beggar. "This is the man everyone talks about so often. He raised that man Lazarus from the dead! This is the Messiah we have been waiting for!" And then turning his attention to the sounds around him, he began to shout, "Jesus, Son of David, have mercy on me!"

"Be quiet!" the crowd shouted back. They were embarrassed by the presence of these undesirable men and tried to block them from the visitors' view.

But Jesus would not be blocked from anyone. He stopped and asked that the two men be brought to him. "You cried out to me. What is your request?"

Bartimaeus groped at the air, as if wanting to touch Jesus. "Lord," he said with a raspy, emotionally charged voice, "I want to see again . . . we want to see again."

Jesus, filled with compassion, stretched out his hands and touched their eyes. It had been a long time since anyone other than their fellow beggars had touched them with kindness, so at first they flinched, expecting a shove or a slap. Instead, they heard Jesus say, "Receive what you desire. Your faith in me has healed you."

Both men shouted out joyfully as they received their sight. Together with the crowds of people around them, they praised God as they followed Jesus into the city.

"I never get tired of hearing this sort of praise from the lips of those who have been touched by Jesus," Simon said to Andrew.

* * *

Many in Jericho had hoped that Jesus would stop and spend some time with them, but Jesus hurried through as if he was needed elsewhere. As the group began to ascend up the path on the other side of the city, they came to a large sycamore tree with quite a broad canopy of dense, dark green, heart-shaped leaves. Townsfolk did not plant sycamores close to their houses as the extensive root system could topple stone walls. To everyone's surprise, Jesus stopped right under the tree and looked up.

"Zacchaeus," Jesus said, apparently speaking to the tree itself. "Come down from your perch. You are to offer us hospitality for the night."

They all looked up. At first nothing happened. Then the leaves of the tree began to rustle as someone started to climb down. A smallish man emerged and dropped to the ground. Some of the locals spat on the ground, hissing, "Tax-collector!"

"Forgive me, teacher," the small man said. "I could not see you over the crowds." He grinned and laughed nervously, "I am short, as you can see. But you are welcome." Then looking at the disciples he quickly added, "You are all welcome."

"I don't believe it," Simon heard a woman say to a man who appeared to be her husband. "He has chosen to stay with that hateful man instead of with any one of us!"

Jesus put his arm around Zacchaeus's shoulders and walked alongside him. As always, Jesus did what most people did not expect. He was associating with what many considered the dregs of society – first a beggar . . . now a tax-collector.

* * *

That evening as they reclined at the table, Zacchaeus suddenly stood up. He had been talking earnestly with Jesus all day, listening intently, and nodding vigorously from time to time. Simon could see that something Jesus had said had touched the small man deeply.

"Lord," he began.

Ah, the first good sign, Simon thought. He has changed the title of address from "teacher" to "lord." It never ceased to amaze Simon how Jesus could focus on one specific individual, as if that individual was the only person in the world at that moment. Jesus also possessed the amazing ability to speak directly into that person's life as if he had known them personally for many years.

"Lord," Zacchaeus continued, "tonight I vow to give away half my possessions to the poor. And for those whom I have defrauded, I pledge to give back fourfold what I have stolen from them as is required by the law, just like King David promised."[8]

At first, no one really knew how to respond. Then Matthew quietly rose from the table and walked over to embrace Zacchaeus. At this, they all cheered loudly and praised God for bringing another son of Abraham back into the fold.

"This is why I came into the world," Jesus said, leaning over to Simon. "I came to seek and to save the lost."

Later, Simon recalled these words . . . words spoken shortly before the momentous events that were soon to take place in Jerusalem. Was Jesus thinking of Zacchaeus while he was on the cross?

* * *

Jesus gestured that they all needed to be quiet. He knew that many people thought he was on his way to Jerusalem to re-establish the kingdom of Israel and he wanted to correct their thinking.

"There was a high-ranking person," Jesus began, "who went overseas to be appointed king over his country."

"That is what Herod Archelaus did," Philip whispered. "He wanted Caesar Augustus to appoint him king."[9]

"Yes," Simon replied, "and that after he slaughtered three thousand people in the temple precincts!"

"But he was later banished to Gaul, wasn't he?" asked Andrew.

"Yes," Philip whispered back, "but only after he had angered many of our people."

"Before the man left," Jesus continued, "he summoned some of his servants, gave each one of them ten coins, and told them to put the coins to good use. But his subjects hated him so much, that after he had left, they sent a delegation stating clearly that they did not want him as their king."

"That's exactly what happened to Herod Archelaus!" Philip said.

"But they were not successful," Jesus continued. "He returned as their king. Then he called his servants to account for the money he had entrusted to them. The first said he had made an extra ten coins."

"Oh, I have heard this story before," Thomas said.

"Yes, but not quite like this," Simon said, shushing him.

"He's going to tell us now that the second servant made five more, and the last servant did nothing with the money because he feared his master."

---

8. Exodus 22:1; Leviticus 6:4–5; Numbers 5:7; 2 Samuel 12:6.
9. See Josephus, *Wars* 1.32.6–8, and *Antiquities* 17.11.4.

"Well done, Thomas," Jesus said. "You remembered. Now, can you remember the point of the story?"

"Yes," Thomas answered. "The coins were taken away from the last servant and given to the first, because . . ." Thomas started to blush. He could not recall the application.

"Because those who are faithful will have more entrusted to their care, while those who are not faithful, will lose all they once had," Andrew filled in.

"Exactly!" Jesus said. "And then, the newly crowned king judged those who had dared to oppose his enthronement."

"I don't think we are talking about Herod Archelaus any longer," Philip whispered.

"What makes you say that?" Thomas asked. "Archelaus did execute many who opposed him."

"True," Philip replied, "but somehow I think Jesus is referring to himself . . . and those who have opposed him for so long. Perhaps we are about to witness the day of reckoning."

"Do you believe that?" Simon asked.

"Well, I know something is about to happen. Jesus is very serious about this trip to Jerusalem . . . it seems that he is planning something big."

"From your lips to God's ears," Simon replied. Perhaps, he is right, he thought to himself. Jesus has been very focused . . . almost as if he is in a hurry to get to Jerusalem. We will just have to wait and see.

* * *

They left early the next morning, shortly after Jesus had returned from his time with the Father. Zacchaeus provided them with more food than they could possibly eat for a week. The small man had already surprised a few of his neighbours with gifts and apologies. It was wonderful to see the joy of his salvation.

Mary, Martha, and Lazarus were thrilled to see Jesus and his disciples again, and soon they were being fussed over by their three dear friends. There were still six days to go before Passover and their compound was abuzz with friends and family who were on their way to attend the feast. The trio were a little concerned as they had heard rumours that the leaders had given strict orders that if anyone knew Jesus's whereabouts, they were to report it to the authorities so that they could arrest him. As always, however, Jesus was at peace.

That evening, as they reclined at the table, Mary took a large container of pure nard – a rather expensive anointing oil – poured it over Jesus's feet, and began to wipe his feet with her hair. It was her way of expressing her gratitude for all he meant to them as a family. The whole house was filled with the rich aroma.

"Oh, so now it is acceptable to be wasteful, is it?" Judas spat out. "That nard costs a fortune! It's worth more than a whole year's wages! We could have sold it and given the money to the poor."

Mary looked startled at the sudden angry outburst. She was hurt and confused. Her eyes brimmed with tears. John looked over at Simon and raised his eyebrows. Something was wrong with Judas.

"Stop it!" Jesus said, clearly annoyed. "Mary saved this anointing oil for the time of my burial. There will be time enough to do good to the poor because they are always around you, but I will not always be with you."

There was a tense silence in the house for a moment. But then they heard the sound of many voices outside the door. People had heard that Jesus was there, and they had come to see him – and Lazarus – because word had spread that Lazarus had been raised from the dead. In fact, rumours were circulating that the leaders were seeking to execute Lazarus as well as Jesus, because many people had become convinced that Jesus was the Messiah because of the miracle.

Jesus stood up and went outside to greet them. No one noticed Judas slinking off into the shadows.

23

The Gathering Storm

It was cool the next morning. The fragrance of the pure nard used by Mary the night before to anoint Jesus's feet still lingered in the air. Simon quietly tiptoed outside. The air was sweet and crisp. The almond trees in Bethany were covered with subtle pink blossoms, a somewhat startling contrast to the blood-red poppies that blanketed the ground. It was slightly overcast and there was a gentle breeze from the west. Simon looked up at the sky. Would it rain? One never knew if it would or would not at this time of year.

Simon noticed that Jesus was standing alone on the far side of the courtyard, praying, hands stretched out, palms facing upward as if to receive a gift. Simon thought that Jesus had seemed overly tense the past few days . . . something was on his mind. He kept on talking about his death as if this was imminent. Even last evening when Judas had challenged what appeared to be a waste of expensive perfume, Jesus referred to it as an act of preparatory anointing for his burial. None of the disciples understood this sudden heaviness. It had shattered the atmosphere of festivity that had filled the room up until that point. To be sure, rumours abounded that Jesus's opponents were plotting to kill him, but that had never seemed to bother him before. Not like now . . .

This sombre mood of Jesus was all the more difficult to understand because there seemed to be every reason for rejoicing. Many people had heard that he had arrived and all sorts of expectant rumours were circulating. Those who had been at the raising of Lazarus continued to spread the word about this miracle-working rabbi . . . and on top of that, this was a very hopeful time . . . Passover. The whole land seemed to be filled with pilgrims. Inquisitive people flocked to see the resurrected Lazarus, and as a result of the miracle, they put their faith in Jesus. This was a threat to the chief priests, of that they were very aware. But Jesus had triumphed over disease, demons, and death itself . . . what were a few threats from the leaders when the crowds were on their side?

"Today we go into Jerusalem." Simon had been so lost in his thoughts that Jesus's sudden speech made him jump. "Tell the others. I need two of you to bring me a colt."

"A colt?" Jesus had never done anything like this before, so the repeated statement in the form of a question did not seem impudent to Simon. Perhaps he had not heard correctly.

"Yes, a colt," Jesus said, "one on which no one has ever ridden. You will find it tethered just as you enter the village ahead of us . . . untie it and bring it to me."

Simon turned to call the others, but he bumped into James and John who had been standing behind him listening to this strange request. The three disciples had become quite close over the past year. By drawing them closer to him, Jesus had drawn them closer to each other.

"If anyone asks you why you are taking the colt, just tell them, 'The Lord needs it and will return it shortly.'"

Most of the disciples had learned not to question Jesus even when they did not fully understand him, because over time, they had learned that everything he did was deliberate and significant. They believed that a constant need for clarity often revealed underlying doubt . . . after all, wasn't that what faith and trust was all about? Didn't the prophet say that the clay should not question the potter?[1]

James and John left immediately and soon returned with the colt, its mother in tow, meeting the rest of the group halfway between the villages. It had happened exactly as Jesus had said. They threw their cloaks over the colt so that Jesus could sit on it. A large crowd was gathering . . . many were coming out of Jerusalem in anticipation of his arrival.

This is it, Simon thought. Today is the day of salvation!

The crowds obviously thought the same as they began to throw down their cloaks before Jesus on the road, just like when Jehu was anointed king over Israel.[2] Some began to chant from the Psalms, "O Lord, deliver us! O Lord prosper us! May he who comes in the name of the Lord be blessed; we bless you from the house of the Lord!" Such expectation! For too long the Jews had been discontent under Roman rule . . . the Jews had longed for freedom ever since the squabble of the Hasmonean brothers had allowed the Roman General Pompey to take over under the guise of arbitration.

---

1. Isaiah 45:9.
2. 2 Kings 9:13.

"Brother!" Andrew had a look in his eyes that Simon had come to recognize as one of profound understanding. Andrew had learned the Scriptures well and could often rehearse whole passages at a time. "Brother, it is the prophecy!"

"What prophecy?" Although he was older than his brother, Simon had much to learn when it came to the memorization of the Scriptures.

"Rejoice greatly, beloved Zion," Andrew quoted from memory, "shout, beloved Jerusalem! Look, your king is coming to you. He is victorious and triumphant, yet humble too, riding on a colt, the foal of a donkey . . . to him all nations shall surrender, and he will rule from sea to sea and from the river to the ends of the world."[3]

"Yes!" Simon nearly shouted. "I knew it! That's why he has been so preoccupied lately! Jesus is openly declaring his right to be king! His time has finally come! Today is the day!"[4] And then he shouted for all to hear, "Blessed is the coming kingdom of our father, David! Save, O Lord! Glory to God in the highest!"

People were now cutting down branches and spreading them on the road before Jesus. Some had even brought palm branches up from Jericho, anticipating this triumphal entry. They truly believed that God's anointed king had come at last . . . come to set the captives free, to set at liberty the oppressed, to proclaim the Jubilee year! They flocked around him, some running on ahead, others dancing on behind.

Some of the Pharisees were indignant. They knew what the people wanted, and they were very afraid. Rome did not look kindly on those who spoke of any king other than Caesar. "Teacher," they shouted, "rebuke your followers! Tell them to be silent!"

Jesus seemed to be amused. "Silent? You want me to tell them to be silent? You don't understand. If they keep quiet, the stones of the walls will cry out!"[5]

They threw their hands up in the air in resignation. "Oh, what's the use?" they said. "Look, the whole world is following after him!"

---

3. Zechariah 9:9.

4. William Lane Craig says: "Jesus is deliberately and provocatively claiming to be the promised king of Israel who will re-establish the throne of David. His action is like a living parable, acted out to disclose his true identity. The Messianic secret is now open news. The triumphal entry shows us Jesus' messianic self-consciousness and who he took himself to be. He identified himself with the Shepherd-King predicted by Zechariah." https://www.reasonablefaith.org/writings/popular-writings/jesus-of-nazareth/the-triumphal-entry/.

5. I believe this statement of Jesus to be reference to Habakkuk 2:11 where the stones cry out in judgment against the rulers of the people.

At that moment, the company crested the hill and Jerusalem lay before them, basking in the early morning sunlight. The view was breathtaking. Simon thought that Jerusalem, glittering in the sun, looked like the snow-capped Mount Hermon. But unlike Hermon, the reflection from the gold of the temple was warm and inviting.

But with a shock, Simon noted that Jesus's expression had changed from mirth to deep distress. Clearly the view did not have the same effect on him as it did the other pilgrims. Indeed, the expression on Jesus's face was one of profound horror. What did he see that they did not?

"O Jerusalem!" Jesus sobbed. "If you, even you, only knew the source of true peace on this day . . . but you do not . . . it is hidden from you."

His whole body shook as he wept. Those who noticed were perplexed and didn't quite know what to do, but many were too emotionally caught up in the excitement of the moment. There was so much noise very few had heard him. "How odd," Simon pondered. "People can be so preoccupied that they fail to see the pain of others right beside them." He instinctively drew closer to Jesus. He didn't know what to do, much less what to say, but in times of grief, he knew that the mere presence of another caring individual could offer comfort. Andrew came to stand at his brother's side.

"O Jerusalem," Jesus said through his tears, "the days will come when your enemies will build a siege mound around you and trap you inside. They will annihilate you . . . you and your children within your walls. Not one stone will be left upon another because you were blind to the truth and did not recognize the time of your visitation!" After he said this, Jesus regained his composure and moved the colt forward once more.

Simon saw the blood drain from Andrew's face. "What is it, brother? What does he mean? Tell me!"

"I can't say for certain, but Jesus's words are similar to those used by Isaiah in his denouncement of Jerusalem. The prophet called for weeping and lamentation because God had pronounced the destruction of the city."[6]

"Surely not," Simon said. "That can't be right, can it? I mean he is the king foretold by Zechariah, is he not? How can his own city be destroyed? We are on our way to crown him king. Andrew, what on earth is going on? I just don't understand."

But the company was moving forward quickly now, down into the Kidron valley, and there was no time for further discussion. It would be a while before the disciples understood what had happened that day.

---

6. Isaiah 22. See especially verse 4 and 12.

Crowds of people were streaming out of Jerusalem to meet Jesus as he approached the eastern gate. There was much laughter and singing and dancing, exactly like the time when David brought the Ark to the city so many years ago. Whatever had happened on the crest of the hill was now forgotten. The people in the city were in an uproar. "Who is this man?" some people demanded. "Jesus, the prophet from Nazareth in Galilee," the jubilant crowd shouted in response.

Jesus now entered the temple precincts. The air was pregnant with a sense of expectancy. Everyone was waiting for Jesus to say something . . . do something . . . exactly what they didn't know, but they waited with bated breath all the same. "This is the day of reckoning," Simon mused. "The day everyone has longed for, yearned for, prayed for . . . but wait! Where is he going? He is leaving! Leaving without having done anything?"

The people also looked confused . . . they felt lost and dejected. They had been expecting something . . . at least some teaching, if not a rallying of the people to overthrow the Romans. But Jesus simply turned around and left without a word. Joyful voices faded away . . . arms dropped . . . branches fell to the ground. They just stood there and watched him leave the same way he had come.

The disciples followed silently, liked whipped dogs with their tails between their legs. They did not dare look the people in the eyes . . . . they did not understand Jesus's behaviour themselves. Simon suddenly felt drained, his emotions had been stretched from one extreme point to the other. He had been filled with such hope . . . such expectancy, but now he felt like they had missed the best opportunity they had ever had. The crowds had been ready . . . all Jesus had to do was say the word and they would have crowned him king. They had already hailed him as such. But now the joyful acclamations had ceased . . . the dust settled on the streets of the city as the people slowly left.

The hoped-for king had left the city, and it seemed, he had left them as well. The twelve silently followed him back to Bethany.

Simon wondered if it was just too late in the day to get anything started. Perhaps tomorrow. In one sense he was right. In another he was altogether mistaken.

* * *

The next morning, Simon still felt an acute sense of disappointment. Had they all been wrong? The crowds had been there . . . why hadn't Jesus declared himself to be the Messiah? Why hadn't he seized the moment like the judges and prophets of old had done . . . or like the Maccabees? He had them all . . .

right in the palm of his hand. He could have asked them for anything and they would have gladly given it . . . they would have even given their lives. Would he ever be able to recover the trust of the crowds?

Simon sensed that someone was watching him as he stood staring at the changing colours of dawn.

"We must return to Jerusalem. Come. We are all waiting for you." There was such tenderness in Jesus's voice . . . as if he understood the battle raging inside of his disciple.

Simon sighed. No, he did not understand, but Jesus had never failed him. He turned and shuffled after the others. All was quiet now. No jubilant, singing pilgrims . . . no foal . . . no spreading of cloaks or branches . . . nothing. Just the usual sounds of creation waking from a night's slumber . . . rooster crowing, sheep bleating, birds singing, donkeys braying, camels rumbling, and people starting their daily routines.

The sun was just beginning to show itself when they left Bethany. They had not had anything to eat as it was still early in the morning, but none of them really felt like eating anyway. No one had even given a thought as to whether Jesus was hungry . . . their disappointment had blinded them to the needs of anyone but themselves. Simon suddenly felt embarrassed when he saw Jesus approaching a fig tree. He's hungry, he thought.

This fig tree was a strange sight. Fig trees usually only begin to leaf at that time of year, but this tree was full of leaves. The dense foliage indicated the possibility of early fruit. It looked very promising, but on closer inspection, they found no fruit. Simon couldn't help but think that this was how he had felt about Jesus yesterday . . . Jesus, like the fig tree, had looked promising, but had not delivered.

Jesus too seemed disappointed. "May no one eat of your fruit again," he said simply and continued to walk towards the city.

They followed the same path they had the day before . . . down into the Kidron valley and up towards the temple mount. But in contrast to yesterday, this time Simon was dealing with thoughts of despondency and despair. Jesus had done nothing . . . none of Simon's expectations had been met. Simon tried to convince himself that he simply did not understand . . . that Jesus had his reasons . . . that he had a better plan . . . But Simon was not totally convinced. His feet felt heavy, as if they were caked with clay, as he trudged up the steps towards the gate.

Like the day before, Jesus entered the temple grounds. The courtyard was bustling, but not with joy-filled crowds singing and dancing and waving leafy branches. Money changers in their stalls were exchanging foreign coinage for the currency used in the temple, and merchants were selling all that was needed for sacrifice and ritual . . . all inside the temple walls.

Simon was filled with revulsion. It wasn't that there was anything wrong with the selling of sacrificial animals or the exchanging of foreign coins for local currency. Travellers, especially those from distant countries, needed to purchase animals and other ritual requirements for the festival, and they also needed to change their pagan coins for what was acceptable for use in the temple. What Simon was upset about was that the leaders were allowing the buying and selling, which was supposed to happen outside the temple precincts, to take place inside. This was the court of the Gentiles . . . the only place where people from non-Jewish nations could gather for prayer . . . but now it was a rowdy marketplace.[7] And then there was the price. They were clearly overcharging those who had no choice but to buy from them. "Thieves," Simon said to himself. "What is the difference between them and highway bandits? This practice surely turned people away from God rather than to him."

Then Simon heard a loud crash behind him and even louder protestations. He turned to see Jesus overturning the money changer's tables and chasing the animals and their keepers out of the court to where they ought to have been in the first place.

"He's doing it again!" Andrew shouted over the commotion.

"Yes, this is it! This is the beginning!" Simon blurted out, his mood suddenly changing. "Just like King Josiah[8] and Hezekiah![9] That's why he was waiting! Cleansing the temple is critical to any form of national revival. Why didn't I see that?"

"And don't forget Judas Maccabeus!" Matthew chimed in. "First the temple, then the nation! Liberty! Liberty, Simon!"

Riveting words coming from a former collaborator with the Romans, Simon thought. Just shows how much Matthew had changed over the years. Liberty! Freedom from taxation . . . freedom from oppression . . . freedom from foreign domination . . . freedom . . . finally!

As the last tradesmen left the court, Jesus turned and faced the wide-eyed priests. "It is written," he boomed, "my house will be called a house of prayer

---

7. G. R. Osborne, *Matthew: Exegetical Commentary on the New Testament* (Grand Rapids, MI: Zondervan, 2010), 761–62.

8. 2 Kings 22–23; 2 Chronicles 34–35.

9. 2 Chronicles 29–32.

for all nations![10] All nations! But you have stolen that from them! You have made this space inaccessible and turned it into a den of bandits!"[11]

Simon saw some movement at the entrance to the court. Would those robbers really dare to return and show their faces? But no. Who were these people? Some were being carried, others led by the hand, to Jesus. They were the blind and lame of Jerusalem . . . those who were often excluded from the temple because of their infirmities.[12] Now Jesus welcomed them with open arms and healed them all.

"See what he's doing?" Andrew said. "Once more he is opening the way for those who have been excluded in the past. The maimed, the blind, the weak . . . not the great and powerful of this world. Like the prophet Ezekiel said: 'I will search for the lost, and I will bring back those that have strayed; I will bandage the injured, and I will nurture the weak; but the fat and strong ones I will destroy. I will shepherd them in the right way.'"[13]

Hope-filled joy slowly began to seep back into the atmosphere. The jubilant praises of those healed were heard far and wide. Children ran into the court and took up the chant that had melted from the lips of those who were disappointed in Jesus's lack of action the day before. "Save, Lord! Praise be to the Son of David!" They skipped and danced about Jesus, laughing and singing as they did.

"Enough!" The chief priests and the scribes stormed up to Jesus. "Do you hear what they are saying?"

The children were startled by the sudden outburst, but Jesus gently took one of them by the shoulder and turned her to face him. He smiled, and the child beamed back at him. He touched her lightly on the cheek and then slowly straightened up to face his irate opponents. "Yes," he said, "yes, I hear them. Tell me, haven't you ever read in the Scriptures, 'From the mouths of nursing infants and children, you have called forth your praise'?"[14]

---

10. Isaiah 56:7.

11. Jeremiah 7:11. It is probable that the charge of banditry had more to do with robbing the Gentiles of their right to pray to God in this court than with financial extortion as Jesus specifically mentions the "nations" in his denouncement. Jesus says as much soon after this event in Matthew 23:13–15.

12. See also King David's rash oath in 2 Samuel 5:6–10 and 1 Chronicles 11:4–6; N. T. Wright, *Matthew for Everyone: Part Two* (Louisville: SPCK, 2004), 71.

13. Ezekiel 34:16.

14. Matthew 21:16; Psalm 8:2. Rabbis would often only quote a part of a passage expecting the hearer to fill in the rest. The verse continues: ". . . you have established a stronghold against your enemies, to silence the foe and the avenger." The songs of the children were an open rebuke against the hard-heartedness and spiritual blindness of the leaders.

Simon thought the leaders looked like fish just out of the water, their mouths opening and closing but making no sound. Without another word, Jesus turned and walked out of the temple grounds.

Just then Philip came up to Andrew. "Andrew, there are Greeks here who want to see Jesus." They had no doubt heard that Jesus had cleared the space allocated for them to pray, and they had approached Philip because he was from Bethsaida and fluent in Greek.

"Come, let's tell him," Andrew replied.

They came up alongside Jesus and told him about the request. Jesus stopped midstride and turned to look at the people around him.

"My hour has come," he said, as if to himself.

His hour, Simon thought. Jesus often spoke about his hour that was yet to come. The first time he had heard Jesus speak of this "hour" was at the wedding in Cana. What did this mean?

"The hour has come for the Son of Man to be glorified," Jesus said, louder this time.

"Yes!" Simon said under his breath. "At last. Now he will restore to us the kingdom!"

But Jesus did not announce his imminent coronation. Instead he returned to the theme of death. "Listen well. If a wheat seed does not die once planted in the ground, it will always only be one seed, right?"

Oh Jesus, Simon thought, not now. This is not the time to speak in riddles. Please, speak plainly before you lose the momentum again.

But people were nodding . . . they seemed to understand the agrarian imagery, even if only superficially.

"But if it dies, it will produce many seeds. In the same way, if a person is overly preoccupied with the preservation of their life in this world, they will ultimately lose it. But those for whom this worldly life holds no attraction . . ." Jesus paused to let this thought penetrate, "they will preserve their lives."

He's challenging us all, Simon thought. Our leaders are not prepared to acknowledge him as king because they fear that the Romans will come and destroy the city and the temple . . . and so in seeking to preserve their lives they will ultimately forfeit their lives. They care more for this life than for the truth! But what about us? Are we prepared to forfeit our lives for the truth?[15]

Jesus continued, "Whoever claims to be my disciple must follow me, imitate me, walk as I walk. That way, my disciple will be wherever I am . . . we

---

15. Cf. John 11:48.

will be as one. When people see my disciple, they will see me. My Father will honour such a person."

That's the image of the multiplication of the wheat, Simon thought. He is the one kernel and we are the seeds he produces. But what does that have to do with dying?

"I am deeply disturbed," Jesus said to his disciples. They could all see an inner strain . . . a struggle . . . it was evident on his face. His shoulders drooped and he sighed softly.

"But what should I say? 'Father save me from this hour . . . from the very reason for which I came to the earth?' Never! No, I have come to do his bidding even to the point of death."

Jesus's demeanour suddenly changed . . . he now had a determined look on his face. "Father," he cried out loudly for all to hear, "glorify your Name!"

There was a sudden rumble in the sky above them. The weather was unpredictable this time of year, so people were not surprised when they heard the sound. They thought it was thunder. But it was not thunder . . . it was a voice!

"I have glorified it, and I will glorify it again!" the voice said.

"An angel has spoken to him," a woman said to her companions.

"No," they replied, "it is just thunder."

"Thunder does not have words!" she shot back.

"This voice was for your benefit," Jesus said, "not mine."

"I told you it was a voice . . ." the woman said, but her companions quickly shushed her. They wanted to hear what Jesus would say next.

"This is the time . . . the time which is ripe for judgment on this world. Now the prince of this world will be driven out."

"What prince?" Simon whispered in his brother's ear. "Does he mean the Caesar?"

"I don't know, brother. That is not a term usually used for an earthly ruler . . . I think he means the evil one. Simon, has it ever occurred to you that he may be talking about something far bigger than what we think?"

"I will drive out the prince of this world when I am lifted up from the earth. Then I will draw all people to myself."[16]

"That sounds like he is saying he will be crucified," Simon whispered in alarm.

---

16. Cf. Exodus 19:4. In my opinion Jesus is using Exodus imagery here . . . God delivered his people from slavery in Egypt, defeated Pharaoh, and then drew them to himself at Mount Sinai.

The crowd was growing restless. People were no longer following Jesus's line of reasoning. Someone shouted out, "We have been told that the Law says the Messiah will remain forever!"

"That's right," someone else added, "so why are you telling us that the Son of Man is going to be lifted up? Besides, just who is this Son of Man, anyway?"

"Listen carefully and understand!" The tone of Jesus's voice was urgent. "The light is with you only for a little while longer. Walk while you have the light . . . before darkness overtakes you and you are no longer able to navigate your way forward. Trust the light now while you still have it . . . that way, you too will be sons of light."

It was a clear call for them to choose. To choose to follow him wherever he led them, whether they understood or not, or to be led astray by their leaders and their desire to maintain their present sense of security, thus giving up their only chance for true liberation . . . for true life. It seemed as if they understood the challenge because they were too stunned to say anything further. With that, Jesus turned and left the city.

This time the disciples did not retreat in silence and shame. To the contrary, they couldn't wait to see what Jesus would do next. He clearly had a plan. Maybe he would reveal himself as king at the feast?

Once more, they spent the night in Bethany with their friends. Simon struggled to fall asleep that night. How could he have been so blind? He should have trusted Jesus as his light. How could he have doubted him? Wasn't this what the prophets had predicted? That people would not hear the message of the Messiah . . . that they would be blind, and their hearts would be hardened? Simon knew that many people in the crowds actually did believe in Jesus, but they were afraid of being expelled from the synagogues. They wanted the people and the leaders to think well of them and were therefore not prepared to take the risk of being marginalized . . . and so they missed the praise of God.

How terribly sad, Simon thought.

Jesus had clearly told the crowds that if they trusted in him, they would be placing their trust in God as well, because it was God who had sent him. In other words, seeing him was seeing the one who had sent him. Jesus had come to bring clarity in the midst of all the confusing teaching of the leaders – like a strong light shining in the darkness so that those who followed him would no longer be stumbling in the dark. Their leaders had added so many extra rules and regulations to the Law that it was hard to know how to live life.

"I will not judge those who hear me but don't keep my words . . . that was not the reason why I came into the world. I did not come to judge but to rescue, to set free, to deliver, to save," Jesus had said. "What will judge you are the very words I have spoken because they are really not my words . . . I only said what the Father told me to say. I have not spoken on my own authority. Whatever the Father commanded me to say I have said . . . and I know his command always leads to life eternal. So, my words are his words. You are rejecting the very words of God."

Simon resolved to never question Jesus's actions again. Looking back later, Simon marvelled at his naiveté that week.

* * *

It had rained during the night and the morning air was crisp and clean. Sunrays sparkled through the droplets on the leaves of the trees and puddles reflected the clear blue of the sky. The disciples were far more animated today as they made their way back to the city. Simon even had a bounce in his step.

"Rabbi!" Simon said amazed, "the fig tree you cursed yesterday . . . it has withered completely."

The sight of the once foliage-laden tree, now dried from the roots up, was in many ways surreal. Jesus's words, "May no one ever eat fruit from you again," had come to pass in a dramatically permanent fashion. The tree would be barren for ever.

"How did the tree wither so quickly?" the disciples asked.

"This is one of his acted-out parables," Simon pondered. "It has to be, otherwise it is arbitrary and makes no sense. But what exactly *does* it mean?"

"Have faith in God," Jesus said simply. "As I told you before, if you have faith in God and do not doubt him, you will be able to accomplish great things."[17]

As they walked on, they crested the mount and gazed once more upon the glory of the city. Surely the temple is one of the wonders of the world! Simon thought. And the city . . . is there any city like Jerusalem? The city of the Great God!

They stood in silence for a while, taking in the beauty of the view before them.

"Do you know," Jesus said, "that if you truly believe and trust God without doubting, not only will you be able to do what was done to the fig tree, but also you can say to this mountain, 'Go and throw yourself into the sea,' and it will be done."

Was Jesus looking directly at the city as he said these words? Simon wondered. Yes, he was . . . or more specifically, he was looking at the temple.

---

17. Jesus used similar words in Matthew 17:20.

Simon turned to Andrew, who was his trusted source for scriptural knowledge. "The day before yesterday, you thought Jesus was pronouncing judgment on Jerusalem and on the temple. Do you think this is what he is saying now? You know the psalm: 'The Lord is great and much acclaimed in the city of our God – his holy mountain – fair-crested joy of all the earth, Mount Zion, summit of Zaphon, city of the great king.'[18] Jesus says the mountain will be cast into the sea. Is he saying that Jerusalem will be taken over by pagans?"[19]

"I don't know, brother, but Jesus's words sound very much like Zechariah's prophecy.[20] Did you know that the fig tree was used by the sages to describe the nation of Israel? . . . and the prophets often spoke about God's coming to seek early figs from us but finding none.[21] This is all similar language, but I really don't know what to make of it."

"And how are we to ask for this judgment? Is Jesus saying we must ask God to pour out his judgment on the city? Will God even listen to such a prayer?"

Simon became aware that Jesus was looking at him. Had he heard what they were discussing?

"If you believe, you will receive whatever you ask in prayer," Jesus said. He smiled sadly and then led them on.

"Jesus is getting more and more difficult to understand," Simon grumbled to himself. "It can't just be me that doesn't understand . . . the others all look confused too."

Once more they entered into the temple precincts and Jesus began to teach those who gathered around him. It wasn't long before the leading priests and elders came to challenge him once more. "By what authority do you do the things you do? Who has given you permission? You have no right . . ."

Jesus looked up at them. For a while he said nothing and just stared at them. Everyone began to feel awkward. Then he said, "I tell you what. Let me ask you a question. If you answer my question, I will tell you from where I get my authority. John the Baptizer . . ."

---

18. Psalm 48.

19. In the Old Testament, the sea was often a metaphor for the pagan nations.

20. Zechariah 14:1–9.

21. "This foundational metaphor for Israel's spiritual health vividly blooms in the prophetic era. The time had come for God's people to yield fruit that would bless the world (Isa 27:6). Several times the prophets describe God as inspecting Israel for "early figs," as a sign of spiritual fruitfulness (Mic 7:1; Jer 8:13; Hos 9:10–17) – but he finds "no first-ripe fig that my soul desires." So in two exiles (Assyrian and Babylonian), God pours out the curse of barrenness (Hos 9:16), and Israel becomes a rotten fig (Jer 29:17)." Cf. https://www.thegospelcoalition.org/article/jesus-curse-fig-tree/.

A murmur went through the crowd at the mention of John's name. The people revered John as a hero . . . more than a hero . . . a prophet. Another righteous martyr. The leaders no longer looked so sure of themselves.

"John's authority to baptize . . . did it come from heaven or was it merely something he did of his own accord . . . something he made up himself?"

The leaders huddled together, talking to each other in hushed tones. One of them said: "If we answer, 'from heaven' then he will ask why we did not believe him." "But," another piped up, "if we say it was merely human . . ." Another completed the sentence, "the crowd will surely stone us. They believe John was a prophet . . . we can't say that."

Simon could not help smiling. Secretly he was overjoyed when Jesus confounded the smug leaders.

"We cannot say," they said, once more facing Jesus.

"Well then," Jesus replied, "I won't tell you by what authority I do the things I do."

The leaders looked shocked. No one ever dared speak to them in this manner and yet there was nothing they could say in response.

"But tell me what you think about this," Jesus said. "A man had two sons. He asked the first one to go and work in the field, but he refused." He paused for dramatic effect. "But later the son relented and went and did what his father had asked. But in the meantime, the father had also asked the other son to go and work in the field. That son had said he would do what his father had asked . . . but then he did not."

The people always loved Jesus's stories, but Simon especially loved them because he knew that there was a hook somewhere . . . like bait for fishing. Somewhere the story would turn and catch the listeners.

"Which one did his father's bidding?" Jesus asked.

One of the leaders scoffed and rolled his eyes. "Always the simple storyteller . . . who does he think we are? We're not the illiterate rabble he loves to attract."

But another replied, "The first."

Jesus nodded at his challengers and stared into their eyes. Oh, those eyes, Simon thought, they bore into your soul!

"Yes, the first," Jesus continued. "Listen very carefully . . . all of you. Corrupt tax-collectors and adulterers will gain access to the kingdom of God before you do, because they believed the message of John the Baptizer. They repented of their wicked ways and changed their lives. But you . . . you did not believe him. And even when you witnessed their changed lives, you still did not follow their example."

Oh, that must have hurt, Simon thought. Like a dagger to the heart.

"Here's another simple story. There was a landowner who planted a vineyard . . ."

"He is going to hit them with Isaiah's song about the Lord's vineyard!"[22] Andrew whispered to Simon. "This is something they will understand and I think many in the crowd will as well. This is a clear rebuke, brother."

"This man did everything necessary for the vineyard . . . he built a wall around it, dug a winepress, built a watchtower for protection . . . everything. When he went on an extended journey, he leased it out to tenant farmers. At the time of the harvest, he sent one of his servants to collect his share of the fruit. But the tenant farmers treated the servant with contempt. They beat him up and sent him back empty handed."

"He is referring to the prophets of old," Andrew said.

"They did the same with every one of the servants the owner sent. All were beaten and then sent back with no fruit," Jesus continued.

"No fruit," Simon repeated as if to himself. "No fruit on the fig tree . . ."

"Finally the owner decided to send his only son, whom he loved dearly. He thought that the tenant farmers would respect his son in the same way they respected his authority. But when they saw the son approaching, they hatched a wicked plan. Because this was the man's only heir, they decided that it was in their favour to kill him and thereby seize the vineyard for themselves."

The silence in the temple court was palpable. No one dared make a sound. Jesus was a master storyteller and he had strung them all along to this climactic point . . . they hung on his words, waiting with bated breath for the application of this shocking story.

"So the tenant farmers grabbed the son, killed him, and threw his body outside the vineyard walls."

"No!" A man in the crowd clearly could no longer contain himself.

"Yes, that's what they did. They murdered his only son. Now, what do you think the owner of the vineyard will do?"

The same man blurted out, "He will come and deal with those wretches himself! He will execute them and lease the vineyard to other more worthy tenants who will give him his share of the fruit!" If the situation was not so serious, this man's indignant outburst might have been comical . . . he was red in the face and spittle flew from his mouth as he spoke.

"Indeed," Jesus said. Then turning to his challengers he continued, "Tell me, have you ever read this in the Scriptures: 'The stone that the builders

22. Isaiah 5:1–7.

rejected has become the chief cornerstone. This is the Lord's doing and it is marvellous in our sight.'?"

"Simon! This statement is from the same psalm that the crowds were chanting as he rode into Jerusalem!" Andrew said excitedly. "He is declaring himself to be the Messiah!"

"He is?" Simon still could not understand why Jesus did not just say so in words that everyone could understand.

"Do you understand what this means?" Jesus asked. "The kingdom of God will be taken away from you and given to people who will produce the required fruit of right living. People who fall on this rejected cornerstone will be broken . . . but those on whom the stone falls will be completely crushed."

Simon glanced over to the leaders. Their faces were white with rage. It was obvious that they knew Jesus had meant they were the wicked tenants. But the leaders also knew there was nothing they could do as long as the crowds were around Jesus.

We are heading for a major collision, Simon thought to himself. The leaders may not say anything here and now, but they are clearly upset. He has exposed them, and they will want revenge. Their plots will continue as long as they refuse to believe in him.

But Jesus had not yet finished teaching. "What is the kingdom of heaven like?" he asked. "I'll tell you. It is like a king who prepared a great wedding feast for his son. You know how that works, right? You send out all the invitations and then when the food is ready, you tell those who are invited to come. Well, they refused!"

"Another retelling of an excellent story," Andrew said.

A collective gasp exploded from the crowd. "How rude," said a few.

"Indeed," Jesus said. He went on to elaborate, sketching the very scene of rudeness before the eyes of their imagination. Everything had been prepared . . . the host seemingly spared no expense . . . but those who were invited ignored the messengers, abused them, and even killed some. Most people in the audience understood that Jesus was talking about the way their ancestors had treated God's prophets in the past.

"The king was furious," Jesus went on. "He sent his army to destroy the murderers and burn down their city."

A hush fell on the crowd. What would the king do now they wondered?

Jesus went on to describe the king's radically changed plan. He told his servants to invite the outcasts, the marginalized, and the disenfranchized, instead. So the king filled his palace with guests most respectable people would not consider inviting into their homes.

"This sounds like what Jesus has been doing, don't you think, brother?" Andrew said under his breath.

Simon smiled. "What? Do you mean me?" They both laughed.

"But," Jesus continued, "when the king came to meet his guests, there was one person who had not received a wedding garment."

"This is a change to the usual story," Simon said.

"The man obviously tried to get in his own way," Thomas said to the others. "He must have bypassed the porters at the door for some reason."

It dawned on Simon that Jesus was once again speaking out against the current leaders of the Jewish people . . . or, at least, those who did not believe in him. As Jesus continued it became clearer to them all. He spoke about the man without the wedding garment being forcibly removed and cast out of the palace into an inhospitable place.

Jesus spoke so much about judgment and yet . . . he did nothing. Simon just could not understand this. He knew that this very direct line of attack was going somewhere . . . Jesus was openly provoking the leaders and exposing them for all to see.

"All are called, but not all are chosen," Jesus declared.

"That's the key," Andrew said. Simon looked at him blankly. "Don't you see? Everyone was called to the feast, but because they refused, they forfeited the right to be present at the wedding. They did not respond to the invitation . . . either the first one or the second one. So, they were not chosen to be present . . . only those who responded were!" Simon still looked blank.

"Make way!" Everyone turned to see a few of the Herodians and some disciples of the Pharisees forcing their way through the crowd. They stood before Jesus in order to ask him a question. The disciples later heard via the Jerusalem grapevine that the Pharisees were trying to trap Jesus into saying something that would get him into trouble with the authorities. Their aim was to find adequate grounds to arrest him.

"Teacher," they purred sweetly.

"Oh, Lord, have mercy," Simon said. "Do they really think this will work?"

One of the Herodians gave Simon a withering look.

"Teacher, everyone knows that you are an honest man and that you teach the way of God according to the truth. You are no respecter of persons . . . you are not concerned with the opinion of others because you are not swayed as other men are by power or status. You are completely impartial."

Here it comes, Simon thought. First the honey, then the poison.

"So, we are wondering . . . what are your thoughts on Roman taxation? Should we pay Caesar or not?"

"You play your parts well . . . play actors the lot of you! Why are your testing me? Show me the coin used for the tax!" Jesus was clearly irritated.

They handed him a coin.

Jesus held the coin up for all to see. It was a Roman coin . . . a denarius. It was not a coin most pious Jews would have on them, not only because it had the image of Caesar on it, but also because of the inscription, "Tiberius Caesar, son of the Divine Augustus." Local coins did not have the profile of the Caesar stamped on them . . . the Jews considered the image on the denarius idolatrous.[23]

"Whose image and inscription are stamped on this coin?" Jesus asked the crowd.

"Caesar's," they shouted in unison. Some spat on the ground in revulsion.

"Well then," Jesus said, handing back the coin, "give to Caesar what is Caesar's. But," he paused for a moment, looking directly into the eyes of the frustrated group, "give to God what belongs to God."

His reply so shocked the leaders that they spun on their heels and left immediately.

But the attacks were not over. The Sadducees also approached Jesus and told him a highly unlikely tale about a woman who married seven brothers, one at a time, with each husband dying before producing an heir. The story was hypothetical, of course, but the challenge was very real – was there a resurrection or not? Simon knew the Sadducees did not believe in resurrection . . . they believed that this life was all there was. This was convenient for them because, if there was no resurrection, then there were no consequences to the way they lived. They also only read the five books of Moses . . . nothing else.

Typical, Simon thought. When you don't want to believe in something that will have an effect on the way you want to live, then simply deny that it exists.

Once again Jesus pointed out their misunderstanding of the very Scriptures in which they claimed to believe. After indicating that marriage was an earthly institution, therefore the rules of marriage would not apply in the hereafter, Jesus simply reminded them that Moses referred to the Lord as the God of Abraham, Isaac, and Jacob . . . and Moses said this long after the patriarchs had died. God, Jesus said, was the God of the living, not the God of the dead.

"Well said, Teacher," the teachers of the law responded. The crowds were dazzled by his teaching, but the Pharisees who overheard the discussion were not at all happy. They had overheard the debate and were still intent on

---

23. Osborne, *Matthew*, 809.

discrediting Jesus. So one of them, an expert in matters of the law, asked Jesus to tell them which one of the commandments was the most important.

How they love to nitpick, Simon thought. Aren't all the commandments equally important? Break one and you break them all. How can one be more important than the other? How can one be "great," and another be "little"[24] when they reflect the mind of God?

But Jesus was not going to be drawn into that argument. He recited the Shema, leaving no door for disagreement. "Hear O Israel! The Lord is our God, the Lord alone. You shall love the Lord your God with all your heart and with all your soul and with all your might!" But there was a sting in what he said next. "The second is like it. You must love your neighbour even as you love yourself. There is no commandment greater than these."

They hadn't asked him for a second, most-important law, Simon reflected. Jesus's addition caught them by surprise. It is relatively easy to make a show of loving an invisible being through pious words and rituals . . . but it is an altogether different thing to demonstrate that love in a tangible way that can be seen and experienced by all.

The law expert seemed at a loss for words. He had prepared himself for some back and forth, but Jesus's reply deflated him. The best response he could come up with was simply, "Well said, Teacher. You are right. There is only one God and to love him with your entire being . . . as well as to love your neighbour . . . is more important than all the burnt offerings and sacrifices."

Jesus seemed surprised that the expert had not countered him. Simon noticed that Jesus was looking into the man's eyes . . . that look . . . those eyes. That look was like having every layer of your life peeled away until there was only the essence of your being left . . . the real you that he could see clearly.

"You have answered wisely," Jesus said. "It is clear that you are not far from the kingdom of God."

For a moment the man looked pleased, but then he became aware of his fellow Pharisees around him and he broke eye contact with Jesus. No one else dared to ask Jesus another question . . . they would have to regroup and devise another devious plan.

"I just don't understand," Simon whispered to his brother. "Why don't they believe? If a thick head like me can see that Jesus is the Messiah, why can't they? They know the Scriptures better than any one of us does . . . besides, Jesus, of course."

---

24. "Jewish rabbis counted 613 individual statutes in the law and attempted to differentiate between "heavy" (or "great") and "light" (or "little") commands," *Archeological Study Bible*, 1650.

"Brother, learning in itself can make one dull . . . especially when all you learn is how to dissect and reinterpret the Scriptures. That's what they do all day long . . . debate the meaning of words and numbers . . . so much so that they miss the real meaning of what they learn."

But before the group left, Jesus had his own question to pose to them. "Tell me," he said, "how is it that you teachers of the Law call the Messiah the Son of David when David himself, speaking under direction of the Holy Spirit of God, said, 'The Lord said to my Lord, "Sit at my right hand while I make your enemies your footstool."' If David refers to him as his lord, how then is it possible for the Messiah to be his son?"

The crowd was delighted because Jesus had floored the leaders again. But Simon was convinced a showdown was coming. These men were powerful, and they were being backed into a corner. Only God knew how long it would be before their humiliation would cause them to act rashly. But maybe that is exactly what Jesus wanted . . . a choice had to be made by everyone whether to follow him or to continue life in their own way . . . a way that, as Jesus was showing them, meant their lives were like broken cisterns that could hold no life-giving water.[25]

The expert on the law no longer looked pleased. He had chosen his side. The Pharisees turned to walk away without even responding to Jesus's last question, but then they stopped as they heard Jesus address the crowds once more.

Jesus launched into a long series of "woe pronouncements," like the prophets used to do long ago. The speech was a long disclosure of the leaders' hypocrisy. They held positions of authority, they did not practice what they preached . . . they simply added burdens to an already overburdened people. Everything they did was for show and while they went to great lengths to obey the law, they missed the essence of the law completely. They were cruel in their religiosity and their hearts did not reflect the mercy of the God they claimed to represent. Jesus likened them to white-washed tombs . . . beautiful to behold but full of unclean things.

Did he just call them snakes? Simon was silently aghast. He had never heard Jesus speak so harshly before. It was shocking. Simon remembered what God had told Abraham about the sins of the Amorites. Their punishment would come in the future because their sins would not have been complete until then.[26] And now, Jesus was laying the collective guilt of the nation on

25. Jeremiah 2:13.
26. Genesis 15:16.

the Pharisees' shoulders. But Simon's mind was reeling . . . he simply did not know what to make of this denouncement.

"Be wary of these teachers of the law," Jesus said. "They like to draw attention to themselves. They dress in flowing robes so that they will be recognized and seen as important in the marketplace. They love to be addressed by titles such as 'Rabbi' or 'Teacher' and they jostle for position in the synagogues and compete for the seats of honour at banquets. Instead of caring for widows they cheat them, and then they dare to make a spectacle of themselves by praying lengthy and wordy prayers. Such duplicity will not go unpunished!"

Just then, a poor widow approached the nearby collection box. Rich people had been depositing their gifts while Jesus was speaking, making a great show of how much they were putting in. But the widow only put in two lepta, which was all she had to give. Pointing to her, Jesus said, "You know what? This widow has given more than all the affluent people put together . . . they gave out of their surplus, but she sacrificed everything she had."

Jesus then stood up. "O Jerusalem . . . Jerusalem . . . you who slaughter the prophets and stone those sent to you. How often I wanted to gather you to myself, as a mother hen protectively gathers her chicks under her wings, but you have repeatedly refused. Now you are exposed to the full force of God's fiery judgment. Your house will be left empty and desolate . . . nothing but ruins."[27]

"Your house?" Simon pondered. "He did not call the temple God's house, but your house . . . maybe he was not talking about the temple at all, but about their order . . . the Pharisees, the Sadducees, and the scribes." It was difficult for him to imagine Jesus pronouncing wholesale destruction of the indescribably beautiful temple structure itself. Surely it was still the house of God?

But Jesus was leaving. He stopped and turned to face the stunned leaders. "You will not encounter me again until you openly say about me, "Blessed is the one who comes in the name of the Lord!"

* * *

The disciples were confused. Had Jesus pronounced judgment on the temple or not? Had he just said it would be destroyed? In an attempt to clarify the issue, they pointed out the temple's magnificence to him.

"Yes," Jesus said, "but I tell you, not one stone will be left upon another . . . every one of those gigantic blocks will be forced off the other and cast onto the pavement below."

---

27. See 2 Kings 21:14; Jeremiah 12:7; 22:5; Ezekiel 8:6; 11:23.

They walked in silence for a while, each one trying to make sense of what they had just heard. Finally, they decided to ask Jesus to tell them when the things he had been speaking about would actually occur. They also asked if there would be any accompanying signs for what Jesus referred to as his coming and the end of the age.

In his reply, Jesus divided the question into two time periods – one filled with signs that would anticipate the destruction of Jerusalem and the temple, the other, the end of the age that would have no signs at all. In the first, he warned them that there would be wars, rumours of wars, famines, earthquakes . . . that they would be persecuted and even put to death. He described the end of the city in such vivid and horrific terms that the disciples shuddered. Jerusalem would be surrounded by armies, Jesus told them, and at that time they were to flee to the mountains. Those who remained in the city would be slaughtered or sent away into captivity. Jerusalem would be trampled.

He told them there would be some who claimed the Messiah had returned, and he warned them not believe them, because his return would be as obvious as lightning. He predicted the overthrow of the whole nation in prophetic terms, using the language of Isaiah, Ezekiel, Joel, and Zephaniah.[28] He spoke of himself as the returning conquering Son of Man described in Daniel,[29] saying that the nation would mourn when he came in judgment. But, like the king in the parable, he would then send out messengers to gather in those who were now invited in the place of those who had refused to come. There was an urgency in his speech as he told them this would all take place within their generation. How little they understood then . . .

But then Jesus spoke of another time . . . the time of the end. Unlike the predicted end of Jerusalem and the temple, he said there were no signs for the end of the age. It would be as unpredictable and unexpected as the flood. Everyone would go about their lives as if there was no coming judgment . . . that was how the end would be. It would be like a thief at night, or like the unknown return of a master who had left his household in the charge of a servant. So they were charged to be watchful because the return of the Son of Man would be when they least expected it.

Just who is this Son of Man? Simon thought, but said nothing.

Jesus went on to tell parables about wise virgins who were ready and foolish virgins who were not ready. He spoke about a man who went on a journey leaving three servants with varying amounts of money to use according to their

---

28. Isaiah 13:10; 34:4; Ezekiel 32:7; Joel 2:10, 31; Zephaniah 1:15.
29. Daniel 7:13.

abilities. The last was as foolish as the virgins and was subsequently judged. He spoke of a time of judgment when the Son of Man would be seated on his throne separating people from one another as a shepherd separates his sheep from the goats. The sheep will be rewarded with eternal life while the goats will be cast into eternal fire.

The images were so graphic, and Simon felt he was so dull . . . this was so hard to understand. What did this have to do with their current situation? Was Jesus going to restore the kingdom of Israel now or not? Why destroy the city and the temple? Why all this talk of judgment and eternity?

But then Jesus made it even worse. "You know the Passover is in two days, right? That is when the Son of Man will be handed over to be crucified."

Simon felt like he had just been punched in the gut. Passover. The slaughtering of lambs. Crucifixion. The Son of Man. What did this all mean? He just did not have it in him to ask any more questions. His head was hurting.

* * *

Unknown to the disciples, dark clouds were gathering and soon a storm would be unleashed on them like they had never known, the origin of which was not of the earth. And yet, as they would learn later, Jesus was in complete control. No one did anything to him that he did not allow. His hour had come, and he followed through in obedience to his Father's will.[30]

The leading priests and elders met in secret at the palace of the Roman-appointed High Priest, a man by the name of Caiaphas. There they plotted together as to how they might capture Jesus secretly and dispose of him permanently. The only thing stopping them from hatching this vicious plan was the Passover itself . . . they knew the crowds favoured Jesus and they did not wish to risk a riot. So they planned and waited for an opportune moment. The forces of darkness would soon grant them their desire.

While the disciples were sleeping, one of their own, Judas Iscariot, snuck out and went to the leading priests and the captains of the temple guard. He agreed to deliver Jesus to them for a price. From that time on, Judas looked for opportunities to betray Jesus . . . to betray them all . . . but in the end, the one he destroyed most was himself.

* * *

Jesus taught in the temple the whole of the next day. The crowds gathered early in the morning, eager to hear what he had to say. Strangely, there were no more confrontations with any leaders. It seemed as if the lines had been

---

30. John 10:17–18; 13:3. Cf. Philippians 2:5–11.

drawn . . . Jesus and his followers were on one side, while the leaders and their followers were on the other.

That evening, the disciples retired to the Mount of Olives with the other pilgrims from out of town. They slept under the clear, ink-blue, star-studded sky. All was peaceful and calm, and Simon drifted off to sleep easily. Although he still struggled with much of what Jesus had been saying since they arrived in Jerusalem, he had decided to trust him . . . who was he, a mere fisherman, to question the Messiah. Even the learned men did not seem to understand.

24

Into That Dark Night

Because the Pharisees and the people from Galilee counted days from sunrise to sunrise, while the Sadducees and the people from Judea counted days from sunset to sunset,[1] Jesus and his disciples celebrated the feast of Passover a day earlier than those holding to the Judean calendar. This suited the priests as it made it easier for them to sacrifice the thousands of lambs needed for such a large crowd.

On the 14th of Nisan, the first day of the Feast of Unleavened Bread according to the Galilean reckoning, Jesus sent Simon and John to prepare the Passover for them.

"Where do you want us to prepare it?" they asked.

"As you enter the city, you will see a man carrying a water jug . . ."

"A man?" Simon interrupted. No self-respecting man would be seen in public carrying a water jug.

"Yes, Simon, a man carrying a water jug. Follow him. Speak to the owner of the house he enters and ask him where the guest room is that has been set aside for the Teacher and his disciples to eat the Passover. He will take you upstairs to a large room already furnished and ready, and there you will prepare the meal."

Simon and John went and found everything just as Jesus had said it would be. They had their Passover lamb slaughtered as was the custom and began to prepare the meal.

* * *

That evening, Jesus and his disciples left the Mount of Olives and came down into the Kidron Valley on their way to the city. As they came to the steps

---

1. William Lane Craig, "The Triumphal Entry," https://www.reasonablefaith.org/writings/popular-writings/jesus-of-nazareth/the-triumphal-entry/.

leading to the gate, people were bathing themselves in the ritual baths as had become customary.[2] Descending into the waters in preparation for the most holy celebration was an act of contrition and a symbol of cleansing. People confessed personal and national sins . . . repented and resolved to keep God's Holy Law . . . and then ascending into newness of life, ready to meet with God in a spiritual sense on the Holy Mountain.

Jesus and his disciples now did the same. The disciples had often engaged in this ritual without much thought as to what they were doing. This time, however, was different, particularly for Simon. The long-awaited king was about to fulfil his dreams . . . not only his, but also the dreams of the entire nation! His self-awareness was acute . . . sharp . . . focused. As he walked up out of the ritual bath, he thought he was ready for anything.

* * *

On the way to the upper room, the disciples began to jostle for position around the table. There were two places, one on either side of the host, which were considered the places of honour. Who would sit on Jesus's right and on his left? Looking back, Simon felt ashamed . . . unknown to them at the time, this night was the darkest hour of Jesus's life, and they had been squabbling about who was to be considered the greatest.

As it turned out, all their arguments were to no avail. Jesus indicated he wanted John to sit on his right and Judas to sit on his left.[3]

Judas! Simon thought. He's not even part of the inner three.

But having thought that, Simon immediately remembered Jesus instructing people to take the lower positions rather than the higher ones. He quickly went to the lowest space, usually reserved for the person who served.[4] But he neglected to do the duty of foot washing . . . in fact, all of the disciples conveniently forgot about this demeaning chore.

After they had all reclined, as was customary since the end of the Babylonian captivity,[5] Jesus said, "I have been wanting to eat this Passover with you prior to my suffering. Hear what I say now: I will not eat it again until the significance of this meal is fulfilled in the kingdom of God."

---

2. *Archeological Study Bible*, 1748, note on 13:10.

3. John 13:23–26.

4. Luke 14:10. In John 13:5–12 it appears that Simon might have been the last to have his feet washed.

5. "Originally the Passover meal was eaten standing (see Exod 12:11), but in Jesus' time it was customary to partake of it while reclining," *Archeological Study Bible*, note on 14:18, 1655.

Simon looked over at Andrew, but it seemed clear that his brother had no idea what Jesus was referring to either.

As the meal was being served, Jesus rose, took off his outer garment and wrapped himself with a towel. He poured water into a basin and began to wash the feet of his disciples, drying them with the towel around his waist. There was an awkward silence as he made his way around the table.

Simon could feel his face burning, as if hot coals had been cast on his head. When Jesus came to wash his feet, Simon could no longer constrain himself. "Lord, are you really going to wash my feet?" he protested.

Without looking up Jesus simply stated, "I know there is much you do not understand Simon, but later it will come to you."

"No, Lord! I simply cannot allow you to wash my feet." Simon felt so ashamed. Why had he not done this loathsome task when he had had the opportunity?

Jesus looked up into his disciple's eyes. "Simon, unless I wash you, you can have no part of me."

"Well, if that is the case . . . then don't just wash my feet, wash every part of me!"

Jesus smiled. "Simon you have already washed your body, remember? All that remains is to wash your feet and then your whole body will be clean. And," he added looking up the group gathered together, "you are clean, though not every one of you."

Had someone forgotten to go through the ritual bath? Simon wondered as Jesus dried his feet. Who could have been so negligent?

When Jesus finished washing their feet, he put on his outer garment once more and returned to his place at the table. He looked at each of them, one at a time.

"Do you understand what it is that I have just demonstrated?" No one wanted to admit that they did not, so they all kept silent. So Jesus continued, "You call me 'Teacher' . . . you call me 'Lord' . . . and you are correct. That is who I am. I want you all to spend a moment contemplating this. If I, your teacher and your lord, have stooped to fulfil the menial task of washing your feet, you too must do the same to one another. I have given you an example to emulate. No servant is greater than his master."

All the disciples nodded in unison, although they were still trying to understand what Jesus was trying to get across to them. Did he mean they should literally wash each other's feet or was this act some sort of acted out metaphor?

230 Breakfast on the Beach

"No messenger is greater than the one who sent him. You will be blessed if you do the things that I have shown you."

Jesus must have heard us arguing along the way as to who would be the greatest among us, Simon thought. That is why he is talking about us serving each other.

"Remember when I told you about the pagan kings . . . that they lord it over their subjects . . . they desire to be seen as benefactors? But it must not be so among you!" Jesus urged them emphatically. "The greatest among you must be the servant of all. The one who rules must be like the one who serves. Who is greater? The one who reclines at the table or the one who serves? The one who reclines at the table, right? But I am here among you as one who serves."

Simon thought he was beginning to understand. As always, Jesus had turned the cultural norms upside down . . . or perhaps it was right side up. But he still wasn't clear as to the practical application of it all.

"You have all stood with me through thick and thin. When others left, you remained. Now I confer upon you a kingdom . . . as my Father conferred the kingdom on me. Because it is my desire that you all eat at my table in my kingdom and sit on thrones, judging the twelve tribes of Israel."

Simon glanced over at his brother. They smiled at each other. This was more like it . . . this was kingdom talk. But then his gaze met Jesus's. Was that sadness?

"I am, of course, not referring to all of you. I know those who are mine . . . the ones I have chosen. But in order that the Scriptures might be fulfilled, 'my ally in whom I trusted, even he who shares my bread, has been utterly false to me,' . . . I am telling you now, before it all happens, so that when it unfolds, you will believe me. Whoever accepts anyone I send, accepts me, and whoever accepts me, accepts the one who sent me."

A dark cloud came across Jesus's face. Something was clearly troubling him. Then he said, "One of you . . . one of the twelve . . . will betray me."

Simon nearly choked on a piece of unleavened bread. All the disciples were looking at each other. Who could it be? Simon motioned to John to ask Jesus which one he meant. John leaned back against Jesus and asked quietly, "Lord, who is it?"

"It is the one to whom I give the bread I am now dipping in this dish." Jesus dipped the bread, gave it to Judas Iscariot and said quietly, "What you are about to do, do it quickly."

Judas took the bread . . . then he sat up slowly, avoiding the eyes of Jesus.

What did Jesus tell him to do? Simon wondered. Was there something we forgot to buy? Where would Judas find anything to buy at this late hour? Perhaps Jesus means for him to give alms for the poor.

After Judas had eaten the bread, he left the room and stepped out into the darkness of the night.

* * *

When Judas was gone, Jesus said, "Now is the time for the Son of Man to be glorified, and God will be glorified in him. And because God will be glorified through the Son, God will bestow upon him his own glory . . . and this is all about to take place, even now."

Simon was still wondering where Judas had gone and why. Was there something he and John had forgotten?

"My dear children, I'm only going to be present with you a little while longer. As I said earlier to the Jewish leaders, so now I say to you all as well . . . you will seek me but not find me because where I am going you cannot follow."

Where is Jesus going now? Simon thought. First he sends Judas off into the night and now he says he's going somewhere too. What on earth is going on?

"I want you all to listen very careful to what I am telling you. I'm giving you a new commandment. Are you listening?"

Simon realized he had not been listening . . . he was too busy trying to understand the departure of Judas and now this talk of departure by Jesus. It was all so confusing.

"I want you to actively care for each other. I want you to love each other in the way same I have loved you. If you love as I love, then others will know that you are my disciples. If you love as I love, you will be like me . . . and that is a witness to me . . . one they can all see."

Simon simply could not stand the suspense any longer. "Lord," he blurted out, "where are you going?"

"Where I am soon going, you cannot follow now . . . but you will follow me later."

"I don't understand. Why can't I follow you now? I am ready to lay down my life for you."

"Simon," Jesus looked at Simon with such great tenderness, "Simon, Satan has asked to sift you all as one sifts wheat . . ." Jesus slowly looked around the room at his disciples. Then his gaze returned to Simon. "But I have pleaded in prayer for you, Simon, that ultimately your faith will not fail, so that, when you do turn back to me, you may strengthen your brothers."

"What? Fail? Me? No, Lord, I am ready to go anywhere with you . . . to prison or to death itself!"

"Really? You are willing to lay down your life for me? Simon, this may be hard for you to accept right now, but what I am telling you is the truth. I am not trying to hurt you . . . I am trying to help you so that when the time comes you will not be taken by surprise. Before the cock crows tomorrow morning, you will have disowned me . . . denied that you even know me . . . not once, but three times."

"Three times, I . . ." Simon did not complete his sentence. He really did not know what to say. He was deeply hurt by what Jesus had just said. Three times? He had never failed anyone in his life. How could he fail the one he had come to believe was the Messiah? Hadn't he shown himself faithful? Disown Jesus three times? . . . What did the rabbis teach about saying something three times? That it would be permanent! And Jesus himself had said that whoever did not acknowledge him here on earth would be disowned by his Father in heaven? If he were to disown Jesus three times, how then would he be able to turn back to him? It would be over . . . forever.

But Jesus had moved on. He took up a piece of unleavened bread, pronounced a blessing on it, broke it into enough pieces for each of the disciples, and then said: "Take this and eat it. This is my body which I am giving for you. Do this repeatedly in remembrance of me."

Remembrance! That was the great uniting theme of Passover. The meal focused on their deliverance from slavery in Egypt . . . it was a reminder that in the same way that God freed them then, he would free them again. But Jesus seemed to be shifting the focus from the past to the present, as if he was going to lead them to freedom and that this would become the new event to remember. Simon decided to put his hurt and confusion aside and focus on what Jesus was saying . . . this was important . . . he did not want to miss anything. Jesus was once more speaking about things he wanted to hear . . . liberation from oppression. That was Messiah-talk and Simon wanted to be in on it all.

The disciples continued eating in silence . . . each one trying to process what was being said. Every now and again, Simon thought he caught them looking at him, but when he looked up, they turned their eyes away. He felt a mild sense of panic well up inside of him.

They think I'm going to deny Jesus! Simon thought. They all think I'm going to fail. What if Jesus is right? No! I will be vigilant. I will guard myself and make sure I defend Jesus, no matter what happens.

* * *

At the end of the meal, Jesus took the last cup of wine and when he had lifted it up and pronounced a blessing on it, he shared it with his disciples. "This cup is the new covenant between God and his people . . . a covenant that is ratified by my own blood . . . which I will pour out as a sacrifice for you all."

He's going to fight! Simon thought. We are going to be part of his struggle to liberate the nation! He's going to fight to the death . . . shed his blood if needed . . . and I'm going to be right there beside him.

"Don't be afraid or discouraged," Jesus said. "Trust God . . . and trust me."

He sounds just like Joshua, Simon thought.[6] Just before the conquest, God told Joshua to be courageous just before they fought to take possession of the land . . . their home."

"There is plenty of space in my Father's home. If this was not true, I would tell you as much. I am about to go to prepare a place for you all . . . and once that is finished, I will come back and take you to be with me so that you may always be where I am. You know the way to the place where I am going."

"No." Everyone looked surprised when Thomas said what they all were thinking. "Lord, we don't even know *where* you are going . . . so how can we know the *way* to get there?"

"Thomas," Jesus looked at him with such compassion, "I AM the way . . . I AM the truth . . . I AM the life. To get to the Father you have to go through me . . . there is no other way. If you really knew who I am, you would know the Father as well. But you *do* know him because you have seen him."

The disciples felt emboldened by Thomas's enquiry, so Philip blurted out, "Seen him? Did I miss something? Lord, show him to us and we will be more than content."

Jesus looked at Philip with sadness. "You've been with me for so long now, Philip . . . don't you know me yet? Don't you realize that if you have seen me, you have seen the Father? So how can you ask me to show you the Father? Don't you believe that I am in the Father and that the Father is in me? Everything I have taught you . . . every word I have spoken . . . they are not just my words, but his also. Everything I have done, every miraculous work, has been done by my Father living in me."

The disciples looked shocked. This was not the first time Jesus equated himself with God, but was he saying that they were actually one and the same? That was what it sounded like to them.

---

6. Joshua 1:9.

Jesus sighed. "You must believe me when I tell you that I am in the Father and the Father is in me. If that is too hard for you to comprehend right now, believe in the evidence of the miraculous works themselves."

That they could accept. God had definitely been working through Jesus. There was no way any ordinary human being could have done what they had seen him do.

"Listen to me. You have seen me doing great things. But anyone who has faith in me will do what I have been doing . . . and even more, because I am returning to the Father. Whatever you ask in my name . . . anything that is consistent with my character . . . I will do so that the Son may bring glory to the Father."[7]

We will do more than Jesus did? Simon wondered. How? How would such a thing be possible?

"If you love me, obey me," Jesus said.

Obedience is the key to doing what Jesus did? But how can we obey when we cannot follow him to where he is going? thought Simon. He was sure the other disciples were thinking the same things.

"I will ask the Father and he will send you another helper. The helper will be with you all for ever. He is the Spirit of Truth."

Another helper? Someone other than Jesus? Simon preferred having Jesus stay than have another helper sent to them.

Jesus continued, saying that this helper would take up residence in each one of them. However, the words Jesus chose seemed to imply that not only were Jesus and the Father one and the same, but also the helper. This made it all so difficult to understand. How could all three be the same?

Jesus also indicated that their lives would be bound up in him, and that love and obedience were the key to this union. Through being in him, loving him, and obeying him they would gain access to the Father's home.

"I know you don't understand all of this now," Jesus said, "but the Holy Spirit, the helper, will make this clear and will bring to remembrance everything I have taught you."

Jesus looked at his bewildered disciples with such intense love. "I am giving you my peace. This is not the same kind of peace the world claims to give . . . it is greater than that . . . it is a peace that remains."

No one said a word now. They did not know what to say.

"Please don't be uneasy . . . don't be afraid. I told you that I will return . . . rest in that reality. If you love me, you will rejoice with me when I say that I

---

7. I believe this is the meaning of "in my name."

am returning to the Father because the Father is greater than I am. I have told you these things, difficult as they are to comprehend now, so that when they happen, you will remember and believe."

This must be as hard on him as it is on us, Simon thought. He tries to make it clear, but the more he speaks the more difficult it is to understand him.

"There is much I still want to say, but time is running out. The ruler of this world is on the move. But don't fret . . . he has no power over me. I am doing what the Father requires of me. Through my obedience, everyone will know that I love and honour my Father. But come. We must be going."

Where? Judas had gone. Jesus said he was going. Now we're all going. Oh, my aching head, Simon grumbled.

* * *

As they walked, they passed by a vineyard. Jesus stopped and turned to the disciples.

"I am the True Vine," he said.

"Do you know who the vine is, brother?" Andrew whispered in Simon's ear.

"Yes, the vine is us . . . Israel."

"So, if he is the true vine, then . . . ?"

"I don't know, Andrew. Could he mean that as the Messiah he is the head of the new nation?"

"And my Father is the vinedresser," Jesus picked up a branch that had dropped in the dirt. "He removes every branch in me that is fruitless, and he prunes those that are fruit bearing so that they may bear even more fruit.[8] Just as a branch cannot bear fruit unless it stays connected to the vine itself, so you too cannot bear fruit unless you stay connected to me. Is that clear?"

The disciples looked at each other. The meal had been too heavy. Right now, all they wanted to do was sleep.

"I am the vine," Jesus tried again, "and you . . . you all are the branches. Those who remain connected to the vine will bear much fruit. Those who do not remain connected . . . well, the branch that is not connected cannot bear fruit. It will be cast aside and burned. If you remain in me and my teaching remains in you, when you ask for anything consistent with what you have learned from me, it will be granted to you. You see, it is to my Father's glory that you bear much fruit."

---

8. I believe Jesus is referencing the prophecy of Isaiah concerning the Lord's vineyard. See Isaiah 5:1–7. The language, both here and in Isaiah, corresponds with Jesus's prediction of the destruction of Jerusalem in Luke 21:5–36.

Jesus went on to explain that the love he shared with his Father was a love demonstrated through obedience. That was why they were to love one another as he had loved them. He told them that the greatest form of love was sacrificial love . . . giving one's life for another. He added that he viewed them as friends and not as apprentices anymore, because he had taught them everything he had learned from the Father. Unlike other rabbis, he had actively pursued them and chosen them specifically to be his followers. He said the reason he had chosen them was so that they might bear much fruit – fruit that would remain. And all of this had to do with love and obedience.

Jesus told them not to be surprised when non-believers rejected them or hated them. Since they hated him and persecuted him, they would hate and persecute his disciples also.

Fair enough, Simon thought. That I can see . . . our association with Jesus will not make life easier. Just as he has been hounded by the unbelieving leaders, so we will be hounded too. If they hate the one, they will hate the other. If the leaders did not change their views after witnessing all those miracles, then how will they believe us?

"When the helper whom I will send to you comes – he is the Spirit of truth and as such he will bear witness of me – with his help, you too must bear witness of me. I've told you all of this so that you will not be led astray when things get difficult. They will throw you out of their synagogues. In fact, they will be so blind that they will think they are doing the will of God by killing you! They will do these things because they do not know me or my Father."

If the disciples had been awake enough, they might have been worried by what he said about them being killed. But they were sleepy and not paying much attention.

"I know you were disturbed when I said that I will be going away," Jesus continued, "but my departure is to your advantage. You must trust me in this. If I do not leave, the Holy Spirit cannot come. And you need him! Only he can convict the world of sin . . . only he can guide you in truth."

Jesus implied that the truth would be consistent with what they had already been taught . . . that Father, Son, and Holy Spirit all spoke from one mind. Then he added, "In a little while you will no longer see me . . . and then after another little while, you will."

The disciples began to murmur among themselves. They did not understand what Jesus meant when he said that they would no longer see him and then later, they would see him. It was all so obscure.

He explained that what he was about to do was like a woman giving birth, in that the delivery was painful and brought much grief, but once the child had been born, the struggle was largely forgotten, eclipsed by the joy of new life. He compared this to what they would go through shortly saying that this would be their time of grief, but soon they would rejoice again. He indicated that a day would come when their confusion would be something of the past. On that day they would believe that he had come from the Father and had entered the world and that he needed to leave the world and return to the Father.

At this point, the befuddled disciples indicated that they now understood and believed.

"You believe?" Jesus asked in response. "Very shortly, every one of you will desert me . . . you will leave me alone. But I am never alone . . . the Father is always with me."

Once more he warned them that they would have trouble in the world, but that they didn't need to fear because he had overcome the world. It was only much later that the disciples understood what he meant.

* * *

Then Jesus turned his face skyward and prayed to the Father. He prayed that the Father might glorify him so that he, in turn, might glorify the Father. He said that the work he had been given was now complete. Then he prayed for his disciples, that they would be one, even as he and the Father were one. He prayed that they would be kept safe, that they would be protected from the evil one as they continued to live in the world, and that they might be made holy by the truth of the Scriptures. He spoke sending them into the world just as the Father had sent him into the world.

Simon remembered the day Jesus chose them to be his twelve close followers. He called us the sent ones. Apostles. But are we ready? he wondered.

Jesus continued to pray, but now he prayed for those who would believe through the witness of his sent ones. The ultimate goal was that the world would know the Son and would believe that the Father had sent the Son. He prayed that there would be unity among all those who believed . . . a unity in love and a unity in him . . . that where he was, they would be also.

Once he completed the prayers, they went to the other side of the Kidron valley. As they walked Jesus turned and said to them, "This very night, all of you will fall away because of what is going to happen to me. It is written, 'Strike down the shepherd and let the flock scatter.' But after I have risen, I will go ahead of you to Galilee."

These words reminded Simon of what Jesus had said back at the table. Simon felt a bitter taste in his mouth. "Lord, even if everyone else deserts you, I never will." Simon meant every word . . .

"Simon, what I said earlier this evening, I will say again. Before the cock crows tomorrow morning, you will have denied me three times."

"No!" Simon almost shouted. "Even if I have to shed my blood with you, I will never disown you. Never!"

All the other disciples agreed.

Jesus turned and led them to an olive grove where they had often stayed on previous visits to Jerusalem. While the other disciples found soft spots to sleep, Jesus called Simon, James, and John closer to him. Simon was still smarting from Jesus's repeated statement regarding his failure to remain true to him, but he went anyway.

Jesus told the others to stay where they were. There was no argument or protestation. Most were already falling asleep.

"I am exceedingly troubled," Jesus told the three. "Stay here and pray with me."

He walked a little further from them and fell with his face to the ground in anguished prayer. They heard him say, "Father, if it is possible, take this bitter cup away from me." He was breathing heavily and it was clear to them that he was in great distress. "Nevertheless, I want your will to be done, not mine."

That was the last they heard until they woke up to find him standing over them. "Couldn't you pray with me for one hour, Simon? You need to be vigilant. The only way you can avoid temptation is through fervent prayer. Your spirit is sincere and willing, but your flesh is very weak."

This was repeated two more times. He prayed, they slept. Then they awoke to hear him say, "Are you still sleeping? My time has come . . . I am being betrayed into the hands of sinners. Get up, quickly. Look! My betrayer is coming."

They heard the sounds of a large crowd trying to move quietly, but not succeeding. Then they recognized Judas as he came up to Jesus and kissed him on the cheek. They learned later that this was the sign Judas had given the leaders so that they would know which one was Jesus.

Things happened so quickly. Jesus began speaking to the crowd, who were armed with swords and clubs. At first they fell back, but then they surged forward to apprehend Jesus. At that moment, Simon lunged forward slicing off the ear of the high priest's servant. But Jesus told Simon off, saying that those who lived by the sword would die by the sword. Jesus added that he had to drink the cup the Father had given him.

What? Simon screamed in his head. What of the talk of bloodshed? Why won't he let me fight? I said I would die for him . . . why won't he let me?

But Jesus simply stooped down and healed the servant's wound.

Then the crowd grabbed Jesus and bound him, and all the disciples fled, just as Jesus had said. One even fled naked into the night leaving his only garment in the hands of one of the mob. But under the cover of darkness, Simon and John secretly followed the crowd at a safe distance.

"They are taking him to the palace of the High Priest," John said to Simon. "Good, the family knows me. I'll go in and try to find out what is going on. You wait outside the gate. I'll see if I can get you in as well."

A large crowd had gathered in the High Priest's courtyard. Some appeared to be drunk. A mob is a frightening thing, Simon thought. It often takes on a life of its own that no one can control. People have been ripped apart by such crowds. As Simon watched, his fear mounted. In his mind, he played out all the possible scenarios over and over again. He almost fainted when the gate suddenly opened.

"You can come in," said the girl who kept watch at the gate. John stood behind her motioning for him to come in, but Simon hesitated. He was afraid, very afraid. But he had promised not to desert Jesus. When he walked through the gate, he felt like he had entered a den filled with ravenous lions.

Simon reeked of fear. Rivulets of sweat trickled down his back even though it was cool that night. He moved closer to the charcoal fire in the courtyard of the High Priest's palace. The pungent smell of burning charcoal filled his nostrils, but the warmth was somehow comforting. He knew he was shivering, so he leaned in to get control over his shaking.

Then he heard it. The short, sharp sound of a hard slap and a body crumpling to the ground. "They are going to kill him," he thought. "They are going to kill us all." His heart was racing, and he was hyperventilating.

That girl at the gate . . . she was walking his way and a sense of horror overtook him. John had asked her to let him in. She knew that he was with John and she knew who John was . . . what was she going to do? She raised her arm and with a crooked smile, she pointed at him. "He's one of them," she said to those around them. Then she spoke to him directly, "Aren't you? You were with this Jesus of Nazareth!"

Heads turned. Simon thought he was going to throw up. "You're wrong, woman!" he heard himself say, "I don't even know him." Simon could hear his pulse in his head . . . pounding, pounding, pounding.

"Leave now!" he reasoned with himself. "Save yourself while you are still able. You can't help him anymore." But he stayed.

There was yelling and Simon heard another slap. This time there was laughter . . . evil laughter. He looked up. Jesus's face was bleeding. They had pulled out his beard. "Oh, sovereign God in heaven! Help!" he prayed silently.

It felt like there were fingers around his throat pressing harder and harder. His hands were cold and clammy. He tried in vain to regulate his breathing. He clenched his fists, digging his nails into his palms, trying to deal with the rising sense of panic.

"Just don't move," he told himself. "Don't even look his way. Breathe normally. Stop shaking!" But he couldn't help himself. He had to look.

There were a few familiar faces in the crowd around Jesus. People they knew . . . people that had once been part of the crowds that followed Jesus. That was the hardest to deal with . . . the betrayal of friends. But how could anyone, friend or foe, laugh at the misfortune of another? Especially one as good and innocent as Jesus? Besides, a trial ought to be orderly and without violence. This was worse than a mockery . . . it was a travesty of justice. A trial at night wasn't even allowed . . . and just before the Holy Day and the Sabbath.

He moved towards the shadows. Why couldn't he bring himself to leave? He could hear Annas, the High Priest, asking Jesus about his followers and what he had been teaching them. Why this line of questioning? Were they trying to trap Jesus, he wondered? Simon knew full well that only the Romans had the right to put someone to death. Maybe they were trying to trick him into confessing to some form of treason? . . . maybe that he had been teaching his disciples things that would amount to sedition?

He could clearly hear Jesus's reply. "Everyone knows what I teach. I have been speaking openly in synagogues and in the temple. I have not spoken in secret. If you want to know what I have been teaching, ask those who have heard me speak. They know what I have taught."

"Indeed, they do," Simon mused. "Many who are gathered around Jesus now have been in the crowds, in the synagogues, in the temple . . . where is that Pharisee named Nicodemus that Andrew had told him about? Why is no one saying anything in Jesus's defence?"

But his thoughts were interrupted by yet another hard slap. The guard had slapped Jesus across the face. "That is no way to address the High Priest!" the brute shouted. Instinctively Simon stepped forward once more, but he stopped short of stepping into the light of the charcoal fire. The shadows kept him from being recognized . . . in the darkness he felt safer.

There was silence for a moment. Simon strained to hear what was happening . . . he did not dare move closer. He could barely see Jesus who was still standing in spite of the vicious blow.

"You must prove if I have said anything wrong," Jesus spoke with difficulty because his mouth was bleeding, and his lip was badly swollen. "Since I am speaking the truth you have no reason to beat me."

It amazed Simon that Jesus did not retaliate. Surely, the man who calmed the storm, who faced a legion of demons, who robbed the grave, could silence these lawbreakers? But when they hurled their insults at him, for the most part, he simply remained silent. Jesus was not acting like a man who was fighting for his life. It was as if he had entrusted himself to another judge . . . one who always did what was right . . . and, in spite of the verbal and physical abuse afflicted on him, he was at peace.

There was a sudden commotion and Simon realized they were taking Jesus to another part of the compound.[9] They stopped before the house of Caiaphas, the Roman-appointed High Priest and there Simon saw the whole Jewish Council assembled. They had, no doubt, been debating the case amongst themselves while Jesus was being detained by Annas. Jesus was now closer to him. Simon could see the blood and the bruises . . . the raw patch of flesh where his beard had been pulled out. He stifled a sob. Sour bile burned his throat. This was his master . . . his teacher . . . his friend . . .

Some men were shouting, "We heard this man say that he would destroy the temple and raise up another in three days!" They were arguing. Some shouted one thing, others shouted something else. They obviously had not understood Jesus's words correctly.

In the midst of this chaos, Caiaphas stood up. "You choose to remain silent, do you? Won't you defend yourself against these accusations?" When he received no answer, he said in a loud voice, "Then tell us this. Are you the Messiah, the son of the Blessed One?"

Oh, Jesus, Simon thought, don't say anything. They will only distort the true meaning of your words.

There was silence for a very brief period and then Simon heard Jesus say clearly, "I AM."

Did he just invoke the name of God? Does he want to die?

Jesus spoke again. "And you," he looked about at all those standing around him, "you will see the Son of Man seated in the place of power at the right hand of God Almighty as he comes with the clouds of heaven."[10]

Simon felt his knees grow weak. There was no going back now. He knew the prophecy from Daniel . . . he did not understand it, but he knew who Jesus had just claimed to be.

---

9. See *Life Application New Testament Commentary*, page 452, commentary on John. Caiaphas lived in the same compound as Annas.
10. Daniel 7:13.

And the High Priest knew too. "Why do we need further witness?" He tore his robe as he thundered out, "You have all heard the blasphemer. Pronounce your verdict!"

"Guilty!" they all shouted. "He deserves to be killed!" At that moment the mob went wild. They spat on Jesus, blindfolded him, and screamed at him. They hit him with their fists and mockingly demanded that he prophesy as to who hit him. The guards too were striking and slapping him. There was no semblance of order anymore. Absolute mayhem ensued.

Suddenly, Simon realized he had inadvertently moved back into the light of the fire. He felt a hand on his shoulder. He almost yelled as he spun round, eyes wide, and mouth open. The man before him had a wicked grin. "You are one of his disciples, aren't you?" The question slithered out of the man's mouth like a serpent. Simon overreacted and pulled away a bit too quickly. "Don't be ridiculous!" he spat out. "I'm not one of the man's disciples!"

"You have a Galilean accent," the man said. "You must be one of them."

Simon felt like he had taken a hard punch to the stomach. His heart was racing once again, and he was breathing rapidly. He struggled to regain control of himself, but before he could recover from the shock and retreat back into the shadows, another person stepped towards him. Simon noticed the guards looking their way and talking to each other, pointing at the group gathering around him. He felt a warm trickle of urine run down his leg. I'm going to die, he thought.

"Didn't I see you out there in the garden with this blasphemer?" Simon recognized the man speaking. He had been in the garden and had seen Simon cut off the other man's ear in his zeal to rescue Jesus. Where had that zeal gone now? At that time, there had been a group of them and Simon had felt confident in their numbers. But now, he stood alone in the face of a group of people intent on killing them all.

"A curse on me if I am lying," he almost shrieked. "I don't even know the man you are talking about!" He clenched his teeth and looked up, but instead of boldly facing his accusers he looked straight into the eyes of Jesus . . . those loving, kind, compassionate eyes that penetrated deeply into his innermost being. There were no words spoken, but Simon felt he could hear Jesus saying, "I have pleaded in prayer for you, Simon. You will come back to me, and when you do, strengthen your brothers."

Then Simon heard the cock crowing and heard the voice of Jesus speaking in his head, "Before the cock crows, Simon, you will deny three times that you even know me." Three times! He had denied that he knew him three times![11] Did this mean he was no longer a disciple of Jesus? Did that even matter now? He had failed . . . failed his friend when he needed him most. But worse! He had denied he even knew him! Jesus had plainly taught that in heaven he would disown anyone who disowned him on earth . . .

To Simon, his act of betrayal went far beyond that of Judas! Self-loathing rose up inside him like sour bile, erasing the fear he had felt only moments ago. He heard himself howl out from a depth he had never plumbed before. He was wailing, throwing dust on his head, ripping at his clothing, whirling about, blindly looking for the gate. Having found the exit and weeping uncontrollably, he plunged into the darkest night he had ever known in his life.

---

11. *Chazaka* – saying something three times makes it permanent: http://www.askmoses. com/en/article/228,503/Why-are-many-things-in-Judaism-done-three-times.html. https:// en.wikipedia.org/wiki/Chazakah.

25

No Greater Love

Simon had hoped that the sun would not rise the following morning, but it did. He couldn't remember a time in his life when he had wept so deeply. He had not even wept like this when his beloved parents had died. The pain he felt in his core being was so intense that it had caused him to vomit several times. His mouth was dry and tasted foul. The fear he had felt at Jesus's trial had been replaced by a deep, inner revulsion.

What kind of a man was he? Jesus had taught that the greatest love anyone could offer was to give their life for another. But last night, he had only sought to preserve his own life. He had valued his present, earthly life most . . . and now . . . now he had lost it. Everything he had longed for . . . everything he had hoped for . . . he had given up in a moment of weakness. Like Esau he felt like he had sold his birthright for a bowl of soup.

What was he to do? He had denounced Jesus. Three times he had emphatically stated that he was not his disciple. Then what was he now? He felt he did not know himself anymore . . . the person he thought he was had vanished. He felt like an empty cloud that looked promising, but in the end did not deliver anything. How would he ever face the others? How would he face his brother? How would he face his wife? Every vow he had ever made would be called into question now. He had broken his word . . . broken his promise.

He wished that the crowd had ripped him apart last night. Then he would not have to live with his failure . . . with his shame . . . with his lowness and cowardice. The scene before the charcoal fire was indelibly burned in his memory. Was forgiveness possible for one who had denied his friend . . . his master . . . his lord?

Simon could see much that was going on from his hiding place. Because of the stone walls, the sounds of Jerusalem were unavoidable. He heard every voice, every awful word of the blood-thirsty crowd and the chief priests and other leaders who egged them on. But who was he to judge them? They did what was natural for them . . . he had done what was unnatural. Was he then not worse than they?

He could hear them drag Jesus off to the governor, that awful man, Pontius Pilate, who had proved himself to be vicious and cruel. It was very early in the morning . . . Pilate was no doubt already in a foul mood. Simon heard the leaders accusing Jesus . . . saying that he had claimed to be the Messiah . . . a king. Pilate then asked Jesus directly if he was the king of the Jews. Jesus did not deny it.

Even now, Jesus? Simon wondered. Even now when you face certain death you maintain that you are our king? The dogs have tasted blood, Jesus . . . they will not let you go now until they tear the flesh off your body.

Apparently, Pilate did not wish to deal with the matter because he pronounced Jesus to be without fault. This simply caused the leaders to become more insistent. They claimed Jesus was instigating riots wherever he went, from Galilee to Jerusalem. When Pilate heard that Jesus was a Galilean, he had him taken to Herod Antipas who happened to be in Jerusalem for the feast.

Simon could barely see the crowd hustling Jesus along to Herod's palace and once they were inside, he heard nothing . . . nothing but raucous laughter emanating from the palace every now and again. What was the fox doing? He must be mocking him. The Herods never did deal kindly with anyone who claimed to be king of the Jews. A little while later, Simon heard the crowd dragging Jesus through the narrow streets back to Pilate.

Pilate once again attempted to dismiss the charges against Jesus, claiming that neither he nor Herod found any wrongdoing in him. He sentenced Jesus to be flogged and then released. At this news, the crowd erupted with a wild howl.

What?! Simon couldn't believe his ears. They are demanding the release of that insurrectionist . . . that murderer, Barabbas! Surely Pilate will not allow that? Even he seems to be at a loss as to why they want to kill Jesus.

But the leaders pressed hard, even accusing Pilate of political unfaithfulness. They said that if he released Jesus, he would be disloyal to Caesar. Pilate tried to appeal to the crowd, but then Simon heard them cry out something so shocking that he doubted his ears. "We have no king but Caesar! Crucify him!"

Pilate then appealed to them using a visible sign . . . the sign of washing blood-guilt from his hands. Perhaps he hoped they would understand their own law . . . that Jesus's blood would be required from their hands.

But the crowd yelled back, "His blood be upon us and our children forever!"

He has no choice now, Simon thought. Pilate is like me, he will do whatever he needs to do to save his own life.

And he was right. Pilate turned Jesus over to them to do whatever they wanted.

* * *

A cry of horror escaped from Simon's lips when he saw Jesus stumbling under the weight of the heavy, cross beam. He hardly looked human. They had flogged him mercilessly with a roman whip that had shredded his skin. There was a plaited crown of thorns on his head and raw patches on his face where his beard had once been. They had abused him almost beyond recognition! Simon began heaving, dry retching, as there was no more food left in his stomach. He wept until he felt he could no longer breathe. Oh, the horror . . . the horror of it all. He had never thought it could possibly end like this.

Then he saw Judas in the crowd . . . wild, screaming and pulling at his hair. Judas. The one who had put this all in motion. But Simon could not bring himself to hate him. His greed had proved to be as powerful as Simon's fear. They had both, in their respective ways, betrayed Jesus. Judas fought against the crowd, moving in the direction of the temple. He had to live with his irreversible error . . . Simon almost pitied him. When the heart is dark, the light may flicker, but not shine.

In spite of the agony that he was experiencing, Jesus still stopped to address the women . . . the very ones who always suffered for the prideful actions of their menfolk. The days were coming, Jesus told them, when the decisions of their leaders would bring unimaginable suffering on them all.

They took Jesus and two other men outside the city walls to a nearby hill. On the way, the soldiers made another man carry the beam when it became evident that Jesus was no longer physically able to carry it himself. Then Simon watched them as they stripped Jesus of his clothing. His body was so bloodied that he resembled a freshly slaughtered lamb.

Lamb! Simon could hear the priests slaughtering the lambs whose cries mingled with the cries of the one the Baptizer had called the Lamb of God . . . the one who would take away the sin of the world. He could hear once again the words Jesus had spoken the night before . . . words he had so misunderstood at the time. "This is my blood, shed for you." Blood . . . shed not by a sword. Jesus was *giving* his life to save theirs . . . greater love. Simon had no more tears to cry . . . he felt empty . . . dry.

He could hear the nails being driven through Jesus's wrists and feet . . . he heard the cross thud into place . . . he heard every word Jesus spoke, as if he was right there beside him. But he wasn't right there, was he? No, he was hiding . . . hiding from the Romans and hiding from the other disciples . . . but he could not hide from himself.

"Father," he heard Jesus cry out, "forgive them . . . they don't know what they are doing!"

Simon dared to look. The soldiers were gambling for Jesus's clothing. They had nailed the charge against him above his head: "This is Jesus, the King of the Jews." The leaders paraded before the cross like triumphant hunters, yelling abuse at him. They had objected to the charge wanting it to read that Jesus *said* he was king rather than that he *was* king, but apparently Pilate had refused to change it. And so, they continued to mock him instead. Yet here Jesus was, praying for their forgiveness. "How many times must I forgive?" Simon had once asked. "Up to seven times?" Oh, how ashamed he felt. How proud and arrogant he had been! The forgiveness Jesus was praying for at that moment had no limits.

Simon saw the Galilean women standing close to the cross. He could not imagine the pain Jesus's mother was suffering. Was that John? Yes, it was John . . . he probably felt safe because he was known to the High Priest. Simon was ashamed that of all the men, John was the only one there. He heard Jesus entrust his mother to John . . . where were Jesus's brothers?

Simon could hear the awful shrieks of the other two men on crosses, one on each side of Jesus. As their lungs filled with fluid, they pulled themselves up, pushing up with their legs, to be able to breathe. One was hurling abuse at Jesus, screaming at him to save them. The other yelled back at him. Simon heard his voice clearly. "Don't you fear God? We are guilty and deserve this sentence of death. But he has done no wrong!" Then the man turned to Jesus and said, between excruciating gasps, "Jesus, remember me when you come into your kingdom."

What? Simon thought. What kingdom? They are all about to die!

Then he heard Jesus's words, "This very day, you will be with me in paradise."

Paradise? What did that mean? Simon wondered. He had been taught about the collective place of the dead . . . a place Jesus also mentioned in the story he told of the beggar Lazarus and the rich man. The beggar rested in "Abraham's bosom" while the rich man suffered in flames on the other side of a gulf. Was Abraham's bosom paradise? What did that have to do with the kingdom?

Suddenly it began to get dark even though it was midday. As first, the onlookers were silent . . . only the anguished cries of the crucified men could be heard. But as the light from the sun quickly faded, people began to tremble in terror. Simon heard Jesus cry out in a loud voice, "My God, my God, why have you abandoned me?"

Simon did not need Andrew to tell him that Jesus was quoting from the Psalms.[1] And he knew that when Jesus quoted the first line of a psalm, he expected them to recall the whole psalm . . . what was the theme of this psalm? Wasn't it deliverance? Was Jesus perhaps echoing the despairing thoughts of his followers at that moment? They all felt abandoned by God and absolutely powerless in the light of what was happening before their very eyes. Perhaps Jesus wanted to encourage them to think through the entire psalm to see that their perception of abandonment was not true . . . that God had not despised their cries and that he had not turned away from them.[2] In so many ways, Jesus hanging on the cross was proof that God had not abandoned them.[3]

He heard some people say that Jesus had called for Elijah. Someone offered Jesus wine on a sponge when he complained of thirst.

Jesus thrust himself up to draw one last breath. Then he cried out again, "Father!" It was a dry, rasping gasp. "Into your hands I entrust my spirit!" As he sank back down, Simon heard him say clearly, "It is finished!"[4] Then there was the awful sound of a death rattle. Simon bit into his fist and cried silently.

But then he heard another sound coming from the temple. The priests were shouting that the veil covering the Holy of Holies had been ripped apart down the middle. The earth itself was now shaking. People were screaming and running to their homes in the darkness. "None of this is possible," Simon thought. "The sun has turned dark. The earth is shaking. It must be the end of the world." But it was not . . . it was only the beginning.

*　*　*

---

1. Psalm 22:1.

2. Psalm 22:24.

3. For a good article on this understanding of Jesus quoting from Psalm 22 see: https://www.truthortradition.com/articles/did-god-really-forsake-jesus-christ-on-the-cross.

4. Jesus's statement is a direct quotation from Psalm 31:5. As we have seen before with Psalm 22, when a rabbi quoted a line from a psalm, he expected his disciples to fill in the blanks. It is no coincidence that the mockery of the leaders is echoed in Psalm 31:6. "He trusted in God. Let him deliver him." The answer to that mockery, meant primarily for the ears of his devastated followers and later readers of the gospel, is made clear in Psalm 31:7–8. But it is the final verse of the psalm that provides comfort and hope in their time of despair. "Be strong, and let your heart take courage, all you who wait for the Lord" (Ps 31:24).

What is so striking about this particular quotation is the compassionate control of Jesus, even to his very last breath. In the midst of excruciating pain and his failing strength, he was still so focused on the will of the Father, as well as the needs of his followers, that with an effort that must have caused great anguish, he pushed himself up one last time to draw the final breath necessary to quote from this particular psalm, for them as well as for us.

There was a commotion at the cross. The centurion was shouting something about Jesus's innocence . . . then he turned and ordered the breaking of the legs of the two criminals. Simon heard some of the leaders say that they were concerned that the crucified men would not die before sunset, thus defiling their Passover celebrations. "What hypocrites," Simon thought. "Do they really think they are undefiled? After shedding innocent blood?"

Then he saw two men approach the huddle of women. They spoke to John. Who are they? Simon wondered. He thought they looked like rich men . . . one looked familiar . . . was he a member of the Sanhedrin? Simon watched silently as they took the lifeless body of Jesus down from the cross . . . so tenderly . . . so lovingly . . . his mother cradling her son as she did when he was a babe. They were in a hurry because it was the preparation day – the day before the Sabbath – and evening was quickly approaching.

The Judeans will be celebrating the Passover tonight, Simon thought, while we will be in mourning. Our Lamb has been slain and is no more.

He watched them wrap Jesus's body in spices and linen. The soldiers were there . . . they went with them to a nearby tomb hewn out of a rock set in a small garden . . . and there they laid his body on the shelf inside. They would return after the Sabbath to complete the rituals properly. As they left, Simon saw the soldiers secure and seal the large round stone. Why? he wondered. Are they afraid we will steal the body? Why would we steal a dead body? Our hopes and dreams have died too . . . they are entombed with him. We have no hope anymore.

With that, he turned away. He had to find the others. He would have to face them sooner or later. It was better for them to be together than apart . . . at least they could comfort one another. He groaned as he rose. First, he needed to clean himself. He stank of sweat and vomit.

* * *

Simon felt unclean. He had bathed himself and washed his clothes the night before, but he wanted to immerse himself in the ritual baths. Somehow, he needed to wash off the awful feeling of betrayal and defeat. He had done what he swore he would never do. He had denied Jesus . . . deserted him . . . abandoned him at the time of his greatest need. How could he have done such a cowardly and wicked thing? Especially since he had protested so vehemently that he would stand with Jesus, even if that meant he would have to die with him. But Jesus had known he would fail . . . he had said as much . . . that before the cock crowed, Simon would have denied him three times. The sense of shame flooded over him.

The other disciples were kind enough when Simon arrived, but the uncomfortable periods of silence that descended on them from time to time brought home the full reality of his failure. His dear wife tried to comfort him, but he could not be consoled. Everyone tried to remind him that they had all failed . . . they had all deserted Jesus. But Simon knew that none of them had verbally denied him . . . and done it three times . . . making the statement permanent. He had denied Jesus and could therefore no longer be his disciple . . . not in his eyes or in the eyes of his friends.

Today was the first day of the Festival of Unleavened Bread, the day following the Passover. It was also the first Sabbath and, as such, it was considered a high day. According to the law, the next day would be the Festival of First Fruits, during which the first sheaf of green barley would be waved in anticipation of the hoped-for great harvest to come. Then the forty-nine-day countdown to Pentecost would begin.[5] The disciples did not plan to participate in any of these holy events – they were too afraid to leave the confines of the compound where they were hiding. As soon as they could . . . as soon as it was safe . . . they needed to leave Jerusalem and go home to Galilee.

Simon thought of Jesus lying in that dark tomb. It was hard to accept that he was dead and gone . . . that they would never see him again, never hear his voice again. His spirit would be in the collective place of the dead by now. He would be with Abraham and all the beloved believers who had passed on before them. Perhaps he would be talking to the poor beggar, Lazarus. Even the rich man would see him and hear him.

Had following Jesus been worthwhile? He had left everything . . . his boat, his business, his home . . . he had left it all because he had mistakenly believed Jesus was the Messiah. But all his fears, prior to being convinced otherwise, had come true . . . except that the disciples had not been killed like the followers of all the other would-be messiahs had been. But they might still be, and so it was imperative that they remain hidden.

5. Pentecost was a word coined in the diaspora and frequently used. For more information see: https://www.christianity.com/jesus/early-church-history/pentecost/where-did-pentecost-come-from.html.

26

All Things New

Simon woke with a start, drenched with sweat. In his dream, his three accusers at the charcoal fire had caused the Roman soldiers to arrest him and he had been led off to be executed with Jesus. The dream had been so real . . . he could still smell the pungent aroma of the burning charcoal.

What was that sound? It was a soft, yet insistent, pounding at the door. Surely if these were soldiers, they wouldn't be knocking. The disciples were all staring at the door now. Simon moved along the wall until he could hear an urgent whisper . . . he leaned forward and put his ear to the crack between the door and the wall.

"Please. Open the door." It was Mary of Magdala, but it could be a trap. Maybe she had been captured and was being forced to betray the disciples. Fear was their constant companion now. The seed of mistrust had been sown by Judas and watered by their own behaviour the night of the arrest. The heart is a fickle thing, Simon thought. Who really knows what is going on inside any human being?

"Please! You must open! They have taken his body away!"

With that, Simon unlatched the door and quickly opened it. "What?!"

Mary and the rest of the women poured into the room all babbling at once. They were clearly distressed . . . their present agitation was not consistent with their usually calm conduct. They had been with the group from the earliest days . . . they had sat at the feet of Jesus just like his male disciples. No other rabbi allowed women into their group . . . they even said that it would be better for the Law to be burned than to be entrusted to a woman! But Jesus was not like any other rabbi, even encouraging the women to accompany them on their many trips. Over time the men had come to see them as equals . . . the women knew the Scriptures as well as they did and could discuss issues with the best of them. In many ways, they were co-workers, even though society would not

253

allow them to openly engage anyone on a religious level.[1] They even provided for the needs of the group out of their own resources.[2]

The women told the disciples that they had left early that morning, even before the sun was up, to go to Jesus's tomb. The start of the Sabbath the day before had prevented them from completing the customary burial rituals. As they were walking, they were wondering who would help them move the huge, sealed stone aside so that they could enter the tomb. They were talking about it when a sudden tremor caused the earth beneath their feet to shake.

That must have been when the soldiers were shaking me in my dream, Simon thought. How strange. This is the second earthquake since . . . since . . . Simon left that thought hanging in the air and continued listening to the women's account.

When the women arrived at the tomb, they saw that the stone had already been rolled aside and the soldiers were nowhere to be seen. Then their stories became wildly fanciful. They said that angels had appeared to them telling them that Jesus was not dead but had been raised to life. One of the angels told them Jesus would go ahead of the group to Galilee.

"That's what he told us while he was with us," Matthew said. "Remember? He told us we would fall away . . ."

"Yes," James chimed in. "Yes, and then he added that when he had been raised, he would go ahead of us to Galilee. I remember. But I must confess that I still don't understand. He is dead . . . are we to follow a spirit? Besides, where is his body?"

"This is all nonsense," Thomas said, indignant that the ten disciples would even entertain such tall tales. "The women are hysterical . . . fear has made them see things."

Without a word, John bolted out the door.

"Simon!" Mary said. "Go with him! It may not be safe!"

Simon ran after John but could not keep up, since John was much younger than he was. So John arrived at the tomb first, but stopped at the entrance, frightened to go any further. Simon on the other hand ran straight in, and only then did John collect himself and follow. They stood, catching their breath, staring at the empty shelf. The only thing that remained was the linen graveclothes . . . the cloth that had covered Jesus's head was neatly folded and placed to one side.

---

1. This is conjecture on my part, but it is based on the fact that Simon Peter took his wife with him on his trips and Paul had many women he called "co-workers."

2. Luke 8:1–3.

"Why would anyone steal a body but leave behind the expensive linen?" Simon asked. "That doesn't make any sense. And where are the Roman guards?"

John was breathing heavily now . . . not because he had been running, but because he was remembering everything Jesus had told them about him rising from the dead. Why was it so hard for them to understand? It was too much to process. He turned to leave. He would think about it later.

Both men left, confused and despondent. How would they explain this to the others? As they went, they passed Mary of Magdala. She had returned, but they did not even ask why.

A little while after they had been back to the place where they were hiding, Mary returned . . . eyes glowing, face beaming. "I have seen the Lord!" she exclaimed, and proceeded to tell them what had happened.

After Simon and John had left the tomb, she had walked up to its entrance and stood by the stone. She simply could not fathom what was happening. She had come that morning, with the other Galilean women, to show one more act of kindness to the man who had freed her from seven demons and had treated her as an equal.

She related how excruciatingly painful it had been to watch Jesus breathe out his last breath . . . with his every cry she felt that her heart was being ripped apart. When he spoke his last words, "It is finished,"[3] she felt it really was all over . . . his life and hers.

She had just wanted to anoint Jesus's body one more time. But as she stood at the tomb, it seemed that even this had been denied her and she was overcome with grief. Sorrow welled up inside her like a gigantic wave and spilled out of her eyes.[4]

"Woman." She heard the voice from within the tomb and stooped down to see who was speaking with her.

"Dear woman, why are you weeping?" Two white-robed angels, like those she had seen with the other women, sat at either end of the shelf.

3. I believe the statement, "It is finished," is new creation imagery, purposefully echoing the words in Genesis 2:1–4. Mary would not have understood that at the time, but I do think later reflection as seen in the Epistles reflects this understanding.

4. In their society women were to be seen and not heard . . . to bear children and serve in the kitchen, but nothing more. They were not even permitted to travel without their husband's express permission. Many women were trapped in loveless marriages, but they endured the constant emotional abuse and humiliation because the alternative was far worse. To be cast out by one's husband was considered a shameful thing, and divorced women were often shunned by even their family members. Many died in poverty.

"Because they have stolen the body of my Lord and I have no idea where they have taken him," she replied, without thinking that it was strange to be having a conversation with angelic beings.

She turned to leave and through her tears saw another person standing close by. She told the disciples that she assumed he was the keeper of the garden, so she asked him to tell her where he had put the body of Jesus if he had taken it away.

And then she heard him speak her name, "Mary." He did not need to say anything else. She held on to him as if she would never let him go. She did not ask any questions . . . she did not need to. She had found what she wanted, and more! She went seeking to anoint a dead body . . . but he was not dead. He was very much alive!

Finally, Jesus convinced Mary to let go of him. He then told her to go and tell the disciples . . . especially Simon . . . that he was alive and would be returning soon to the Father.

The disciples stared at her. They did not doubt her . . . they knew she was telling the truth. Her story matched what Jesus had been telling them all along. But they wondered why he had chosen a woman to be the herald of his resurrection? Simon and John had both been at the tomb. Why didn't Jesus show himself to them? Why Mary?

"It is fitting that the undoing of the curse be announced by a woman," Philip said.

They all looked at him blankly.

"The curse came through the words of Eve, correct? Adam believed his wife and took of the fruit. Well, here Mary brings us the words of life. She is a sign that the curse has been broken."[5]

If Jesus had not included women from the beginning of his ministry, Philip's statement might have been a struggle for the disciples. But Jesus had never done anything according to their expectations . . . his anticipated kingdom was radically different from anything they had ever heard of before, including the status of women. Unlike the rabbis and religious leaders, Jesus had always treated women with profound respect and as equals. In many ways,

---

5. Again, this is speculation on my part, but the fact that the Gospel writers did not hesitate to tell the story as it happened, that a woman was the first witness to the resurrection, indicates that they believed that Jesus's choice was significant. There are also many parallels between Eve and Mary Magdalene such as both events take place in a garden, in both cases God speaks, and angels are present . . . but the one is the herald of death whereas the other is the herald of life. This is not an original thought on my part. A few Pre- and Post-Nicene Fathers noted this, Augustine being one of them.

it seemed that the kingdom Jesus spoke of was a return to the original state of creation, where men and women, both created in the image of God, were to serve together as his vice-regents over his world.

Mary, the one sent to the "sent ones," was the sign of the beginning of that return . . .

* * *

That evening, all the disciples gathered together to discuss the monumental events witnessed by the women, especially Mary. By this time, Jesus had appeared to Simon as well, but try as they might, they could not get much information out of him. Rumours were flooding in of long-deceased relatives roaming the streets of Jerusalem.[6] It was as if the place of the dead itself had been plundered . . . that those held captive by death had been resurrected with Jesus.

Some of those who believed in Jesus were linking these resurrections to the Festival of First Fruits. They were saying that like the sheaf of green barley, Jesus was the first fruits, but not only of those who had passed on before . . . he was the green sheaf offered in anticipation of a great harvest of souls yet to come.[7]

Two other disciples were on their way to Emmaus when Jesus appeared to them as well. At first, he was disguised as a stranger, and chastised them for their lack of understanding. But then he began to explain the Scriptures to them as they walked along the way. When they arrived at Emmaus, they persuaded him to stay the night and as they began their meal together, he revealed himself to them when he broke the bread. He then suddenly disappeared. They had immediately returned to tell the others.

There they were, all gathered together except Thomas, meeting behind locked doors because they still feared a backlash from the Jewish leaders. They were deeply engaged in discussion when suddenly Jesus stood before them. The shock rendered them speechless.

"Peace be with you," Jesus said simply.

No one moved except Simon . . . he slowly backed up into the shadows. He was still struggling with feelings of shame and guilt . . . like Judas and yet unlike Judas. He had heard about Judas . . . they had all heard about Judas. Apparently, he had felt terrible for what he had done and had gone to the temple leaders in a vain attempt to undo his wicked deed. But what was done was done . . . there was no undoing the past. Simon knew that only too well.

---

6. Matthew 27:52–53.
7. 1 Corinthians 15:20–23.

Judas had thrown back the silver coins and had rushed out to put an end to his miserable life . . . he went and hung himself. But his dead weight had later proved to be too much for the tree and his swollen body had crashed to the ground, splitting open where it fell. That ground was now cursed. Simon wondered what the leaders would do with that piece of land now.

From the shadows, Simon watched as Jesus stepped forward into the dim light and showed them his pierced wrists and feet. His wounds were still clearly visible . . . it was clear that this was no imposter.

Again, he said, "Peace be with you. I am sending you out into the world, just as my Father sent me out into the world." And then, just like God had breathed over Adam, Jesus breathed over them. "Now receive the Holy Spirit."

He is showing us who he is, Simon thought. He is God. This act is surely nothing less than an act of re-creation . . . a reversal of the effects of our ancestor's disobedience. This is the age that was to come, spoken of by all the prophets. And Jesus is now giving us the power we need to do what he has been doing.

"If you forgive the sins of any, they are forgiven. If you do not forgive them, their sins remain." Jesus looked over to where Simon was sitting, his eyes piercing the darkness.

Forgiveness, Simon thought to himself. A wonderful thing to receive to be sure, but can it reverse what I've done? I denied him three times, so I cut myself off from being a disciple. I revealed what was in my heart . . . what I knew all along . . . that I am a sinful man and not disciple material. I should never have left my boat.

After having eaten with them, Jesus opened their minds to understand what the Scriptures said about him. It was a night of study they never forgot. From Moses through the prophets and the writings, Jesus showed them where what had transpired during the past few days had been predicted.

"It was also written," Jesus continued, "that the Messiah would suffer and die and rise from the dead on the third day, and that this message of salvation through my death and resurrection would be proclaimed to all nations . . . beginning here in Jerusalem. There is forgiveness of sins for all who repent and believe in me. You are eyewitnesses of all I have said and done. So, you must tell the world. But as I promised, I will send the Holy Spirit who will guide you and empower you to be my sent ones."

Simon stayed in the shadows. This was not for him, he thought. He was no longer a sent one. He would quietly return to his old vocation.

Jesus then left the same way he had come . . . one moment there, the next gone. Simon simply went to bed.

* * *

"I don't believe you," Thomas said. "You are all deluded by your own wishful thinking. Unless I see the nail prints myself, put my fingers in them, and put my hand into the spear wound in his side, I will not believe."

Thomas had not been with them when Jesus had appeared, and no amount of persuasive speech could sway him.

"He is dead! It is over! He is never coming back! Our misguided messianic dream has faded away. We will simply have to get used to the fact that the Messiah is still yet to come."

Eight days later, they were all gathered together in the same place again when suddenly Jesus stood in their midst. Just as before, the doors were locked, but the new resurrected body of Jesus was different from what it had been . . . they could touch him and feel him, he could eat and drink, and yet he could appear and disappear at will.

"Peace be with you," Jesus said. Then he turned to Thomas.

Simon thought the doubting disciple was about to faint from fright. He pitied him. He knew what it felt like to be so very wrong.

"Put your finger here, Thomas," Jesus said. "Look at my hands. Put your hand in my side."

But Thomas did not move.

"Faith, dear Thomas, that is what it takes. So, believe."

Thomas crumpled before him like a wet rag . . . he fell on his knees and wept. Through his sobs he exclaimed, "My Lord! My Lord and my God!"

They had all come to believe that Jesus was God by that time . . . there was no other feasible explanation.

"Thomas," Jesus looked at his disciple with such tenderness, "you believe because you have seen. Those who believe without seeing are truly blessed."

Then he turned to the disciples and said, "Meet me in Galilee." And with that he was gone.

Galilee, Simon thought. Yes, it is time to go home.

27

Breakfast on the Beach

Blisters. He actually had blisters on both his hands. It had been a long time since he had handled the nets. Too long. His body ached all over. In the humid predawn, rivulets of sweat streamed down and collected in little pools at his feet in spite of the fact that he had stripped earlier on in the evening. Had he lost it? Had he lost the ability to catch fish? When he was younger, he could fish all night long and then still stay up until his nets were washed and mended. But what was he thinking? He was still young . . . it was just over three years ago that he had left his nets to follow . . . no, he didn't want to think about that. It was too fresh . . . too painful. It just deepened his sense of failure . . . that he did not measure up to his own expectations, not to mention the expectations of others, for that matter. And he thought he knew himself so well! How could he have been so mistaken? He was once so sure of himself . . . now he only had doubts and confusion.

Simon looked out over the lake. It was still fairly dark, but he could see the shoreline. The lake always brought back memories . . . myriads of memories, some good, some not so good. Like the memory of one night in particular . . . that night when he called him to come to him on the water. At first there was nothing but certainty . . . he didn't even think twice. Why did he take his eyes off him? Why did he look down? Maybe he ought to have walked away then and saved himself the humiliation of . . . no, he was not going there. He was sure that if he thought about this more recent awful night he would sink into darkness and never resurface.

He had once been so sure . . . so sure of everything he did . . . but now? Now he couldn't even catch a single fish. Failure. Nothing but a failure.

What was that sound? Was someone shouting to them? Yes, there was a voice coming from the far shore. He could just see the outline of a man standing on the beach. The others gathered around Simon and strained to hear what the man was saying. "Children, have you caught any fish?" The voice sounded familiar . . . was it one of their regular customers?

"No," they shouted back.

Another failure, Simon thought . . . another disappointment. What kind of a fisherman can't catch a single fish?

What was that? Did the stranger tell them they should to cast their nets on the right-hand side of the boat? Yes. That's exactly what he had said. "Then you will catch some," he said. Really? Simon looked at the water . . . he couldn't see anything moving beneath the surface. Aside from that, the sun was about to crest the mountain . . . it was getting too late for a catch. But a certain resignation overcame him. Why argue? He was so tired . . . tired of trying to prove himself . . . tired of always trying to be right . . . tired of always trying to be better. Just do what the man says. Besides, what did he have to lose?

And then . . . the nets had hardly sunk down when the water began to bubble and swirl. Fish! Lots and lots of fish! Instinct kicked in and Simon began to pull at the ropes. As they emptied the net into the boat, fish flapped furiously all around him, drowning in oxygen. Thinking back later, Simon could not quite recall when it dawned on him that something about this event felt ever so familiar . . . as if this had happened before. And then he heard John say, "Simon, it is the Lord!"

The Lord? The Lord! Simon suddenly felt naked . . . exposed. That voice! In some sense, Simon felt that the voice was indirectly calling out to him. "Simon, where are you? Simon, what are you doing here?" Simon was the one who had tried to convince the others to return to their old vocations. There was nowhere to hide. This awkward meeting was unavoidable. He felt trapped . . . and yet . . . he felt elated as well. Yes, elated and somehow free . . . he had already hit the bottom of the deepest pit in his life. What could be worse than that? He threw on his outer garment, plunged into the sea, and swam to the shore where Jesus was waiting for him.

Simon stumbled out of the water and straight into the arms of his Lord. For a moment he simply clung to Jesus since he was completely out of breath after the swim. The others were still struggling with the fish-laden nets.

There was already a fish on the fire along with a piece of bread. How did he . . . where did he . . . ? Simon thought.

"Simon, bring some of the fish you have just caught," Jesus said.

The fish he had caught? If it wasn't for Jesus, he would still have had an empty net!

He climbed back into the boat to help drag the net to shore. It was full of fish . . . one hundred and fifty-three in total. But astoundingly . . . the net was not torn or damaged.

"Come," Jesus called to them from near the charcoal fire, "let's have breakfast."

Breakfast on the beach? How wonderful. I'm famished, Simon thought.

He did not yet know that it would be a breakfast that would change his life completely.

* * *

As Simon walked closer to Jesus, carrying a fresh fish for breakfast, he saw and smelled the charcoal fire. In the shadows of the pre-dawn light, the embers glowed. But the sight was not a cheerful one. To Simon it was ominous. In that moment, he was transported back in time to that horror-filled night in the compound of the High Priest. He stood, motionless, reliving the terror and the shame. The sounds of beating, the wicked laughter, the sight, the smells, the fear . . . they all came flooding back. In the coals, he saw the eyes of his accusers . . . burning into him. He saw the soldiers looking at him . . . he tasted bile in his throat. They were coming for him . . .

"Brother?" Andrew took Simon by the arm.

"No!" Simon shouted. "Let me go!" Everyone looked up at him, startled. Everyone, but Jesus.

"Forgive me, brother . . ." Andrew stammered. "I didn't mean to . . . that is, I . . ." Andrew noticed his brother was trembling . . . his eyes were fixed on the glowing charcoal fire. "Brother, the fish . . . you are bruising the fish."

"What?" Simon turned to look at his brother. He was breathing hard and fast.

"The fish," Andrew said. "Your grip is too tight. You are bruising it."

"Oh, . . . yes, I'm sorry. I was . . ." Simon was trying hard to regain his composure.

"Here, let me take the fish," Andrew offered.

"Thank you," Simon said shakily. His legs felt weak. He knew he needed to sit down, so he made his way to where the other disciples had gathered around Jesus and the fire. His mouth was dry. He needed a drink of water. He looked around but seeing nothing, he looked back at the group . . . straight into the eyes of Jesus. It was still not light enough to distinguish his features, but Simon knew those eyes . . . those eyes that penetrated the very depths of one's soul.

"Come," Jesus said, "have a piece of fish."

Simon took the piece Jesus offered him and bit into the juicy flesh, grateful for anything moist at that moment. The disciples' mood began to lift, and soon they were all chatting away merrily.

Turning to face Simon, Jesus said suddenly, "Simon, son of John." He used the same term of address as when they first met, close to Bethany beyond the Jordan.

"Yes, Lord," Simon said, vividly remembering that initial introduction, when the Lord first called him "Cephas." It seemed like ages ago.

"Simon," Jesus's voice was filled with tenderness, "is your dedication to me greater than that of my other followers?"

Silence descended on the group. They all knew that Jesus was referring to Simon's rash declaration that even if everyone else deserted Jesus, he never would. But it was not a question meant to embarrass or even expose him . . . that much Simon knew. It was a question that revealed to him the limitations of his own human strength, and therefore the futility of boastful declarations.

"Perhaps not *more* than . . ." Simon began. "That is to say, I . . . I mean . . . yes . . . yes, Lord, I am dedicated to you."

Jesus smiled. "Good, because I need you to look after my community."

After a while, Jesus looked back up at Simon and said, "Simon, son of John. Search your heart. Are you truly dedicated to me?"

Again there was a lull in the conversation. Simon thought back over the years he had walked with Jesus. Yes, there were times when he had been filled with confidence . . . when he thought he knew himself well . . . when he thought nothing would every prevent him from following Jesus wherever he led them. But the recollection of the incident at the charcoal fire was still fresh in his mind. What did his denials reveal about his resolve? Was he as dedicated to Jesus as he had thought? Obviously not. In the beginning he had worried he was not disciple material – he had said as much, asking Jesus to look for someone else. Back then he knew his limitations, but somewhere along the line, he had begun to think more highly of himself. And yet . . . deep down in his heart he knew who Jesus was . . . that he could not deny. He looked back up at Jesus . . . it had seemed as if the silence had lasted for a lifetime.

"Yes, Lord," Simon said, "you know I am dedicated to you."

"Simon," Jesus took hold of his hand, "I really need you to watch over my community."

Some of the other disciples had returned to the boat. Perhaps they felt the conversation was becoming more personal and that Jesus and Simon needed to be alone. Andrew began to extinguish the fire, pouring moist sand onto the embers. John stood close by, wanting to help . . . wanting to encourage

Simon . . . wanting to show some form of support for his hurting friend, but he said nothing.

"Simon, son of John," Jesus said, turning, once again, to face Simon. "Look at me."

Simon looked up. In the eyes of his Lord he could see only love and compassion.

"Simon, son of John . . . I want you to answer me from your heart. Are you dedicated to me?"

Simon felt the hot tears burning his eyes. Jesus had not given up on him . . . no, he was as relentless as ever. He knew full well that Simon needed to reaffirm his commitment three times . . . once for every denial . . . each positive reply cancelling the negative declaration. It was like a hammer and chisel breaking through the hard shell of guilt brought on by failure.

He has already searched my heart. He knows everything about me, Simon thought to himself. He even knows my thoughts. Before I speak, he knows what I am about to say. He knew me before I was formed in my mother's womb . . . he made me . . . he knew every single day of my life before there was one of them.[1] He knows me better than I know myself. He knows my strengths . . . he knows my weaknesses . . . and yet, he loves me. I have given him every reason to reject me . . . every reason to give up on me . . . but here he is, wooing me back to him . . . healing my brokenness and restoring my dignity.

"Lord," Simon's voice broke, "you know my heart. You know everything about me. You know that in spite of myself, I am dedicated to following you."

Jesus stood up and helped Simon to his feet. With one fluid movement, he embraced his sobbing disciple and held him close.

When Simon's weeping subsided, Jesus said to him. "Simon, I need you to lead my community once I am no longer with you all. Will you care for them as I have cared for you?"

Simon could not speak. He could only nod his assent.

"Come, let us walk for a bit," Jesus said.

As they walked, Jesus spoke about the personal cost of following him. He told Simon that a time would come when he, too, would be arrested and executed for his faith. As they walked, Simon noticed John trailing behind them. Curiosity overcame him and he dared to ask if John would meet a similar fate.

Jesus smiled. "That's not for you to know, Simon," he said. "The outcome of the lives of others is not your concern. It makes no difference to you if I

1. Cf. Psalm 139.

want John to remain alive until my return. You need to focus on following me yourself."

With that he placed his arm around Simon's shoulder and said, "Call the others . . . all the others. I will meet you on that mountain over there."

"I will gather them all, Lord. And thank you. Thank you for not giving up on me."

But Jesus was already gone.

Strangely, Simon now felt he was finally ready to live as Jesus lived. This encounter, however painful, had taught him that, like Jesus, he needed to walk closely with the Father and not trust in his own strength or rely on his own understanding. If he was to succeed in the kingdom, he had to know the mind of Jesus, who was so focused on the will of God, that even though hell itself should bar the way, he pressed on through in obedience . . . even obedience to martyrdom . . . until every knee had bowed and every tongue had confessed that Jesus Christ is Lord, to the glory of God the Father.[2]

---

2. Philippians 2:5–11.

Part IV

Reproduction and Replacement

" . . . you will do even greater things than I have done."
John 14:12

28

Bearing Much Fruit

There he is!" Mary of Magdala almost shouted with glee. She ran the rest of the way and fell at his feet in worship. Some of the people who had not been with them in Jerusalem at the crucifixion stayed on the fringes of the group . . . they were not quite sure what to make of this new Jesus. But after a while, they realized that he was no apparition or ghost, and so they came closer to listen to him giving them more instructions as to their future roles.

It was a clear day and from their vantage point on the top of the mountain, it was as if they could see to the very ends of the earth.

"I am all that Adam ought to have been," Jesus began. "But as I am both God and Man, and as the head of the new creation, I have now been given authority over all things, both in the heavens and on the earth. So now, I tell you as my community of followers, wherever you may go, be fruitful . . . multiply . . . make more followers of me. Bring them under my authority through baptism in the name of the Father, and of the Son, and of the Holy Spirit. Train them to walk in obedience . . . to follow faithfully all I have taught you. But always remember that I am with you . . . walking right beside you . . . even to the end the age."

With that he turned to Simon and in front of the whole group, he said, "Simon, you are now ready to bear the name I gave you when we first met. You are Cephas . . . Peter . . . the rock. Lead this community of mine now."

To the group, he said, "Meet me in Jerusalem with the rest of the community there."

They were about to ask when and where, but he had already vanished from their sight.

"I suppose we need to leave right away," Simon Peter said.

* * *

It was the most joy-filled trip they had ever made to Jerusalem. They were praising God in both word and song all the way to Bethany. There they collected Martha, Mary, and Lazarus, and together they went to the house of Mary, the mother of John Mark, in Jerusalem, where they had stayed before. Jesus was already there, waiting for them in the Upper Room.

That evening, as they enjoyed a meal together, Jesus said, "Do not leave Jerusalem until you have received the gift . . . the gift I told you about at Passover . . . do you remember? The counsellor who is like me. The Holy Spirit. In a few days he will come upon you all."

The following morning, long before sunrise, Jesus led the group of one hundred and twenty followers, that included Jesus's mother and his siblings, to the area of Bethany. On the way, some who still did not quite understand, asked him if this was the time when he would restore the kingdom to Israel.

Jesus did not rebuke them. He simply smiled and said, "It really is not for you to know these sorts of things . . . days and dates and when things will be fulfilled . . . things that God the Father alone has the right to determine. You must trust that the Father has these things well in hand. Your responsibility is not to speculate about the future, but to bear witness to me in the present . . . starting here in Jerusalem, moving out into Judea and Samaria, and not stopping until you have reached the very ends of the earth. But you must first wait for the infilling of the Holy Spirit. He will give you the power and the authority to do all that I have commanded you."

As he was still speaking, a bright cloud enveloped him. He disappeared into it, and it lifted him up into the heavens.

"The cloud, Peter!" John said. "It is just like our time on Mount Hermon!"

"What happened on Mount Hermon?" Andrew asked.

"Ah, yes," Simon Peter replied. "Remind me to tell you about that."

They were still staring at the remnant of cloud in the sky when they became aware of two angels standing beside them.

"Why are you staring into space, Galileans?" they asked. "Jesus has returned to the Father as he told you he would, to be seated as the reigning king at his right hand. But he will return one day just as he has gone now." And then they disappeared from view.

"Come, let's return to Jerusalem," Simon Peter said. "Jesus didn't mean for us to stand around. We need to be actively waiting for what he has promised."

"What is the Holy Spirit, Peter?" Philip asked.

"I'm not sure, Philip," Simon Peter replied, "but this much I know. Jesus said the Spirit is like him . . . he will remind us of everything Jesus taught us . . . he will give us the strength to do what Jesus did – to do even greater things than Jesus did. Remember, Jesus was only one man . . . a man filled with the Holy Spirit, but still only one man. He could only be in one place at a time. But, think about it! We are many, and we will become many more if we make more disciples. So, if he is the same Spirit that rested on Jesus, the same Spirit who led him and gave him the ability to do the wonderful things he did, the same Spirit who raised Jesus from the dead, I, for one, can't wait to meet him."

"Me too," said Mary of Magdala, "me too."

TO BE CONTINUED . . . in Simon Peter's life and yours.

Appendix

Timeline

PART I: PREPARATION AND PLANTING

Chapter 1: Tilling and Sowing

1. The Pre-Existence of Christ
   John 1:1–18 – The Word Made Flesh
   Luke 1:1–4 – The Preface of Luke
2. The Christ of Prophecy
   Genesis 3:15
   Deuteronomy 18:15
   2 Samuel 7:14
   Psalms 2; 16; 22; 34; 69; 110
   Isaiah 7:14; 8:14; 8:23–9:1;
   9:6–7; 11:12; 28:16;
   52:13–53:12
   Jeremiah 31:15
   Ezekiel 37:24, 26–27
   Daniel 9:24–27
   Hosea 11:1
   Micah 5:2
   Haggai 2:6–9
   Zechariah 9:9; 12:10
   Wisdom 2:12–20 (Apocrypha)
3. The Genealogy of Christ
   Matthew 1:1–17
   Luke 3:23–38
4. Zechariah, Elizabeth and John the Baptist
   Luke 1:5–25
5. The Conception of Christ
   Matthew 1:18–25
   Luke 1:26–38
   John 1:14
6. Mary and Elizabeth
   Luke 1:39–56
7. The Birth of John the Baptist
   Luke 1:57–80
8. The Birth of Christ
   Luke 2:1–7
9. The Shepherds and the Angels
   Luke 2:8–20

10. The Circumcision and Presentation of Christ in the Temple
    Luke 2:21–24
11. Simeon and Anna
    Luke 2:25–38
12. The Visit of the Magi
    Numbers 24:17–19
    Isaiah 60:1–3
    Daniel 2:48
    Matthew 2:1–12
13. Herod the Great
    Matthew 2:13–15
14. The Flight to Egypt and the Infants of Bethlehem
    Matthew 2:16–18
15. Archelaus: Herod the Ethnarch
    Matthew 2:19–23
    Luke 2:39
16. The Return from Egypt to Nazareth
    Matthew 2:19–23
    Luke 2:39
17. The Infancy and Childhood of Christ
    Luke 2:40–52
18. Tiberius
    Luke 3:1–2
19. Pontius Pilate
    Luke 3:1–2
20. Herod the Tetrarch
    Luke 3:1–2
21. Annas and Caiaphas
    Luke 3:1–2
22. John the Baptist
    Matthew 3:1–12
    Mark 1:1–8
    Luke 3:1–20
23. The Baptism of Christ and the Descent of the Spirit
    Matthew 3:13–17
    Mark 1:9–11

   Luke 3:21–23a
   Acts 19:1–5
24. The Temptation of Christ
    Matthew 4:1–11
    Mark 1:12–13
    Luke 4:1–13
25. John's Testimony about Himself
    John 1:19–28
26. John's Testimony about Jesus as the Lamb of God
    John 1:29–34, 36

Chapter 2: First Impressions

27. Jesus's First Disciples
    John 1:35–51
28. The Wedding in Cana and the First Stay in Capernaum
    John 2:1–12

Chapter 3: Misgivings

29. The First Cleansing of the Temple and Early Response to Jesus's Miracles
    John 2:13–25
30. Nicodemus
    John 3:1–21
31. John the Baptist Exalts Christ
    John 3:22–36
32. On the Way to Galilee
    John 4:1–4
33. The Samaritan Woman, Harvest and Sychar
    John 4:5–42
34. Arrival in Galilee
    John 4:43–45
35. The Healing of the Nobleman's Son
    John 4:46–54
36. The Pool of Bethesda
    John 5:1–47
37. Jesus's Departure from Judea
    Matthew 4:12 – John's (1st?) arrest

Bibliography

Adeyemo, Tokunboh, ed. *Africa Bible Commentary: A One-Volume Commentary Written by 70 African Scholars.* Nairobi: WordAlive Publishers, 2006.

Bailey, Kenneth E. *The Good Shepherd: A Thousand-Year Journey from Psalm 23 to the New Testament.* Downers Grove, IL: IVP Academic, 2014.

———. *Jesus through Middle Eastern Eyes: Cultural Studies in the Gospels.* Downers Grove, IL: IVP Academic, 2008.

———. *Poet & Peasant and Through New Eyes: A Literary-Cultural Approach to the Parables in Luke (Combined Edition).* Grand Rapids, MI: Eerdmans, 1983.

Barrett, C. K. *The Gospel according to St. John: An Introduction with Commentary and Notes of the Greek Text.* London: SPCK, 1967.

Bartholomew, Craig G., and Michael Goheen. *The Drama of Scripture: Finding Our Place in the Biblical Story.* Grand Rapids, MI: Baker Academic, 2014.

Bartholomew, Craig G., Mary Healy, Karl Moller, and Robin Parry. *Out of Egypt: Biblical Theology and Biblical Interpretation.* Grand Rapids, MI: Zondervan, 2004.

Blizzard, Roy B. *Mishnah and the Words of Jesus.* Texas: Bible Scholars, Inc., 2013.

Bock, Darrell L., and Gregory J. Herrick. *Jesus in Context: Background Readings for Gospel Study.* Grand Rapids, MI: Baker Academic, 2005.

Bockmuehl, Markus. *Simon Peter in Scripture and Memory: The New Testament Apostle in the Early Church.* Grand Rapids, MI: Baker, 2012.

Brandes, Yochi. *The Orchard.* Jerusalem: Gefen Publishing, 2018.

Brown, Raymond E., Karl P. Donfried, and John Reumann. *Peter in the New Testament: A Collaborative Assessment by Protestant and Roman Catholic Scholars.* Eugene, OR: Wipf & Stock, 1973.

Bruce, A. B. *The Training of the Twelve.* ReadaClassic, 2010 (1871).

Capewell, Phil, James Martin, John Kerr, et al. *Fisherman to Follow: The Life and Teaching of Simon Peter.* Swindon: Hayes Press, 2015.

Card, Michael. *A Fragile Stone: The Emotional Life of Simon Peter.* Downers Grove, IL: IVP Books, 2003.

Clark, Helen. *Simon Peter: Challenging Times.* Leominster: Day One Publications, 2009.

———. *Simon Peter: The Training Years.* Leominster: Day One Publications, 2009.

Clarke, Ken. *Going for Growth: Learning from Peter.* Leicester, UK: Inter-Varsity Press, 2011.

Cohen, Abraham. *Everyman's Talmud: The Major Teachings of the Rabbinic Sages.* New York: Schocken Books, 1949.

Complete Apocrypha, The. Columbia: Covenant Press, 2018.

Cullmann, Oscar. *Peter: Disciple, Apostle, Martyr.* New York: Meridan Books, 1958.

Edersheim, Alfred. *The Life and Times of Jesus the Messiah, Volumes 1 & 2.* CreateSpace Independent Publishing, 2015.

Ellsworth, Roger. *Simon Peter: Encountering the Preacher at Pentecost.* Leominster: Day One Publications, 2007.

Elton, Godfrey. *Simon Peter: A Study of Discipleship.* London: P. Davis, 1965.

Forbes, Greg W., and Scott D. Harrower. *Raised from Obscurity: A Narratival and Theological Study of the Characterization of Women in Luke-Acts.* Eugene, OR: Pickwick, 2015.

Franzmann, Martin H. *Follow Me: Discipleship according to Matthew.* St. Louis, MO: Concordia, 1982.

Gallaty, Robby. *The Forgotten Jesus: How Western Christians Should Follow an Eastern Rabbi.* Grand Rapids, MI: Zondervan, 2017.

Gray, Tim. *Peter: Keys to Following Jesus.* Greenwood Village, CO: Ignatius Press-Augustine Institute, 2016.

Helyer, Larry R. *The Life and Witness of Peter.* Downers Grove, IL: IVP Academic, 2012.

Hengel, Martin. *Saint Peter: The Underestimated Apostle.* Grand Rapids, MI: Eerdmans, 2010.

Hill, David. *The Gospel of Matthew.* London: Oliphants, 1978.

Huntsperger, Larry. *The Fisherman: A Novel.* Grand Rapids, MI: Revell, 2003.

Josephus, Flavius. *The Complete Works of Josephus.* Grand Rapids, MI: Kregel Publications, 1981.

Lane, William L. *The Gospel of Mark.* NICNT. Grand Rapids, MI: Eerdmans, 1974.

Martin, Hugh. *Simon Peter.* London: Counted Faithful, 2017.

Neusner, Jacob. *A Midrash Reader.* Minneapolis, MN: Fortress Press, 1990.

Nicoll, W. Robertson. *The Expositor's Greek Testament.* Peabody, MA: Hendrickson, 2002.

Osborne, Grant R. *Matthew: Exegetical Commentary on the New Testament.* Grand Rapids, MI: Zondervan, 2010.

Perkins, Pheme. *Peter: Apostle for the Whole Church.* Minneapolis, MN: Fortress Press, 2000.

Pixner, Bargil. *With Jesus through Galilee according to the Fifth Gospel.* Rosh Pina: Corazin Publishing, 1992.

Pryor, Dwight A. *Behold the Man! Discovering Our Hebrew Lord, the Historical Jesus of Nazareth.* Dayton, OH: Center for Judaic-Christian Studies, 2005.

———. *Unveiling the Kingdom of Heaven: The Origins and Dimension of the Kingdom Concept as Taught by the Rabbi Jesus.* Dayton, OH: Center for Judaic-Christian Studies, 2008.

Ran, Nachman. *Journeys to the Promised Land.* London: Studio Editions, 1989.

Ray, Stephen K. *Upon this Rock: St. Peter and the Primacy of Rome in Scripture and the Early Church.* San Francisco, CA: Ignatius Press, 1999.

Spader, Dann. *Four Chair Discipling: Growing a Movement of Disciple-Makers.* Chicago: Moody Press, 2014.

Spangler, Ann, and Lois Tverberg. *Sitting at the Feet of Rabbi Jesus: How the Jewishness of Jesus Can Transform Your Faith.* Grand Rapids, MI: Zondervan, 2009.

Temple, William. *Readings in St. John's Gospel.* London: Macmillan, 1950.

Walker, Peter. *In the Steps of Jesus,* 2nd edition. Oxford: Lion Hudson, 2018.

Wiarda, Timothy. *Interpreting Gospel Narratives: Scenes, People, and Theology.* Nashville, TN: B&H Academic, 2010.

Wigram, George V. *The Analytical Greek Lexicon of the New Testament.* Peabody, MA: Hendrickson, 1983.

Wright, Christopher J. H. *Knowing Jesus through the Old Testament.* Downers Grove, IL: InterVarsity Press, 1992.

———. *The Mission of God: Unlocking the Bible's Grand Narrative.* Downers Grove, IL: IVP Academic, 2006.

———. *Old Testament Ethics for the People of God.* Downers Grove, IL: InterVarsity Press, 2004.

Wright, N. T. *John for Everyone: Parts One and Two.* Louisville: SPCK, 2004.

———. *Luke for Everyone.* Louisville: SPCK, 2004.

———. *Mark for Everyone.* Louisville: SPCK, 2004.

———. *Matthew for Everyone: Parts One and Two.* Louisville: SPCK, 2004.

———. *The New Testament and the People of God.* Minneapolis, MN: Fortress Press, 1992.

Wylen, Stephen M. *The Jews in the Time of Jesus: An Introduction.* New York: Paulist Press, 1996.

Bibles Consulted

Africa Study Bible. Edited by John Jusu. Oasis International, 2016.

The Greek New Testament, 3rd Edition. Edited by Kurt Aland, Matthew Black, Carlo M. Martini, Bruce M. Metzger, and Allen Wikgren. Stuttgart: United Bible Societies, 1983.

The Interlinear Bible. Edited by Jay P. Green Sr. Grand Rapids, MI: Baker Book House, 1985.

JPS Hebrew-English Tanakh: The Traditional Hebrew Text and the New JPS Translation, 2nd Edition. Philadelphia: The Jewish Publication Society, 2000.

NIV Archaeological Study Bible: An Illustrated Walk through Biblical History and Culture. Grand Rapids, MI: Zondervan, 2005.

New International Version. Grand Rapids, MI: Zondervan, 1984.

New Living Translation. Carol Stream, IL: Tyndale House, 2015.

A Reader's Hebrew and Greek Bible. Edited by Richard J. Goodrich, Albert Lukaszewski, A. Philip Brown, and Bryan W. Smith. Grand Rapids, MI: Zondervan, 2007, 2008.

The Passion Translation. Edited by Brian Simmons. BroadStreet Publishing Group, 2018.

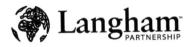

Langham Literature and its imprints are a ministry of Langham Partnership.

Langham Partnership is a global fellowship working in pursuit of the vision God entrusted to its founder John Stott –

to facilitate the growth of the church in maturity and Christ-likeness through raising the standards of biblical preaching and teaching.

Our vision is to see churches in the Majority World equipped for mission and growing to maturity in Christ through the ministry of pastors and leaders who believe, teach and live by the word of God.

Our mission is to strengthen the ministry of the word of God through:
• nurturing national movements for biblical preaching
• fostering the creation and distribution of evangelical literature
• enhancing evangelical theological education
especially in countries where churches are under-resourced.

Our ministry

Langham Preaching partners with national leaders to nurture indigenous biblical preaching movements for pastors and lay preachers all around the world. With the support of a team of trainers from many countries, a multi-level programme of seminars provides practical training, and is followed by a programme for training local facilitators. Local preachers' groups and national and regional networks ensure continuity and ongoing development, seeking to build vigorous movements committed to Bible exposition.

Langham Literature provides Majority World preachers, scholars and seminary libraries with evangelical books and electronic resources through publishing and distribution, grants and discounts. The programme also fosters the creation of indigenous evangelical books in many languages, through writer's grants, strengthening local evangelical publishing houses, and investment in major regional literature projects, such as one volume Bible commentaries like *The Africa Bible Commentary* and *The South Asia Bible Commentary*.

Langham Scholars provides financial support for evangelical doctoral students from the Majority World so that, when they return home, they may train pastors and other Christian leaders with sound, biblical and theological teaching. This programme equips those who equip others. Langham Scholars also works in partnership with Majority World seminaries in strengthening evangelical theological education. A growing number of Langham Scholars study in high quality doctoral programmes in the Majority World itself. As well as teaching the next generation of pastors, graduated Langham Scholars exercise significant influence through their writing and leadership.

To learn more about Langham Partnership and the work we do visit **langham.org**

Lightning Source UK Ltd.
Milton Keynes UK
UKHW020643020721
386508UK00005B/171